'This book will very quickly and deservedly become a well-thumbed and leading reference point for everyone interested in nineteenth-century crime. Johnston has produced an eminently readable and engaging review of how society perceived, rationalized and responded to criminal activity during this period. The text expertly and seamlessly synthesizes the existing literature with real-life case studies and archive material, creating a rich and vivid narrative. Johnston has truly earned her place amongst the elite writers in this field.'

Kim Stevenson, *Professor of SocioLegal History,*
Plymouth Law School, UK

'This valuable and wide-ranging study illuminates changing public and official attitudes toward crime, criminality and offenders across the long nineteenth century. It charts the evolving English criminal justice system through attention to provincial offenders and local prisons, as well as the increasing penal reach of central government. The detailed and often poignant case studies of individual adult and juvenile offenders add depth to our understanding of offenders' lives and behaviour and of the wider impacts of summary justice, penal servitude, transportation and capital punishment.'

Vivien Miller, *Associate Professor, American and Canadian Studies,*
University of Nottingham, UK

'This is a comprehensive, accessible and well-written text, which links effectively the different sectors of the nineteenth-century English criminal justice system. The author offers a multidimensional analysis, highlighting the impact of changing contexts and attitudes, engaging with key areas of historical debate and presenting evocative, in-depth case studies in each chapter. The latter in particular will help bring the nineteenth-century criminal justice system and its impact on individual offenders to life. In addition, this book includes a fascinating range of primary source examples and images, always supporting arguments made with plenty of evidence. This book will provide an excellent introduction to the nineteenth-century criminal justice system in England and its impact on those who were subject to its mechanisms.'

Alyson Brown, *Professor of History,*
Edge Hill University, UK

CRIME IN ENGLAND 1815–1880

Crime in England 1815–1880 provides a unique insight into views on crime and criminality and the operation of the criminal justice system in England from the early to the late nineteenth century.

This book examines the perceived problem and causes of crime, views about offenders and the consequences of these views for the treatment of offenders in the criminal justice system. The book explores the perceived causes of criminality, as well as concerns about particular groups of offenders, such as the 'criminal classes' and the 'habitual offender', the female offender and the juvenile criminal. It also considers the development of policing, the systems of capital punishment and the transportation of offenders overseas, as well as the evolution of both local and convict prison systems. The discussion primarily investigates those who were drawn into the criminal justice system and the attitudes towards and mechanisms to address crime and offenders. The book draws together original research by the author to locate these broader developments and provides detailed case studies illuminating the lives of those who experienced the criminal justice system and how these changes were experienced in provincial England.

With an emphasis on the penal system and case studies on offenders' lives and on provincial criminal justice, this book will be useful to academics and students interested in criminal justice, history and penology, as well as being of interest to the general reader.

Helen Johnston is Senior Lecturer in Criminology at the University of Hull. Her research interests lie in the history of crime and punishment, particularly in the penal system and offenders lives during the nineteenth and early twentieth century. She is the editor of *Punishment & Control in Historical Perspective* (Palgrave Macmillan, 2008) and co-editor of *Prison Readings* with Yvonne Jewkes (Willan, 2006).

History of Crime in the UK and Ireland
Series editor: Professor Barry Godfrey

Rarely do we get the opportunity to study criminal history across the British Isles, or across such a long time period. *History of Crime in the UK and Ireland* is a series which provides an opportunity to contrast experiences in various geographical regions and determine how these situations changed – with slow evolution or dramatic speed – and with what results. It brings together data, thought, opinion, and new theories from an established group of scholars that draw upon a wide range of existing and new research. Using case studies, examples from contemporary media, biographical life studies, thoughts and ideas on new historical methods, the authors construct lively debates on crime and the law, policing, prosecution, and punishment. Together, this series of books builds up a rich but accessible history of crime and its control in the British Isles.

CRIME IN ENGLAND 1815–1880

Experiencing the criminal justice system

Helen Johnston

Routledge
Taylor & Francis Group

LONDON AND NEW YORK

First published 2015
by Routledge
2 Park Square, Milton Park, Abingdon, Oxon OX14 4RN

and by Routledge
711 Third Avenue, New York, NY 10017

Routledge is an imprint of the Taylor & Francis Group, an informa business

British Library Cataloguing-in-Publication Data
A catalogue record for this book is available from the British Library

Library of Congress Cataloging-in-Publication Data
Johnston, Helen
Crime in England 1815–1880: experiencing the criminal justice system /
Helen Johnston.
page cm.—(History of crime in the UK and Ireland)
1. Criminal justice, Administration of—England—History—19th century.
2. Crime—England—History—19th century. I. Title.
HV9960.G72E548 2015
364.941'09034—dc23
2014033238

ISBN: 978-1-84392-954-3 (hbk)
ISBN: 978-1-84392-953-6 (pbk)
ISBN: 978-1-315-76940-0 (ebk)

Typeset in Bembo
by Book Now Ltd, London

MIX
Paper from
responsible sources
FSC
www.fsc.org   FSC® C013056

Printed and bound in Great Britain by
TJ International Ltd, Padstow, Cornwall

CONTENTS

For Eleanor Devey

ILLUSTRATIONS

Box

Figures

Table

ACKNOWLEDGEMENTS

I would like to take this opportunity to thank the following people with whom I have worked in recent years on various projects: Yvonne Jewkes, Barry Godfrey, Heather Shore, Dave Cox and Jo Turner, together with my colleagues and friends in the Centre for Criminology and Criminal Justice at the University of Hull, especially Simon Green, Louise Sturgeon-Adams, Peter Young and Karen Harrison. I am lucky enough to have been taught and shared research interests with some great people at Liverpool John Moores University and Keele University during my own studies and since; thanks to Joe Sim, who helped me find the history of punishment, as well as Anna Souhami, John Locker, Bronwyn Morrison and Michael Fiddler. Sections of this book originated in my doctoral thesis; thanks to Roger Swift and Richard Sparks for their comments on the earlier research. The case studies of convict lives were compiled as part of a larger study on The Costs of Imprisonment (RES-062-23-3102), and I am grateful to the Economic and Social Research Council for funding this research. Thank you to the criminology team at Routledge and to Heidi Lee for her patience. I am grateful to Tyne and Wear Archives for permission to reproduce the images from Criminal Registers on the cover of this book and to Shropshire Archives for the plan of Shrewsbury prison reproduced in Chapter 6. Also thanks to Logaston Press for the permission to reproduce an adapted version of part of H. Johnston (2005) 'Policing, punishment and social institutions in the nineteenth century: the role of the Shropshire magistracy', in D. J. Cox and B. S. Godfrey (eds), *'Cinderellas and Packhorses': A History of the Shropshire Magistracy*. Finally I would like to thank Christian, my Mum and Dad, and family and friends for their love and encouragement. Also thank you to Jessica, my daughter, whose arrival provided an immovable deadline.

Helen Johnston, *University of Hull*

ABBREVIATIONS

HO	Home Office
NA	National Archives
PCOM	Prison Commission
PP	Parliamentary Papers
QA	Quarter Sessions Administration
QS	Quarter Sessions
RCP	Reports of the Commissioners of Prisons
SA	Shropshire Archives
VJR	Visiting Justices Reports

INTRODUCTION

This book covers a relatively well-trodden time period in the history of crime and punishment. The period under examination, 1815 to 1880, encompasses some of the major transitions in, and the establishment of, what might be called the 'modern' criminal justice system and, in the broader sense, is one that overlaps with what is often referred to as the 'Age of Reform' in Britain. The aim here is to examine the causes of crime, views about offenders, and the consequences of these views for the treatment of offenders by the criminal justice system from the late Hanoverian period to mid-late Victorian England. This book brings together original research through the use of case studies and synthesises the existing literature; the material covered is a reflection of the author's research interests, and this therefore influences the perimeters of the discussion. It will explore the perceived causes of crime and concerns about particular groups of offenders, such as the 'criminal classes' and the 'habitual offender', the female offender and the juvenile criminal. It will also examine the development of policing, the systems of capital punishment and the transportation of offenders overseas, as well as the evolution of both local and convict prison systems. The discussion deals primarily with how those people who were drawn into the criminal justice system were dealt with and both the attitudes towards and the mechanisms used to address the perceived problems of these groups of offenders. Overall, the emphasis throughout will be on views about crime, criminality and offenders and the results and consequences of these views for the policies and practices of policing and punishment.

The discussion presented here is concerned primarily with what people thought about crime and criminality and what they did to try to address the problems that crime posed for English society during the nineteenth century. It is not a quantitative study of these questions but, rather, attempts to illuminate qualitatively the offender and the experience of the machinery of the criminal justice system; it is concerned not with an accurate picture or measure of crime but with those people who were drawn into, processed and administered by this changing system. Largely, the history of crime is a 'history of how better-off people disciplined their inferiors; of how elites used selected law-breakers to sanction their own authority'; it is also about 'how public fears about change and disorder were displaced onto "criminals", even when criminals were the inappropriate objects of those fears', and not about real levels of law-breaking (Gatrell, 1990: 245–6). The book is influenced by such sentiments; therefore the quantitative questions in the discussion are overarching and not an exact measure of 'what was happening, but of what people believed was happening' – the picture of crime with which nineteenth-century society thought they were confronted and how they reacted to it (Sindall, 1986: 34–5). Most of my research to date has been in the field of punishment, and as a result there is a greater slant than the reader might find in other books on this period towards the ways in which these views played out in the penal system.

The period in question has also been the subject of much theorising by historians and criminologists on the changing nature of criminal justice, policing and punishment. Research on the major institutions of criminal justice in the nineteenth century have examined, explained and interpreted the transitions in these areas. This is not to say that these developments and transitions did not have a longer history, either before or after this period, but these will be examined within the period set for this contribution to the History of Crime in UK and Ireland series in which it is published. The theoretical explanations put forward for such changes in criminal justice and punishment are set down here and will be returned to the concluding remarks. Traditional or Whig accounts, frequently based on the views of the reformers writing at the time, tend to see these transitions – the decline in bodily punishments; the organisation and development of 'modern' policing; the decline of the death penalty and systems of transportation; and the increased use of imprisonment as a means to change offenders' behaviour – as progressive. The changes are often seen in linear terms: the practices of the past were barbaric, inefficient, ineffective and haphazard, whereas the 'new' system would be measured, rational and effective in dealing with the problem of crime. More broadly, these changes, which resulted in a more orderly and organised criminal justice system, are located within the progressive development of a modern civilised society – the march of progress – and were led by enlightened, benevolent humanitarian campaigners and reformers. For example, since the ineffective parish constables could not deal with the problem of crime in a rapidly urbanising and industrialising society, a 'new' police was needed to bring safety and security to the populace (Critchley, 1978). Brutal public displays in which the masses would observe the infliction of bodily punishment or the death and dissection of capital felons were barbaric and excessive; they needed to be replaced by a new system which was more measured, which executed only certain offenders (and then in private, away from the eyes of public), and which would ultimately lead to the total abolition of the death penalty (Cooper, 1974; Hibbert, 1957). This system of punishment would be replaced by the prison, not the disorderly and diseased gaols of the past but a new prison: an orderly and functional environment where prisoners were given the basics for survival – food, shelter and sanitation – were put to labour and were given religious and moral education through which their behaviour could be altered (Webb and Webb, 1963; Whiting, 1975; Stockdale, 1977).

The alternative approach to understanding these changes and transitions, the revisionist accounts as they are known, have taken apart many of the claims summarised above. Primarily, the revisionists have been concerned with power and social control, many of the early accounts emerging from or influenced by the Marxist social histories of the 1970s. Collectively, these accounts explore questions of power and power relations; they seek to understand the economic and philanthropic motives of 'reformers' as well as the interests of the governing class, state power, authority and regulation. The law has been one focus of attention, and scholars were concerned with the operation of the law and the criminal justice system. They argued that class interests predominated and that, despite appearing universal, there was a deep class bias in the law, as exemplified in cases of capital punishment and the operation of mercy (Hay, 1975; Linebaugh, 1975, 1993; Gatrell, 1990, 1994).

Similarly, when it came to the new authority of the police, the role of magistracy and processes of prosecution and law enforcement, scholars such as Philips (1980, 1983), Storch (1975, 1976) and Gatrell (1990) all examine changes during the nineteenth century in light of these roles and the nature of state power. How was law enforcement governed? Who wanted the new police and why? Whose interests did the police serve and who were the subjects of these new methods of policing? Philips (1980) argued that, by the 1830s, a new system of prosecution had developed. This encouraged prosecution for all offences within a modern system of law enforcement and administration, through the paid, bureaucratic new police as well as via the extension of the powers of magistracy and the range and number of criminal offences, though there was significant resistance to the police over a long period. Storch (1975, 1976) explored working-class hostility and resistance to the new police, documenting both the nature and the extent of such resistance through riots and the extension of the state through the police as domestic missionaries, so curbing working-class life and leisure with a view to reshaping morality. Gatrell (1990) argued that, as the state took increasing control of the criminal justice system, a 'policeman-state' emerged; the police were placed at the centre of a new disciplinary enterprise (though not unchallenged) for order through the law, as yet more bureaucratic control was needed to solve the perceived problems of crime.

Philips (1980, 2003) examined the class interests and motives of the police and criminal justice reformers, most recently to explain how these 'moral entrepreneurs' used the available evidence to construct the problem of crime in such a way as to achieve their own ends. This approach was also taken with regard to punishment by Ignatieff (1978, 1983), Rothman (1990), Platt (1969) and Cohen (1985), all of whom have questioned and examined the motives and ideology of the reformers and philanthropic endeavours rather than taken their views at face value. These authors have questioned the motivations and the consequences of the 'reform' measures that were implemented and the degree to which the former can be viewed purely in terms of benevolence.

A number of revisionists saw a connection between the movement away from bodily punishments and the rise of monolithic prison institutions and the emergence of broader changes in social control. Foucault (1991), Melossi and Pavarini (1981), Cohen (1985) and Cohen and Scull (1983) all located the changes and development of the prison within this broader understanding of social control. Melossi and Pavarini (1981), building on an earlier account by Rusche and Kirchheimer (1939), examine punishment through the prism of labour and the capitalist mode of production. While locating the origins of these relations in the sixteenth century, they see their pinnacle manifested by the nineteenth century in the invention of the penitentiary and its machine-like operation, where, in the interests of capitalist society, the inmates were taught and had instilled in them the habits of discipline and labour.

Foucault's (1991) graphic account of the execution of Damiens in 1757, followed by the timetabled and minutely detailed account in 1838 of the juvenile reformatory Mettray, just outside Paris, set up his discussion of this transition. Although this is a historical example, Foucault is not a historian so, while we can be picky about the details, this is not really what he was trying to achieve with this example. Foucault's aim is to look at the emergence of power and to understand the formation of what he terms 'disciplinary society'; the shift from bodily punishment to incarceration exemplifies what he is trying to understand in the present. Disciplinary society is underpinned by a range of institutions on the 'carceral continuum' which operate with similar techniques – the prison, the asylum, the hospital, the army, the school – institutions that train, control and regulate the population. Foucault challenges the notion that punishment within the prison was less severe than the barbaric public punishments of the past. Indeed, he argues that the objective of punishment changed, from avenging the crime through the body infliction of punishment towards altering the offender through the internal prison regime. In order to change or reform the individual offender, the disciplinary prison operates through the use of experts from the fields of medicine, psychiatry and criminology to gain knowledge of their character and background.

Since the revisionist accounts there have been more nuanced narratives. Garland (1985, 1990, 2002) has discussed a range of ideas that locate changes in penality within broader social structures, notably in the early-twentieth century 'penal-welfare' complex, and also sought to understand contemporary issues in crime and justice through a history of the present influenced by the approach taken by Foucault. Dobash et al. (1986) and Sim (1990) have taken Foucauldian approaches to the history of the punishment of women and the development of the prison medical service. Work on the former in the nineteenth century, particularly in England, remains comparatively sparse – Dobash et al. (1986), Zedner (1994) and Bosworth (2000) – though contributions have come from Ballinger (2000) and Seal (2010) on the capital punishment of women in the twentieth century and from Barton (2005) on semi-penal institutions. Many have also been influenced by the work of Rafter, primarily on the punishment of women in the US (Rafter, 1982, 1983, 1985).

Some scholars have been influenced by more cultural approaches (for example, Wiener, 1994; Smith, 2008) or those inspired by the work on the civilising process by Norbert Elias. This is most obvious in the contributions of Spierenburg (1984, 1991, 2005) but also in those by McGowen (1983, 1986, 1994, 2000) and Smith (2008) and in John Pratt's *Punishment and Civilisation* (2002). Questions of civilisation have also been prominent in the history of crime through the recent body of work on violence (Spierenburg, 2001; Wiener, 2004; Wood, 2004; Emsley, 2005).

Criminal statistics

In 1805 the government had begun to collect statistical information on crime, patchy at first, largely related to the death penalty. However, for a few years from 1810 annual returns, also somewhat erratic, were made on the number of serious offences and executions as well as those committed for trial; these were revived in 1827. In the 1830s criminal statistics were organised into six different categories: offences against the person, offences against property (divided between those involving violence and those that did not), malicious offences against property, offences against currency, and miscellaneous offences (Rawlings, 1999; Emsley, 2010; Godfrey, 2014). In 1836 returns on the numbers of prisoners were also collected, coinciding with the recent establishment of the Inspectors of Prisons (see Chapter 6). In 1856 the courts and police from across the country began to compile statistical returns on committals, summary cases, convictions and the numbers of those imprisoned, which were published annually by the Home Office. These returns tell us about the offences or the people who were drawn into, prosecuted and dealt with by the criminal justice system and those punished by the penal system. They do not provide a complete picture of the amount of crime in nineteenth-century society, but they do tell us about the activity of the criminal justice system.

Moreover, we must also note that prosecutions at this time were led by the victims, who prosecuted the offender themselves in the courts and paid the costs of doing so. This would evidently have been a deterrent for those who could not afford to pay – wives who were victims of domestic violence being the most obvious – but for many petty offences the prosecution costs were relatively low. Some victims may not have wanted to prosecute on account of the severity of the law, though if the offender was not apprehended the case would have fallen away.

The criminal statistics were substantially revised in 1892 when Home Office statisticians set about a major overall of their compilation after nearly fifty years of use. The main problem identified was the different ways in which police forces collected their information, but there were also deficiencies noted in the reporting, accounting, and collection of the number of both offences and criminals, as well as more general inconsistencies (Godfrey, 2014).

Quantifying the amount of various types of crime in the period 1815 to 1880, given the nature of statistical collection at the time, has been estimated and debated by a range of crime historians (for example, Gatrell and Hadden, 1972; Gatrell, 1980; Emsley, 2010; Sindall, 1986; Godfrey, 2008; Godfrey *et al.*, 2008), and that exercise will not be repeated here. Rather, this book will examine the views about criminality and offending which resulted from this growing social enquiry and the quantification of the problem of crime. Once information about crime was being collected and estimated, the data, however partial, influenced views about the nature of crime and criminality as well as the government response to the problem. The task here, then, is to examine these views about crime and to illuminate the responses to, and consequences of, such opinions for the lives of those who were arrested, prosecuted and punished by the criminal justice system.

Case studies: offending and prison lives and provincial criminal justice

The case studies in the book illuminate the wider discussion of criminality, offending and criminal justice through the use of two types of research: offending and prison lives, and provincial criminal justice. The first provide an understanding of the experience of criminal justice and its institutions through the people who were subjected to it. These 'whole life' histories, a methodology created by Godfrey *et al.* (2007, 2010) and recently applied to convict imprisonment and release by Johnston and Godfrey (2013a; see also Cox *et al.*, 2014) examine the offending, personal histories and institutional experiences of those who went through the courts and systems of punishment. The individuals chosen as case studies have been selected from hundreds that were reconstructed in a recent ESRC-funded project, 'The Costs of Imprisonment, 1853–1940' (Johnston and Godfrey, 2013a). Research began with an analysis of the penal records and licensing documents held in NA/PCOM 3 and 4 (partially available online at www.ancestry.co.uk). From this main source we traced the whole life of an offender and constructed a narrative. We also drew on census returns (1841–1911), which detailed residence, family status, and occupation; online birth, marriage and death indices; the British Library Nineteenth Century Newspapers Online, *The Times* Digital Archive, and *The Guardian* Digital Archive, which provided coverage of the trials; the Old Bailey Proceedings Online; the Home Office Criminal Registers (HO26 and HO27), which supplied details of offenders between 1805 and 1892; and other Prison Commission documents.

The second set of case studies are concerned with provincial criminal justice and understanding how local areas – in this case, Shropshire – experienced some of the transitions in criminal justice and punishment that are the focus of this book. To this end, the establishment of the new police, the use of public execution, the development of the county prison in Shrewsbury and the responses to the problem of juvenile crime in Shropshire will all be examined. Shropshire, the largest inland county in England, remained a relatively rural and agricultural county throughout the nineteenth century. It was geographically close to the rapidly industrialising Black Country and the Midlands and on the route both to Wales, in the west, and the expanding areas of Manchester and Liverpool, to the north. Provincial understandings of criminal justice administration through the Quarter Sessions courts make an important contribution to our knowledge, as, 'for most people, the justices, rather than central government in London, represented public authority as they would experience it in their daily lives' (Philips, 1976: 161). It was not only the economy that remained stable in Shropshire; the social composition of the magistracy and the attending magistrates at Quarter Sessions was also relatively constant. There were 140 to 150 magistrates on the Commission of the Peace between the 1830s and 1880s, of whom between 30 (fewer in the 1840s) and 40 regularly attended the sessions (Baugh, 1979; *Kelly's Directory of Shropshire*, 1863, 1870; Johnston, 2005b, 2005c). The magistracy in Shropshire remained the preserve of the landed gentry for much of the nineteenth century, with only a few professional people or tradesmen being introduced gradually by the end of the century (Johnston, 2005b). The county did not experience the magisterial revolution of nearby industrialising areas such as Wolverhampton or as occurred in Lancashire, where the middle classes began to attend the bench (Swift, 1992; Foster, 1974).

Chapter outlines

Chapter 1 looks at the perceived causes of crime during the period 1815 to 1880. Throughout these years the causes of crime were rooted in notions of individual morality. People became criminals because they were immoral, were poorly educated, lacked religion, and were influenced by the examples around them – others in the community, cheap literature and low entertainment as well as drink. The chapter will draw on commentators' views from the time, illuminating the ways in which they discussed the problem of crime and how to address it. It will also examine the problem of drunkenness and its association with certain communities (the Irish) as well as problems of poverty and 'less eligibility' and its relationship to crime and punishment. The final section will focus on crime in rural communities; using predominantly the example of poaching, it will provide the context for examining the life history of Enoch Swift, the first case study in the book. While Enoch did experience long-term imprisonment in the convict system, he was a petty offender who regularly found himself in trouble with the law for poaching and related offences. With the exception of one offence, like the overwhelmingly majority of the people processed by the criminal justice system, Enoch committed summary offences and received as punishment fines or, in lieu of payment, short terms of imprisonment.

Chapter 2 focuses on the development of the idea of a 'criminal class' and the increasing concerns about 'habitual offenders'. The concept of a criminal class was influenced not only by the activities and views of criminal justice reformers but also by social commentators who drew attention to this perceived group. The criminal classes were not casual offenders who, due to some mishap, fell foul of the law; they were thought to live through criminal activity. Views about this group will be examined, as well as wider concerns about street violence and the decline of transportation to Australia, which influenced the responses to this problem. By the 1860s and 1870s the term 'habitual offender' had come to mean a repeat offender who needed to be monitored and surveyed by the state, and formed an administrative category in the criminal justice system. The development of legislation and the systems of monitoring, surveillance, identification and photography which followed will also be discussed. Annie Greenfield is the subject of the case study provided in this chapter, and her story sheds light on the system of monitoring in place when offenders were released on licence from the penal system. Annie is one example of an offender whose licence was revoked after she was arrested and charged with being drunk and disorderly.

Chapter 3 examines the establishment of the police. Even before the early nineteenth century there was increased discussion of the role and effectiveness of the police in dealing with the perceived 'problem of crime' in a rapidly industrialising and urbanising society. The chapter will detail the key changes that occurred, from the discussions leading up to the Metropolitan Police Act in 1829 to the establishment of police forces across the country through the implementation of the County and Borough Police Act of 1856. Policing was also subject to growing intervention by the government as it sought greater control over the bureaucratic administration of criminal justice. The case study used in this chapter will look at the early development of the county police in nineteenth-century Shropshire. This will provide a picture of provincial policing and contribute to a wider understanding of policing outside London or the rapidly urbanising or industrialising areas such as Lancashire and the Midlands. This will not only illuminate how a relatively rural and agricultural county saw the problem of crime and made decisions about policing but also reveal why Shropshire was one of the first counties to initiate a 'new' police force.

Chapter 4 examines public punishment, focusing largely though not exclusively on the use of public execution, its decline and its subsequent removal from public view. The chapter begins with a discussion of public punishments such as the pillory and whipping and the decline or privatisation of their infliction by the early decades of the nineteenth century. It then turns to the death penalty, considering both the way in which executions were dealt with by the criminal justice system and the reduction in the severity of the law, as well as the execution day. From the late eighteenth century, the carnival of public execution had been increasing curtailed, and by the late 1860s this resulted in its abolition. From 1868 onwards all executions were held inside local prisons, though by this time the only people executed were those who had committed murder. The case study in this chapter examines public execution in nineteenth-century Shropshire, drawing on a number of executions carried out in the county town of Shrewsbury between 1815 and the 1860s.

Chapter 5 deals with the system of transportation. By the early nineteenth century the banishment of convicts overseas was in what might be termed its second phase. Transportation to the colonies of America had roots in the seventeenth century, but this came to an end during the outbreak of the American War of Independence in the 1770s. Transportation to Australia was already well established by 1815 and peaked in the 1830s, when over 5,000 offenders per year were being sent there. The chapter examines the route that offenders took to Australia via the hulks moored in English ports and (if they made it past that experience) then on the journey and to a life on the other side of the world. It will look briefly at convict life in Australia, the transportation of juvenile offenders and the prospects for reform for those sent abroad. The case study concerns George Pobjoy, originally from Somerset. After committing a number of serious offences, George was sentenced to seven years' transportation, and his story highlights one man's experience of this punishment.

Chapter 6 is a detailed study of local prisons between 1815 and 1880. Although criminology and the history of crime often focuses on the more serious offenders and offences, the everyday experiences of those who committed and were punished for relatively minor crimes are sometimes overlooked. Local prisons, historically as today, hold the overwhelming majority of prisoners who are serving short sentences. In the late eighteenth into the early nineteenth century, there were hundreds of gaols and houses of correction spread across the country. Estimates of their number at the time range between that in the 1770s by the prison reformer John Howard, at 244, and that in 1812 by the reformer James Neild, who claimed 317 in his survey of prisons. By 1865, when the terms 'gaol' and 'house of correction' were replaced with the collective term 'local prison', there were about 130 of these institutions and by the time the government took over the administration of these prisons in 1877 there were 113. After the closures at centralisation there were 69 local prisons (Brodie *et al.*, 2002).

Local prisons played a crucial role in the system, holding those on remand awaiting trial or sentence, prisoners serving sentences of up to two years, and those awaiting the death penalty or removal to the hulks for transportation (or, later, to the convict system). Chapter 6 examines the development of disciplinary regimes in local prisons from the reform period through to the debate between the systems of separate and silent imprisonment and the more deterrent regimes apparent from mid-century. It also examines the deterrent philosophy of punishment that dominated prison regimes until at least the end of the century and the centralisation of the local prisons in 1878. The case study reveals the transformation of imprisonment in one local prison, Shrewsbury, from the late eighteenth century onwards.

Chapter 7 considers the establishment and development of convict prisons and the experience of penal servitude. The convict system was constructed to hold offenders sentenced to longer periods of imprisonment – over three years. Convict prisons were built or adapted during the 1850s and the system expanded throughout the middle decades of the century as transportation to Australia was wound down. Although prisons already existed in England, these served a new function in the system of long-term imprisonment known as penal servitude. With the exception of those having committed murder (although sentences of death were also sometimes commuted to long terms of imprisonment), serious offenders could now expect a lengthy period of incarceration rather than death or transportation overseas. It would also mean that, for the first time, offenders who had served long sentences would be released back into English society after completing the required terms. This was a source of great anxiety to the public and social commentators, but it also put in place mechanisms which began, albeit very basically, to consider how to release offenders from prison and how they might be supervised or monitored on their release. Towards the end of our period, there were ideas about the kind of support that offenders might need on release from prison in order to prevent their return. The case study contained is the life history of John Baines, convicted of fraud and related offences, who was sent to prison for five years and allocated to 'star class'; this was a new category used from the late 1870s to identify first-time prisoners.

Chapter 8 examines women, crime and criminal justice in the nineteenth century. This chapter will discuss the perceived causes and explanations of female criminality and the ways in which women were dealt with by the criminal justice system, especially the penal system. While the social controls of perceived feminine conduct, family and the double burden of work both in and outside the home meant that the majority of women did not come into contact with the criminal justice system, those who did fall foul of the law were often seen in particular ways. Not only were their crimes gendered, but so too were the responses to such infractions. Women were overrepresented in certain categories of crimes – theft and offences under the Pawnbrokers' Acts, prostitution, poisoning and infanticide. Responses to such crimes varied. Many women, like men, experienced the revolving door of the local prison, and from the mid-century onwards a smaller proportion of women experienced the convict system. Throughout the period under study there was also a range of semi-penal institutions – homes, refuges, retreats, asylums, and the like – that either housed criminal or destitute or 'deviant' women through 'voluntary' admission or were used after or instead of imprisonment. The life of Alice Ann Rowlands is the case study here. Alice began offending in her early teens, and after a five-year sentence in a juvenile reformatory she again came before the courts for petty offences and received short sentences of imprisonment. Following a longer sentence for housebreaking, she was charged with larceny from the person and received five years' penal servitude. Alice served two years and three months in the convict system before she was released on conditional licence to a refuge, where she continued in custody until July 1887. This proved to be the final contact she had with the criminal justice system. She returned to Liverpool, where she married and had children, and does not appear to have offended again during her lifetime.

Chapter 9 examines the problem of juvenile crime and the mechanisms established to deal with the young offender. In previous centuries, juvenile crime had not been seen as a separate social problem, but by the nineteenth century it began to attract the attention of philanthropists and social commentators, and it was recognised that the problem required a response. While young offenders were sentenced to death, to transportation and, most frequently, to short periods of imprisonment in local prisons, by the mid-nineteenth century we see the development of separate penal policy and establishments – reformatories and industrial schools – to manage and contain the juvenile offender.

And so we will begin with a discussion of the causes of crime as they were understood in nineteenth-century England.

1

THE CAUSES OF CRIME

This chapter opens with a discussion of the perceived causes of crime and criminality in the period between 1815 and 1880. Most contemporary views were based on the perceived individual immorality of the offender, and this remained largely unchanged across the period. Crime was thought to be caused predominantly by sinfulness; lack of religion; immorality and vice; bad parenting and neglect; and alcohol. Drawing on views of contemporary commentators, we will focus on a number of examples and themes.

Such views were often put forward as explanations of all types of crimes, but of course the most visible crimes are those for which most people were drawn into the criminal justice system. As will be discussed in Chapter 2, particular types of offenders elicited the concern of the public, frequently those thought to be dangerous or violent. However, the activity of the criminal justice system in the nineteenth century, and today, is focused overwhelmingly upon the more 'ordinary' or lower-level, mundane offenders committed to and processed by the magistrates courts (or petty sessions, as they were known). Their crimes were the ones that most affronted the population of England, as they were the most visible, and these were the offences that were most frequently policed (see Chapter 3). The 'ordinary' offenders, such as Enoch Swift, the subject of the case study at the end of this chapter, were the people who filled the petty sessions courts and went in and out of the local prisons. Swift was largely a petty recidivist, regularly brought before the courts for game and game-related offences across at least thirty years of his life. To provide a little context for this discussion, the chapter will also examine crime in the rural community, focusing particularly on poaching and the game laws. This will not only highlight poaching as a contested offence in which custom and criminal law were drawn into direct conflict but also contribute to our wider knowledge of crime in more rural or agricultural areas. First, we will examine more closely the perceived causes of crime and criminality in nineteenth-century England.

The causes of crime

In the early to mid-nineteenth century the causes of crime were rooted in classical explanations of free will and rationality. Put simply, classical explanations asserted that people chose to commit crime. The criminal law was supposed to operate as a balance to this decision-making by counteracting such a choice. In theory, the criminal justice system would operate in such a way that the capture and inevitable punishment of offenders would be enough to outweigh the benefits of committing a criminal act. These classical explanations were put forward in particular by theorists such as Cesare Beccaria and Jeremy Bentham. Both drew on the Enlightenment thinkers of the seventeenth and eighteenth centuries who advocated new ways of thinking about the world based on ideas of rationality and reason.

As the century wore on, the belief continued that free will and immorality was the determining factor in a decision to commit crime. In some sections of society there was a growing awareness of the links between poverty and criminal behaviour and the effects of rapid social and economic change on the social conditions in which people lived. This can be seen in the division between those considered as the deserving and the undeserving poor, or perhaps between those described by Mary Carpenter as the 'perishing' classes as opposed to the 'dangerous' classes (Carpenter, 1851). These dichotomies were not necessarily new for the nineteenth century and would also continue into the twentieth, but the activities of some social reformers drew increasing attention to the distinctions as the century progressed. Despite 'a recognition that many criminals lived precarious lives in deprived parts of Britain's towns and cities, this was seen more as a *consequence* rather than a *cause* of their criminality' (Taylor, 2010: 77–8; original emphasis). Immorality, vice and idleness, and their consequences, crime and delinquency, were overwhelmingly viewed as features of the lives of the poor and the labouring classes.

The rapid development of the cities and towns and the huge movements of population from rural to urban areas caused a great deal of anxiety in the early to mid-nineteenth century. While the Victorians saw such developments as a symbol of the progress and civilisation of the nation, this was moderated by the fear of an undercurrent in society – a pernicious feature that could undermine the great advances that had been made: crime. Then as today, crime was seen as a social barometer – a measure of the health of the nation – and, as the increasing collection of statistical information on crime and the criminal justice system told people, crime was all around them.

Criminals and, as the century wore on, the 'criminal classes' (see Chapter 2) were seen as products of the urban environment, born and bred into the immorality and vice in deprived and densely populated areas of the expanding cities and towns. Writing in 1849, Jelinger Symons (a barrister and inspector of schools (Shepherd, 2008)) claimed that crime in London had reached its climax. Crowded communities and moral neglect allowed crime to be easily concealed in the urban environment. The chief origin of crime, he thought, was 'the debasement caused by large communities in a small space, and the absence of improving agencies, of which, as regards the poor, London with all its established charities, able preachers and philanthropists, is sadly deficient' (Symons, 1849: 39). Across the country, the rapidly expanding towns and manufacturing districts, the result of much industrialisation and urbanisation in the nineteenth century, were viewed as similarly uncivilised:

> Great cities multiply crimes by presenting easier opportunities … by collecting thieves and robbers into the same neighbourhoods, enabling them to form communications and confederations that increase their art and courage, as well as strength and wickedness; but principally by the refuge they afford for villainy, and of subsisting in secrecy, which great towns afford.
>
> (Paley, cited in Symons, 1849: 49)

Towns and cities were seen as places in which criminal associations were made and criminal practices shared; offenders, it was thought, would then carry these practices back to rural districts. In this respect, lodging-houses were a source for concern, and calls for their suppression were based on claims that they were filled with thieves and prostitutes. One prisoner giving evidence to the Constabulary Force Commissioners stated that 'Lodging-houses are a very great evil. I have known as many as ten men and ten women lying indiscriminately on the floor. A lad who has overrun his parents is sure of a home there, where he is picked up by some unknown prig [thief]; and, after being once there, *there is little chance of reclaiming him*' (PP, 1839: 36: emphasis added). Another stated: 'I have often heard thieves talk in the lodging-houses of what they have done, and make up partnerships. Any lodging-house keeper can readily find a fence [a receiver of stolen goods]' (ibid.).

Poor or bad parenting or the lack of moral guidance was also a perceived cause of criminality. Children brought up in families where their parents had been convicted of crimes were seen as being 'bred into crime'. Parents who sent their children out to forage to support the family income were also seen as setting them on a potential route to criminality, even if this was not the specific intention. Family economic circumstances were often difficult; children were left to fend for themselves because their parents were working long hours or, given mortality rates, could be orphaned and have no other family. The *Report of the Committee for Investigating the Causes of the Alarming Increase in Juvenile Delinquency in the Metropolis*, published in 1816, saw crime as a problem evolving from the poorer sections of society; witnesses to the committee blamed 'vicious and abandoned parents' for the increase in juvenile crime. Juvenile delinquents, it was thought, mixed in bad company; they frequented public houses filled with prostitutes, thieves and vagabonds and they were poorly fed, clothed and educated. Crime was the result of parental neglect. Samuel Day, writing about juvenile crime in 1858, thought parents not only neglectful but out for personal gain and lacking in any natural affection for their children. He cited evidence for this from the chaplain of Liverpool prison, who claimed that hardly any parents inquired, when they were incarcerated, about the welfare of their children:

Children, as soon as they are well able to crawl, are driven into the streets for the purposes of begging or stealing, in order to support the profligate authors of their being in idleness and dissipation; often receiving severe bodily chastisement if the amount of the days spoils does not come up to the required standard.

(Day, 1858: 35)

Symons believed that the physical causes of crime were rooted in spiritual and educational destitution. Quoting evidence from both the *London City Mission Magazine* and the *Ragged School Magazine*, he estimated that

in London 12,000 children are trained in crime; 3000 are receivers of stolen goods; 4000 are annually committed for crimes; 10,000 were addicted to gambling; 20,000 to begging; 30,000 live by theft and fraud; 23,000 are found helplessly drunk in the streets; 150,000 are habitual gin drinkers; 150,000 live in systematic prostitution and profligacy.

(Symons, 1849: 42)

The roots of criminality were also to be found in the examples of immorality and vice that the poor and the labouring classes had around them. Immoral behaviour in its many forms was thought to influence criminal behaviour; sinfulness, the lack of religion, lewd or indecent behaviour, vice or sexual promiscuity and drunkenness were all considered to result in crime. One such area was entertainment of low quality, such as cheap literature, which carried the exploits of well-known or popular criminals, or theatres and music halls where bawdy songs and lewd behaviour prevailed, provided examples of the type of moral turpitude and degeneracy that led to a life of crime.

Reverend John Clay, the chaplain of Preston House of Correction between 1823 and 1858, used narratives from interviews with prisoners to support claims of the evil effects and demoralising and corrupting nature of cheap literature. Prisoner J. A., aged 18 and convicted of housebreaking, stated:

Now I will speak of a few words about reading bad books. There is a book called the '*Newgate Calendar Improved*'. It contains the lives of the greatest vagabonds that ever was. I used to call it my catechism; and I read in that book until I began to think that honesty and industry was a great shame. The book is a '*straight-line*' for a young thief to work upon, and the first foundation and beginning of evil. I first began reading these bad books until I thought it was a sin to be honest.

(Clay, 1846: 50–51)

Similarly, J. M., a 17-year-old prisoner sentenced to transportation, said:

I began very *soon to read the Newgate Calendar, and all such like books as them, – Jack Sheppard, Turpin and different kinds of romances, – this*, with the advice of wicked men, *made me inclined to follow some of their examples, and to try if I could to imitate some of their evil deeds.*

(Ibid.: 51; original emphasis)

James Greenwood, author of *The Seven Curses of London* (1869), also condemned the promotion of 'gallows' literature as a 'hideous vice'. These penny weekly publications, which included such titles as *The Skeleton Band, Tyburn Dick, The Black Knight of the Road, Dick Turpin, The Boy Burglar,* and *Starlight Sall,* he claimed were poisonous papers which promoted the daring exploits of thieves and murderers. For Greenwood, it was not so much the 'glorification of robbers and cut-throats' that worried him as the reliance on lewdness and the effect of this on the minds of young people. He saw this literature as a

contagious disease, just as cholera and typhus and the plague are contagious, and, as everybody is aware, it needs not personal contact … A tainted scrap of rag has been known to spread plague and death through an entire village, just as a stray leaf of 'Panther Bill' or 'Tyburn Tree' may sow the seeds of immorality among as many boys as a town can produce.

(Greenwood, 1869: 142–3)

Further, he argued that, for children who were not the offspring of thieves, pernicious literature did 'much to influence them towards evil courses', as the confessions of juvenile prisoners demonstrated:

It is a fact that at least fifty per cent of the young thieves lodged in gaol, when questioned on the subject, affect that it was the shining example furnished by such gallows heroes as 'Dick Turpin' and 'Blueskin', that first beguiled them from the path of rectitude, and that a large proportion of their ill-gotten gains was expended in the purchase of such delectable biographies.

(Ibid.: 177)

Cheap or low theatres and music halls were also perceived as corrupting influences. Not only were the performances, plays, songs and stories seen as immoral, but the tales and exploits of Jack Sheppard or Dick Turpin, as well as the bad company and drinking that prevailed at these venues, were thought to encourage the emulation of similar activity. Many commentators considered that young people would steal money or commit petty crime in order to obtain the fees to attend such entertainments (Tobias, 1967). Crone (2012) notes that censorship records in London demonstrate the ways in which some of the excesses of the theatres were curtailed from the mid-nineteenth century onwards. Plays which re-created too closely the actual events of recent murders or similar cases, content which was too offensive or violence that was too gruesome were changed, reflecting the attitudes of censors and the views concerning the effects of such material on the viewing public. But it was not just cheap literature or penny dreadfuls that concerned Greenwood (1869).

Among the other pernicious influences were refreshment bars, 'snuggeries', gambling, betting and, of course, drink, which we will examine more extensively later.

How these played out in the eyes of those who worked in the criminal justice system is demonstrated by extracts from the chaplain's reports on those who had recently been committed to the prison at Shrewsbury in the 1850s; they show the ways in which views about the individual morality and vice of offenders manifested themselves and give a flavour of the kind of details chaplains wrote about those they encountered (see Box 1.1).

BOX 1.1 Selection from reports of prisoners by the chaplain at Shrewsbury prison, October 1856 (SA, QS/13/1)

1 Thomas Campbell – labourer, single, Irish parentage, born in Wolverhampton, of no religious persuasion, never goes to any place of worship – knew a few facts in religion – could read very imperfectly. Convicted in Jan 1851 of stealing a watch got 6 weeks. Acquitted Jan 1853 of stealing pair of trousers.
P.S. Had been drinking for three days before found in Barn in July – Drunken.

2 Ellen Games– Servant, Rhuabon, single, – a very quiet ignorant girl – In [family] way expects to be confined in December. Her father is a platelayer on the Hereford line – gets £1–10.0 per week wages – is a good scholar in himself – but has badly neglected his family.

3 Margaret Hughes – Alias Carr – single, born at Malpas, could read well and write imperfectly, acquainted with some facts in religion – never attends any place of worship – A Prostitute – Had two children. Was convicted in Feb 1856, under 18 & 19 Vict. of stealing a gown – and got one month – once in Chester.

4 Thomas Price – Brickmaster – born at Manchester – married – never attended any place of worship except when in prison – or during the few months he was in Militia – A Very Bad Character – spends a great part of his time with Prostitutes – his mother and two sisters being bad characters – In this prison 6!!! times before – A Sound flogging would benefit him.

5 Henry Walker – Sailor, Tramp, born at Ely – single – very good scholar, knows some facts in religion.

6 George Cooper – Stoker, Tramp, born in London, single – could neither read nor write – ignorant on religious subjects.
N.B. Walker said he sailed on board the 'Cruiser' and that she carried 175 men and had no chaplain, Cooper said that he sailed on board the same vessel but that she carried 260 men and her chaplain's name was 'Stevens'.

7 Alfred Roberts – Chimney Sweep, Tramp, born in Manchester. Never attends any place of worship – a pretty good scholar – acquainted with some facts in religion – an intelligent lad – had been apprenticed to his

Uncle, a fisherman at Hull – I hope to prevail on him to go back after his discharge from prison.

8   Mary Steen – Hawker, born in Birmingham, Roman Catholic, could read fairly, acquainted with some facts in religion. Her father is a respectable hawker residing in Birmingham.

9   Mary Williams – Hawker, born at Huddersfield, a Roman Catholic of Irish parentage – could read very imperfectly – but has improved in reading and writing while in prison. Acquainted with a few facts in religion. Conduct in prison good.

   ...

12   Thomas Jones – Tramp – he said he was born in Bilston, could read and write imperfectly – an intelligent man like most 'travellers' – an accomplished thief. Conduct good.

13   Mary Jones – Real name Eliza Brompton – Alias 'Hereford Liz'. This woman wanted me to write for her marriage lines to the English Ambassador, Paris – where she was married 22 Jan 1846 – Under the name Elizabeth Flowers to Geo: Archer – the man now in prison with her.

14   George Shaw – Labourer – born at Hertfordshire – single – could read imperfectly – has improved in reading and learnt to write while here – acquainted with a few facts in religion. Brought here from Stafford prison, where he underwent two months imprisonment for two charges.

Drink and drunkenness

Although legislation which targeted the problems of habitual drunkenness and individual offenders who committed crime while drunk did not appear until the latter part of the nineteenth century, concern about the relationship between drink and crime was prevalent throughout the century and before. The Select Committee on Drunkenness, reporting in 1834, thought that, while intoxication among the middle and higher classes had decreased, its prevalence among the labouring classes had increased. They regarded the problem as one not just for seaports and manufacturing districts but also for agricultural areas, where men, women and even children were all affected. They blamed the increase in drunkenness on the spread in the preceding years of drinking establishments, claiming that there was one establishment for every 20 families, and on the reduction in duty on and cost of liquor. Among the many ways in which intoxication affected the nation, the committee said, was that it spread crime in all its forms, transforming a mass of human beings into 'excrescences of corruption and weakness, which must be cut off and cast away from the community ... the innocent population thus made criminal, being, like the grain subjected to distillation, converted from a wholesome source of strength and prosperity into a poisoned issue of weakness and decay' (PP, 1834: vi). The evidence, Symons stated, was all around:

> of all the proximate causes of crime none is more fearfully powerful than that of drink, ... and temptations to it which the law permits, most disastrously for the morals and welfare of the people. No statistics are needed on this subject: every town swarms with beer-houses and public-houses, the majority of them being ill-conducted, and in towns some are the haunts of thieves, prostitutes and gamblers.
>
> (Symons, 1849: 64)

Arguing for more severe penalties for drunkenness, he thought that 'If there be not some check given to the dreadful extent of drinking and drunkenness among the people, there is slender hope of the reformation of our adult population, and ... the rising generation will fall victims to this moral pestilence' (ibid.: 66). Similarly, Greenwood advanced that 'no sane man will contest the fact that drunkenness has wrought more mischief than all other social evils put together. There is not a form of human sin and sorrow in which it does not constantly play a part' (1869: 332).

Many commentators recognised the 'revolving door' of short-term imprisonment, particularly for those offenders who committed drink-related crimes. Clay reported to the Magistrates of Lancashire in 1846 that, although the prison had been successful in the reform of some prisoners, there remained

> a sordid residue – a few whose moral state is so completely disordered that neither penal nor reformatory treatment can effect a cure. These disgraceful and dangerous pests – not confined to one sex – are perpetually moving between the beer-shop, public house, or other public curse, on the one hand, and the prison, on the other.
>
> (Clay, 1846: 4)

The visibility of crime and disorder also meant that the police and the courts dealt with a regular supply of people charged with offences relating to drunkenness. Throughout the century, the criminal justice system was filled with drunkards, and many experienced the 'revolving door' of local imprisonment as they were committed for short periods after failing to pay fines imposed. Most of the regulations imposed, though, were on the sale of alcohol, the opening hours of beer-shops and public houses – importantly, the Licensing Acts of 1872 and 1874 – and were dependent for their enforcement on a sometimes unwilling police constable (Taylor, 2010).

Drunkenness was also seen as a manifestation of the brutal and uncivilised activities of the poor and of the past. As the nineteenth century proceeded, the Victorians increasingly valued self-control and restraint and saw alcohol as the root of many of the problems of the working classes (Taylor, 2010; Wood, 2004). Excessive drinking and the availability of alcohol were seen as the root causes of violent behaviour (Archer, 2011). Drink was an issue of national concern by the end of the century, when a number of pieces of legislation were passed in order to try to address the problem of the 'habitual drunkard'. Prosecutions for drunkenness had climbed steadily from the late 1860s, to around 200,000 by 1883 (Godfrey, 2014). At the same time, by the end of the century drunkenness was increasingly medicalised (Johnstone, 1996; Harding and Wilkins, 1988; MacLeod, 1967), and legislation was passed to confine those with multiple convictions for being drunk and disorderly or committing serious crimes under the influence of alcohol to specific reformatories for the inebriate (Morrison, 2005, 2008, Hunt *et al.*, 1989).

The problem of drunkenness was associated with negative stereotyping of certain ethnic communities, and in the nineteenth century the most prominent example was the Irish community. Large-scale and rapid migration of the Irish population to England, and the British Isles in general, early in the century only increased after the Irish famine. At its peak, in 1861, there were 806,000 Irish-born migrants, located overwhelmingly in the towns and cities, who were frequently seen as exacerbating urban squalor (Swift, 2005). Moreover, the view of the innate criminality of the Irish, often seen as part of the 'criminal classes' (see Chapter 2), was widespread. The Irish, in particular the poor, were seen as disorderly, drunken and violent, more criminal than the English, and the 'villains' of Victorian society (Swift, 1997). Studies of the contribution made by the Irish to the crime rates in the nineteenth century demonstrate the representation of this group in the criminal statistics, but also that these numbers were disproportionate to their numbers in the community, especially for violence and drunkenness, and they were also more likely to face prosecution (Swift, 1985, 2005; Archer, 2011). Characteristic offences were being drunk and disorderly, assaults, to a lesser degree petty thefts and vagrancy, and altercations with the police, such as resisting arrest. While these may 'fit' the stereotype, they were the very crimes for which most poor and working-class people were arrested and prosecuted; the Irish added to crime because they were poor, often the poorest in some areas, not because they were Irish. In addition, poor communities were the particular focus of the police (Godfrey *et al.*, 2008; Archer, 2011), as will be demonstrated in Chapter 3.

Poverty, 'less eligibility' and the criminal justice system

Poverty was recognised as an influencing factor in the commission of crime, as was unemployment or the poor labour market, but, as we have seen, this was often viewed as a consequence rather than a cause of crime. Intrinsic to the relationship between poverty, crime and punishment as it played out in this period was the notion of 'less eligibility'. Put simply, people should be deterred from seeking support provided by the state either in workhouses or in prisons by their better material conditions. Underpinned by notions of the deserving and undeserving poor, views of this nature had existed before the 1830s but became government policy in the stricter regulations of the Poor Law Amendment Act 1834. From the 1830s, the new poor law made a clearer distinction between state support or relief given in the home (outdoor relief) and commitment to the workhouse (indoor relief). As such, the conditions in the workhouse needed to be unfavourable when compared with those experienced by the poor honest labouring person living outside. Of course, the workhouse was for the destitute poor and not the criminal, and therefore conditions in the prison had to be more severe than those in the workhouse (Johnston, 2008a; McConville, 1981; Tomlinson, 1978a).

From at least the 1830s onwards, these points were constantly argued in relation to prison conditions across the country. As we shall see in Chapter 6, these beliefs were instrumental in government views about uniformity in local prisons; prison conditions should be the same in Durham as they were in Liverpool, Hull, Oxford or Portsmouth. Criminals or vagrants should not view any one prison as 'better' or comparatively 'easier' than any other; neither should they be encouraged to commit crimes in order to be committed to the local prison, under the impression that the diet or conditions there were better than those in their current circumstances. The quality and amount of food received as well as medical treatment in prison were two aspects which most concerned the inspectors of prisons. Indeed, William John Williams, one of the inspectors, stated in 1837 that

> One of the most serious and increasing obstacles to good discipline is the common practice of tramps and prostitutes, when infected with foul diseases (not admitted into public infirmaries), committing some slight offence for the purpose of obtaining medical treatment in prisons. Their committals are generally for one or two months to hard labour, which they seldom or never under-go, often-times passing the entire of the term in hospital; and many of the females are scarcely discharged a month, ere they return again for surgical care. Such prisoners are more disorderly in behaviour, more pernicious in example, and more difficult to control, than any other class.
>
> (Cited in DeLacy, 1981: 184–5)

Across the country, it was claimed that criminals committed offences to get sent to prison or that they smashed the windows of the local workhouse in the belief that the conditions in prison were better. As DeLacy (1981) has shown in her study of nineteenth-century Lancashire, imprisonment may well have been attractive to some sections of the population, particularly during the winter months, as sentences were often short and basic food and free medical care was provided. The suitability of the prison diet was hotly debated. While it needed to be at a minimum for the purposes of less eligibility, prisoners did need enough food to endure long hours of hard labour. When the prison inspectors William Crawford and Reverend Whitworth Russell issued new dietary scales for local prisons in 1843, they wanted to avoid extravagance but did not wish to see the diet used as a form of punishment (Tomlinson, 1978a).

Renewed interest in the prison diet came in the 1850s and 1860s when a shift towards a more deterrent penal philosophy and regime was emerging (see Chapters 6 and 7). Committees of doctors and medical men wrangled as to the minimum that could be given to prisoners. Using a more scientific approach, they tried to balance the general poor state of inmates (complaints about diarrhoea, dysentery, scurvy, scrofula, boils and carbuncles were common) with the need for the body to endure long hours of hard labour without affecting health (Tomlinson, 1981a; *Convict Prison Dietaries*, PP, 1864). Tomlinson (1978a) concludes that the prison diet that emerged from the 1860s probably offered greater quantity than the average poor labourer but had less variety. We may also need to set that against the short sentences in local prisons which ensured that, from the 1860s onwards, the overwhelming majority of prisoners spent their time under the meanest conditions possible because they didn't qualify to move through the progressive stage system (McConville, 1995, 1998a).

Greater recognition of the problems of poverty would come at the end of the nineteenth and early in the twentieth century, when social investigators such as Charles Booth highlighted their scale and persistence. By this time, though, these problems were seen very much as ones that could be dealt with only by the greater intervention of the state, and as such we begin to see the development of a basic welfare state and welfare provision (Garland, 1985).

Crime in the rural community

Large-scale industrialisation and urbanisation in the nineteenth century has often placed the 'city' or the 'urban' at the centre of the perceived 'problem of crime' – on the one hand, a beacon of progress and development, innovation and employment but, on the other, a place of danger or fear, a place where people became criminals or victims (Emsley, 2010). Yet crime occurs in all types of environments, and the causes for concern in the market towns and rural communities were often similar: public offences that affronted the community, drunkenness, prostitution, theft, visible crimes on the street. Moreover, there were crimes that occurred in these locations that were particular to the rural or agricultural environment or activities that were less likely to be found in urban areas, sometimes referred to as 'rural' crimes. A notable example was poaching, which will be discussed further in the following section, but we can also add to the list other crimes, such as animal maiming, arson or other forms of revenge crimes – for example, threatening letters. In addition, there were widespread disturbances relating to the price of wheat in particular parts of the country in the early nineteenth century, known as food riots (Archer, 2010, 2000, 1989; Stevenson, 1989, 1992).

Arson, the sending of threatening letters and some forms of animal maiming were used as forms of personal attack or revenge. Arson could be very serious and remained a capital offence until the 1830s; destruction of property could be extensive in rural areas where fire-fighting resources were scarce and farms were isolated (Archer, 2010, 1989). Farmers or employers could be targeted particularly in trade disputes but also by disgruntled domestic servants or employees (Emsley, 2010). In the early nineteenth century arson became associated with the countryside, especially in eastern England, and in Norfolk and Suffolk there were around 2,000 recorded fires, likely to be an underestimate given that not all fires were reported in the local press. Most were cases of revenge: attacks against poor employers who treated their workers badly, farmers who dismissed workers or those who acted for the poor law. These incidents were not without public support – and in some cases explicit support, such as refusing to put fires out, assaulting firemen or cutting water hoses (Archer, 2010). Similarly, revenge, protest and feuds were motives in the crime of animal maiming. The posting on doors of heads of sheep or skins of animals, the cutting of tails off horses and cattle, or the burning or killing of a whole range of animals, from cattle and sheep to game, cats and dogs, shocked the victim and the entire community (Archer, 2010, 1989).

As Archer's fascinating research has pointed out, poaching was 'the long, bitter and persistent war of the nineteenth century' (2010: 147). The game laws in England decreed that poaching was very serious; the Night Poaching Act 1816 persisted with transportation as the punishment for those who were armed, and some argue that this only escalated the tension and bitterness between poachers and gamekeepers. But what was most important was that many people in rural communities did not believe that poaching should be a crime at all, and this caused considerable friction between landowners and the community (Archer, 2010; Mingay, 1994). As such, 'had the game laws not existed, the history of crime in rural England would have been a very different story. Poaching was the most constant and most common method employed by the poor of snubbing the tenets of the wealthier classes' (Archer, 2010: 148).

Even as they were relaxed as the nineteenth century progressed, and the common punishments for offences meted out by the petty sessions court were often fines or a short period of imprisonment in lieu, the game laws demonstrate the persistence of poaching throughout the period. In 1862, Sir Baldwin Leighton, chairman of the Quarter Sessions in Shropshire, advocated a new Bill in Parliament – the Night Poaching Prevention Act – which would allow the police to search premises merely on the suspicion of poaching. Returns of the convictions under the game laws for the year 1869 demonstrate that they were overwhelmingly for such summary offences under the 1862 Act as 'trespassing in the day-time in pursuit of game', 'night poaching', 'illegally buying or selling game' and 'destroying game'. The more serious offences dealt with on indictment were going out poaching while armed and taking game, and assaulting gamekeepers, but these were very much in the minority. Out of 10,345 convictions in England and Wales in 1869, only 83 were for indictable offences; the overwhelmingly majority of the cases – 8,894 – were for trespassing in pursuit of game (Game Laws (Convictions), PP, 1870).

While poaching could be undertaken by a highly organised group, it could also be carried out by a person in poverty needing food for the family or for sale for financial gain. Economic cycles, seasonal employment and opportunity were of course all elements which played a part in crimes such as poaching (Archer, 2010, 1999). As has been noted, those offenders found guilty in the petty sessions courts for summary offences are often difficult to trace in the historical record, but one such offender, Enoch Swift, has come to our attention because of a single serious offence (there is a detailed case history of one sentence of penal servitude). However, what we can see in the case study of Enoch's life is the significance of poaching and related offences within his criminal career. After his spell in the convict system, Enoch returned to life in South Yorkshire, but it was then his persistence in petty offending that led to his notoriety in the local courts and newspapers.

Case study: Enoch Swift (NA, PCOM 3, licence no. 93039/22606; Convict Registry Office no. 5068; local/county prison register no. 8436)

Enoch Swift was born in Lancashire in the 1830s, but during his childhood the family moved to South Yorkshire. By the 1851 census, when he was about seventeen years old, he was working as a puddler and living with his parents and two brothers in Greasbrough. It appears that his first brush with the law came in 1858 and was rooted in a family disagreement. Enoch appeared in court having been charged by his father for stealing a clock. He had been caught climbing out of the chamber window of his father's house by his father and brother. The *Sheffield and Rotherham Independent* reported that he had been living in the family home until a few months before and that this had been his second attempt to obtain the clock. Enoch claimed the clock was his property, stating that he received it as a prize in a raffle. His father claimed that, as he had paid the shilling for the winning raffle ticket, the clock was his property. The magistrates dismissed the case, stating that they had no power to decide questions of disputed rights (22 May 1858; note that the newspaper report has the names of the father and son the wrong way around).

Three years later, in 1861, Enoch appeared twice in court. In April he was charged with 'trespass in the pursuit of game' and was sentenced to a fine of £2 or two months' imprisonment. He must have been able to pay the fine, as only five weeks later he was back in court. This time he was charged with stealing boots, and the Sheffield court sentenced him to twelve months' imprisonment. By 1864 Enoch had got married to Catherine, and in the same year they were both convicted of minor offences. Enoch served a seven-day sentence in prison for being drunk and disorderly, and in the following month Catherine was charged with the theft of a veil and was sent to prison for three weeks.

In 1865 Enoch was charged with a more serious offence, one that would draw him into the convict system, providing the detailed information that enabled his life history to be compiled. At the Pontefract Sessions, Enoch and Catherine faced charges of larceny; they were both charged with stealing a game cock and five hens, and Enoch was additionally charged with stealing two sacks and a spade. Apparently, the fowls had been discovered missing and, acting on information they had received, the police had searched the Swifts' home. Two of the hens and the game cock were discovered nearby. Inside the Swifts' house the police found the sacks and spade, together with boots that matched the boot marks at the scene. Catherine was acquitted, but Enoch received a sentence of seven years' penal servitude; the court was well aware that he had offended several times in the past.

Enoch was held at Wakefield House of Correction for a couple of months until his transfer to the convict prison system (see Chapter 7). During this period the government rented a number of cells at Wakefield for use in the convict system, and so Enoch served the first part of his sentence under separate confinement at the Yorkshire gaol. His conduct was described as good; he worked at mat-making in his cell and made considerable progress at school. In January 1866 he was moved down south to Portland prison and set to labour on public works. Public works formed the longest stage of a sentence of penal servitude, and Enoch was put to work in a quarry. Throughout his time in prison his conduct was good and his education progressed, as he moved from being able only to read to being able to write as well. In October 1866 he was punished for his only offence while he was in prison – 'wrangling with another prisoner' – and lost 42 remission marks. After serving just under five and half years in the convict system, in September 1870 Enoch was released on licence. He had nineteen months of his original sentence to serve and remained subject to the licensing conditions for this period.

By the time of the 1871 census, Enoch was living with his parents and nephew in Greasbrough and was working as an iron puddler. He was described as unmarried. While this may indicate he was living apart from his wife, by the following census, in 1881, he and Catherine were living together. In the intervening years he had apparently also resumed his relationship with the criminal justice system; in November 1872 he was acquitted by the Bradford Sessions of a charge of larceny, but in May 1875 Rotherham magistrates found him guilty of trespass in the pursuit of game, and he was ordered to pay £1 fine or serve a month in prison.

Moreover, throughout the 1880s and into the early 1890s Enoch continued to break the law. Almost all of the offences with which he was charged with were game related – trespassing in the pursuit of game or assaulting a gamekeeper or police constable. He regularly received fines or, if unable to pay, served short periods in the local prison (see Chapter 6). It is not always clear from the records whether he was able to pay the fine or whether he served the prison sentence instead. He certainly went to prison again for one month in January 1886, but on the other occasions he must have paid the fines. In 1891, when he was described as an 'old offender' by the *Sheffield and Rotherham Independent*, the court noted that Enoch had been before the bench 29 times for poaching, and probably before other benches as well, and the penalties were very heavy; the chairman said that 'if the cost of the prosecution were added they would amount to such a sum as would buy a cottage, and the wages the defendant must have lost during the time he had been poaching would have furnished the cottage' (6 January 1891). However, since all of these offences were committed after the end of the licensing period, they were dealt with summarily, and Enoch was not recalled to the convict system.

Despite his long sentence of penal servitude, during which Enoch appeared to be a 'good' prisoner, this period of incarceration had little effect on his future offending. He continued to commit a large number of crimes. Nor did his marriage to Catherine have any effect on his behaviour. Contemporary criminologists have suggested that a stable relationship or marriage can contribute towards an offender's movement away from criminal behaviour (Farrall and Calverley, 2006). However, Enoch's case seems to bear out historical research suggesting that marriage did not, in the nineteenth century, have the same effect on halting crime that it may do today (Godfrey *et al.*, 2007, 2010). Enoch continued to be a repeat minor offender over the course of at least thirty years. His activities appear to have to been related to the environment and culture in which he found himself; most were offences related to game. Whether he was a poacher for need or greed, or because he viewed game as freely available, we will never know, but he maintained a cycle of offending, repeat court appearances, paying fines or serving short periods of imprisonment for a considerable portion of his life.

2

THE CRIMINAL CLASSES AND THE 'HABITUAL' OFFENDER

Identifying and recording the criminal

As we have seen in Chapter 1, the rapidly expanding towns and cities of England were viewed as sources for the production and spread of criminality. One notable feature of the industrialisation and the anonymous sprawling urban environment was thought to be crime and criminality, and contemporary commentators frequently associated criminality in urban areas with the notion of a 'criminal class'. These were not casual offenders but those who were believed to be living by crime. This chapter will discuss the idea of the 'criminal class' by drawing on the views of nineteenth-century commentators and examine the ways in which the public came to be aware of this apparent threat. It will then focus on the responses to these perceived problems through an examination of the 'habitual' offender – a term which developed around the mid-nineteenth century and became a criminal or legal category by the late 1860s. A raft of legislation and a bureaucratic system of registration and surveillance was established to control the danger posed by the 'habitual' criminal. Through such measures the government attempted to respond to the problems of recidivism and to public protection concerns regarding the release of prisoners, this included the identification and monitoring of offenders.

The 'criminal classes'

By the mid-nineteenth century, Victorian views about criminality were firmly rooted in the notion of a 'criminal class'; use of the term was at its height in the 1850s and 1860s, although it was popular throughout the period (Emsley, 2010; Beier, 2005; Bailey, 1993). The 'criminal class' was thought to be a section of the population in society who lived largely through criminal activity in the rapidly expanding cities and towns – a feature of the urban environment (Emsley, 2010; Gray, 2013). As the Recorder of Birmingham, Matthew Davenport-Hill, put it in 1839, the criminal class was 'a class of persons who pursue crime as a calling' (cited in Bailey, 1993: 236). Widely publicised writings by social investigators and commentators had influenced views about the lower classes and the poor; it was no longer the case that all of the poor and the working class were regarded simply as potentially criminal or dangerous. Instead, there was growing recognition of differences among the poor and, although not entirely new categories for the nineteenth century, the idea they could be divided into those who were 'deserving' and those who were 'undeserving' (Stedman Jones, 2013; Davis, 1980; Himmelfarb, 1984).

One leading commentator and social investigator, Henry Mayhew, had contributed to a greater understanding of the lives of the poor and working classes in published works such as *The London Labour and the London Poor* (1851). He was a co-founder of the satirical journal *Punch* and frequently wrote, and undertook research for, the *Morning Chronicle*. Mayhew and other commentators saw it as their task to document and measure the perceived problem of crime, and as such the Victorian reading public were more likely to encounter the 'criminal classes' in the pages of their newspapers and periodicals than on the city streets (McGowen, 1990). Mayhew found that, while the poor lived in squalor and poverty in overcrowded conditions in the rookeries and slums of Victorian London, they were not all criminal. Many he interviewed were destitute, uneducated and dirty but lived an honest life, working hard to make ends meet in precarious conditions. Although this brought some understanding of social conditions, his assertions also helped solidify views about the 'good' and the 'bad' poor. As Mayhew put it, 'the predatory class are the non-working class' (cited in Himmlefarb, 1984: 381) – 'those who would not work'. Some of his descriptions illuminate the key elements associated with the idea of a 'criminal class':

> Shortly after[,] I came up to London, and became acquainted with a gang of young thieves in Ratcliffe Highway. I lived in a coffee-house there for about eighteen months. The boys gained their livelihood picking gentlemen's pockets, at which I soon became expert. After this I joined a gang of men, and picked ladies' pockets, and resided for some time at Whitechapel.
>
> (Mayhew, [1865] 1985: 498)

As this description notes, it was often asserted that certain districts and communities were rife with crime and immorality, that people were trained into crime by their associates, gaining expertise and experience, and progressing from petty crimes such as handkerchief stealing to larger more financially lucrative thefts. They were seen as embedded in a network and associations of what would later be called a 'criminal underworld' (Shore, 2010). A typical view of the period is presented by a correspondent from *The Times*, who stated that criminals were numerous in London but abundant in the alleys of the Borough:

> Here are to be found, not only the lowest description of infamous houses, but the very nests and nurseries of crime. The great mass of the class here

is simply incorrigible ... They have been suckled, cradled, and hardened in scenes of guilt, intemperance and profligacy. Here are to be found the lowest of the low class of beershops in London, and probably in the world, the acknowledged haunts of "smashers", burglars, thieves and forgers ... There are people who have been convicted over and over again, but there are also hundreds of known ruffians who are as yet unconvicted, and who, by marvellous good luck, as well as by subtle cunning, have managed up to the present time to elude detection. It is the greatest error to suppose that all or even a majority of the criminal classes are continually passing through the hands of justice.

(Cited in Greenwood, 1869: 175–6)

Accepting the contemporary commentators' views, the historian J. J. Tobias noted that 'entry into the criminal classes was a means of finding support; it was entry into an association, informal but none the less real, members of which could be found almost everywhere' (1967: 108). These observations fostered the idea of a network of criminal associations, 'flash-houses' circulating stolen goods, and an urban environment which both facilitated crime, through increased opportunities, and protected the criminal, hiding offenders and their associates in the anonymous, densely populated districts. Such ideas about criminality were reproduced in fictional examples of criminality of the time, in the Newgate novels and most obviously in the work of Charles Dickens – for example, in Fagin's gang in *Oliver Twist* (Shore, 2010; Himmelfarb, 1984).

Within the supposed criminal classes, Mayhew constructed five main headings of criminals and subdivided them into over a hundred different categories, from burglars, sneaks and common thieves to mudlarks, embezzlers, sharpers, beggars and cheats. This classification or categorisation also helped to distinguish between those who had committed crime as a result of some unfortunate circumstance and those who lived a life of crime – a key element in recognising a member of the criminal class. Though we ought to be cautious about taking Mayhew's sketches at face value (Smith, 1979; Himmelfarb, 1984; Beier, 2005; see also Thompson and Yeo, 1971), his collection of knowledge was seen by many as a way to document and understand criminals and their activities with a view to dealing with the problem. As Holland, writing in the *Cornhill Magazine*, commented in 1862:

In the vast aggregate of criminals there are many who are only occasional and temporary offenders. These are obviously neither the most difficult, the most injurious, nor the most costly section of the criminal class: that distinction is enjoyed by habitual, or professional, thieves. How numerous the class of professional thieves is, it would be impossible to say. They count by many thousands. Scattered throughout the country, they form a net-work of veins by which all criminal knowledge circulates. In prison and out of it ... they develop and increase criminal tendencies, and spread criminal knowledge.

(Holland, 1862: 640)

Similarly, the prison chaplain Reverend William D. Morrison, writing at the end of the nineteenth century, said:

> There is a population of habitual criminals that forms a class by itself. Habitual criminals are not to be confounded with the working or any other class; they are a set of persons who make crime the object and business of their lives; to commit crime is their trade; they deliberately scoff at honest ways of earning a living, and must accordingly be looked upon as a class of a separate and distinct character from the rest of the community.
>
> (1891: 141–2)

Harriet Martineau argued that these descriptions of 'Life in the Criminal Classes' 'at last supplied us with the material needed to qualify us so to understand the conditions of a life altogether unlike our own, as to enable us to perceive what sort of minds we have to deal with in our attempts to guard society from the evils of lawlessness' (1865: 337). The criminal classes formed a distinct group written about and perceived as a group apart – the 'other'. Whether they did indeed exist as a 'distinct' class has been a point of debate. Tobias, writing in 1967 and commenting on the above quotation from Morrison, stated that the concept of the 'criminal class' had developed gradually from 1815 and charts the growing use of the term to distinguish between those with the habit of criminality as separate and distinct from the orderly and honest poor. He argues that, from the 1830s for many commentators, the idea that criminals formed a separate section of the community was general and axiomatic. Thus the 'Victorian "underworld" is vicariously lived through the writings of the middle-class social investigators who recorded the lives of criminals and dangerous classes, through the gaslit lens of Whitechapel, circa 1888' (Shore, 2010: 120; for the later nineteenth century, see Walkowitz, 1992; Gray, 2013).

Tobias and other historians, such as McGowen, note that the descriptions of the activities and the views on the existence of a criminal class were to some extent self-fulfilling. Tobias, though, regards the concept 'as an acceptable explanation of the phenomena of the time ... couched almost entirely in terms of such a class, and must be discussed in those terms' (1967: 70), thus appearing to be rather more accepting of the existence of a criminal 'class'. McGowen (1990) approaches the question in a slightly different way, arguing that the Victorians believed in the existence of a criminal class and that their representation in newspapers and periodicals contributed to the construction of this reality. These works then played an important role in how the problem of crime was conceived. The growing collection of criminal statistics, the passing of the Metropolitan Police Act 1829, and the activities of various philanthropists and reformers in the criminal justice system from the early nineteenth century all drew attention to the 'crime problem', making it more visible and contributing to the need to examine and categorise it. As Coleman and McCahill observe, 'these early developments in synoptic surveillance carved out "knowledge" of the "crime problem" and limited this to the lower orders. In enabling the many (law-abiding, responsible citizens) to see the few (criminals), contradictory attributes ensued over what was seen and how what was seen was understood' (2011: 44). Indeed, Philips (2003) argues that the 'moral entrepreneurs' contributed to, exaggerated and utilised this image of criminality to serve their own purpose in campaigning for police reform (see Chapter 3).

What the views of contemporary commentators reveal, McGowen (1990) argues, is not the reality of the criminal class, let alone proof that such a class existed, but the manner in which the Victorians came to believe that it was real. These were not mere representations but contributed to the construction of this social reality. More specifically, the 'fears' of the propertied classes were located and identified in the criminal or dangerous classes, not just in England but in other European countries, particularly France (Foucault, 1991; Lee, 2007), though there is some debate as to the differences between the perceived politically charged motivations of the working classes and the fears of political uprisings in these different national contexts (Bailey, 1993). As Emsley argues, though, the 'notion of a criminal class was, indeed remains, a convenient one for insisting that most crime is something committed on law-abiding citizens by an alien group. The more historians probe the reality of such a class, the more it is revealed to be spurious' (2010: 183). In understanding the experience of the criminal justice system, it is important to note that, 'even if the criminal class was a constructed reality, it was one that was very real in its consequences for those at the sharp end of prosecution and punishment' (Beier, 2005: 501–2). The construction of the problem of crime and the perceived perpetrators of offences would also come to prominence during the 1850s and 1860s on account of a widespread panic about violent street crime.

Garrotting, the media and the ticket of leave men

The widespread readership of journalistic accounts, such as Mayhew's, contributed to a broader knowledge of the lower sections of society and provided a window into their daily lives. But the media also contributed to another aspect which focused public attention and fear on the 'criminal classes', the violent offender and public safety, and this was the 'garrotting panic'.

On 17 July 1862, the Member of Parliament for Blackburn, Hugh Pilkington, left the House of Commons and made his way along Pall Mall towards the Reform Club. While walking along this main thoroughfare he was assaulted by two men, who struck him on the head, choked him and stole his watch (Davis, 1980; Sindall, 1987, 1990). This assault was described by the press at the time as a 'garrotte' attack, and during the 1850s and 1860s the crime of 'garrotting' and fears about violent street crime were to dominate discussions of criminality. As Davis points out, the newspaper reaction to this event was 'immediate and intense … [and] the sense of alarm over the safety of the metropolis expressed in the press throughout July and the following months was shared by much of London and indeed, England' (1980: 90). This was perhaps the second wave of panic over violent street crime in mid-nineteenth-century England.

Concern about violent street crime had begun a few years earlier, in the winter of 1856. A *Times* editorial that November encapsulated the prevailing view that Londoners were unable to walk the streets safely day or night. Even in areas 'inhabited by a numerous and respectable population', men could not walk 'without imminent danger of being throttled, robbed, and if not actually murdered, at least kicked and pommelled within an inch of his life' (10 November 1856, cited in Sindall, 1987: 351). In both 1856 and 1862, the street violence in question was 'garrotting' or garrotte robberies. Garrotting was described as an assault which involved the crushing of the throat, leaving the 'victim on the ground writhing in agony, with tongue protruding and eyes starting from their sockets, unable to give the alarm or to attempt a pursuit' (*Annual Register* 1862, cited ibid.: 352). Commentators such as Holland, writing on 'The Science of Garotting and Housebreaking' with evidence from the 'lips of the criminals themselves', claimed that garrotting was

> a scientific operation, abundantly cruel, but not absolutely murderous; the *intention* was neither to kill nor to maim. The audacity of the system, its novelty, and the difficulty of guarding against it, terrified the public; and this terror gave the very best testimony that could be borne to the merits of a practice already too inviting a crime.
>
> (1863: 79)

He claimed the method was first learnt on convict ships, where it was used by prison guards to put down disruptive prisoners, easily quelling their behaviour, with little injury. As such, convicts

> practise on each other frequently before they venture into the streets – not only to acquire the art of garrotting in every possible position and attitude, but that they may learn how long and with what degree of force they may hug their victim's throat without endangering his life or seriously injuring him.
>
> (Ibid.: 80)

This description of the act as 'putting a hug on' was taken up by various newspapers, including *Punch* magazine (Pearson, 1983; Alker, 2014).

As Sindall (1987) outlines, during 1856 increasing numbers of reports and commentaries about garrotting appeared in the press – 38 pieces were published in *The Times* alone – and by the November of that year two men convicted of a garrotte attack had been transported for life. The perceived perpetrators of this violence were 'ticket of leave' men; these were convicted men who had served a proportion of a sentence of penal servitude (long-term imprisonment began to replace transportation from 1853 onwards; see Chapter 5) and who had been released on licence (an early form of parole) or what was then called a 'ticket of leave'. The 'ticket of leave' system had been used in Australia as a form of early release and to encourage employment, family life and the foundations for an honest living. After transportation had largely come to an end in the 1850s, the ticket of leave or licence period was incorporated into the sentence of penal servitude for continued use in England (see Chapter 7).

After the newspaper reports in 1856 declined, the panic waned, though the lack of severity in the penal system was seen as a root cause. This was to have consequences in subsequent years which will be discussed later. However, the differing element of the garrotting panic of 1862 was the assault on a high-profile person (Sindall, 1987). In both periods attention was drawn to the geography of the violence. While this kind of crime might occur in the poor or working-class districts, the threat had come ever closer: the criminals 'no longer confine their operations to the by-lanes but attack us in the most frequented thoroughfares of the metropolis' (*The Times*, 23 December 1856, cited ibid.: 353). More broadly, the expansion of newspapers in the mid-nineteenth century is also worthy of note; Archer and Jones argue that newspapers from this time have been significant in 'creating the public's awareness and perception of violent crime' (2003: 17). They note that it was not just an ever-widening readership but the language, tone and layout of news about violent crime 'in which sensation and fact intertwined to generate and arouse interest, fear and concern in equal measure' (ibid.).

Reflecting on both periods of street violence, in the mid-1850s and in 1862, Holland stated:

> A few years ago the garotte broke out suddenly, like a new plague, infested the streets with danger, infected the community with half-shameful apprehensions, and disappeared without leaving a hint to settle our bewilderment. Winter after winter passed, and the garotter came not again ... The long summer nights had scarcely ended ... when we were surprised by the most inclement ruffianism that ever disgraced a nineteenth century. Once more the streets of London are unsafe, by day or night. The epidemic has come upon us again, and we are just as helpless as before ... and the public dread has almost become a panic.
>
> (1863: 79)

The garrotters were seen as something 'other' than respectable society and were frequently described as 'hot blooded' and 'un-English', entirely foreign to the national character, or, drawing on a connection with a supposed notorious sect who attacked multitudes of travellers in India, as 'Thuggees' (Emsley, 2005). As *The Times* expressed it:

'When the outrages first commenced, it was doubted whether the crime was not of foreign importation ... but the ruffians who have been arrested are of pure English breed', and, later, 'Our streets are actually not as safe as they were in the days of our grandfathers. We have slipped back into a state of affairs which would be intolerable in Naples' (7 November 1862, cited in Pearson, 1983: 130).

As Davis (1980) points out, previous historians have described the 'garrotting panic' as an understandable if exaggerated reaction to a spate of violent street robberies; however, her point of departure from these views is that the increase in street robberies came only after the panic had already begun. Her analysis of the recording of such incidents shows that, in 1862, there were 97 robberies with violence in the

Metropolitan Police returns, with only 33 in 1861 and 32 in 1860, but, importantly, between January and June only 15 incidents were recorded (a similar number to those in 1861 and 1860). Therefore the sharp increase in the recorded number of robberies with violence actually took place after the garrotting of Hugh Pilkington. Davis therefore argues that this event is more significant than previously thought and meets the conditions of what has been called a 'moral panic' (Cohen, 1972; Young, 1971). Understanding violent street crime in this way, as an event orchestrated by the media, demonstrates the manner in which this problem was amplified and used to promote new measures of control. Davis (1980) maintains that the 'garrotting panic' and the subsequent changes in penal policy which established more deterrent prison regimes and more punitive treatment of criminals can only be understood through the use of Cohen's model. The panic over garrotting has been described as the first 'moral panic' (Sindall, 1987, 1990) but other authors, taking a longer view, have noted the importance of examining the continuities in moral panics about violent street crime from the mid-eighteenth to the late twentieth century (King, 1987, 2003).

In addition, Davis (1980) maintains that the moral panic over garrotting contributed to the 'creation' of the criminal class. For Davis, it fuelled the belief in the 'criminal class' and coincided with other distinctions about the working classes, such as deserving and undeserving, respectable and disreputable, and skilled and unskilled, demonstrating the way in which this 'outcast' group were defined by policy-makers and officials. Bartrip (1981) agrees that public opinion influenced the views of criminals and the subsequent legislation, but instead argues that it was the end of transportation to Australia that was of much greater concern to the Victorian middle classes (also see Smith, 1982). The growing opposition to transportation in Australia from the 1840s forced a discussion about what to do with offenders and, most importantly for public opinion, what was going to happen when they were discharged from prison in Britain. For Bartrip, though, the end of transportation was a

> far more important shock to respectable Victorian society ... the feature ... which most affected the public was the ticket-of-leave system, for it brought the public into contact not simply with discharged criminals, but with serious offenders of the type that were widely thought to have been hitherto shipped overseas, who had not served out the full sentences passed on them by the courts.
>
> (1981: 175)

'When that "wastepipe to the antipodes" was almost completely closed in 1857, it was as if the country had suddenly been invaded by "thousands tainted, stigmatised, corrupted by crime, its slovenly habits and horrid associations"' (*The Times*, 1856, cited in Radzinowicz and Hood, 1980: 1310).

Sindall (1987) argues that, while the moral panic about garrotting led both to fear and anxiety among the middle classes and to hasty legislation, the police showed little sign of alarm. He also shows that the garrotting panic had a metropolitan bias.

Taking the statistics at face value, robbery and attempts to rob were higher elsewhere than in London; while he observes that this was possibly on account of differing police definitions, there were more cases in Lancashire, particularly in Manchester and Liverpool.

Recent contributions by Archer (2011) and Alker (2014) have examined the ways in which violence and street violence was received in Liverpool. Both of these authors argue that the definition of garrotting and of violent street crime were crucial in the response to such violence. Archer argues that violent street robberies were 'neither particularly newsworthy nor especially threatening to the middle class readership' (2011: 111) of the Liverpool press. Brutal street violence often occurred in poor areas of the city or at the docks, where the victims were other poor people or recently paid sailors. Neither of these elements meant that the situation was important enough to warrant concern among the local middle class, who were unlikely to venture into these areas. The garrotting panic of 1862 is discussed in the Liverpool press, but primarily as a threat in the London area, and local robberies with violence were not defined as 'garrottings' (Alker, 2014; Archer, 2011). In Liverpool, the cornermen and roughs, who banded together on the streets with apparently little fear of the police, especially in the north end of the city, drew fear and concern. The vicious attack and murder of a man in the presence of a large crowd of people on Tithebarn Street in 1874 attracted national attention and 'gave Liverpool a reputation for being a violent town, inhabited by people who, if not brutalised themselves, were fearful of bearing witness against these brutal men' (Archer, 2011: 114).

Importantly, the garrotting panics would also contribute to the nature of penal policy in the second half of the nineteenth century. The panics were media fuelled, views on the 'criminal classes' were already cemented, and the public anxiety about the decline of transportation to Australia was also a significant factor. Whether any one event takes precedence is less important, perhaps; they were all influencing factors. However, the consequences of these events are clear, particularly on the operation of the penal system and disciplinary regimes. The immediate effect of the panics was the passing of the Security Against Violence Act 1863 (known as the Garrotters Act), which allowed for robbery with violence to be punished with flogging. In terms of the reach and depth of such powers, perhaps more important were two subsequent areas of legislation – the first relating to prisons and the second to the registration and monitoring of released prisoners and habitual offenders. Prison legislation will be discussed more fully in Chapters 6 and 7, but suffice to say that the Penal Servitude Act 1864 and the Prisons Act 1865 were both aimed at increasing deterrence in the system through long-term and mandatory minimum sentencing for repeat offenders, monitoring and surveillance by the police, and harsh prison regimes based on isolation, hard labour, minimal diet and sparse conditions. But the failure of the reformatory project inside prisons and the debates on the separate system should also not be overlooked as an influential factor in the shift towards greater deterrence (Henriques, 1972; Johnston, 2006).

Monitoring the 'habitual criminal'

By the 1860s the belief in the idea of a criminal class and concerns about the repeat offender or recidivist generated criminal justice policy that was directed at the 'habitual criminal'; the 'dangerous' offenders and the threat they posed were seen as significant, and such individuals needed to be identified, recorded and monitored by the police (Pratt, 1997; 2002; Radzinowicz and Hood, 1979, 1980). Legislation came in the form of the Habitual Criminals Act 1869 and the Prevention of Crimes Act 1871, known collectively known as the Habitual Criminals Acts. The 1869 Act sought to reduce crime through the monitoring and supervision of two types of serious and repeat offenders. The first were convicts released on licence from prison (see Chapter 7) and the second were those who had multiple convictions for felony but had not served a sentence of penal servitude. The latter were defined as 'habitual criminals' and subject to seven years' supervision by the police. The rationale behind this legislation was to focus on repeat offenders – to register and monitor those who had committed previous crimes. Before we turn to the operation of the Acts, it is important to note that perhaps the legislation's 'greatest contribution ... was to create and sustain a huge bureaucracy' (Godfrey *et al.*, 2010: 217), much of which can be used by criminologists and historians today (see, for example, Godfrey *et al.*, 2010; Johnston and Godfrey, 2013a; Cox *et al.*, 2014).

The terms of the Habitual Criminals Act were quite far reaching and were open to interpretation; those offenders discovered by the police and thought to be 'obtaining a livelihood by dishonest means', 'about to commit or aid in committing a crime', 'waiting for the opportunity to commit or aid in committing a crime', or being unable to account for their presence could find themselves guilty of an offence and subject to a maximum of one year's imprisonment, with or without hard labour. If taken in by the police on such accusations, the onus was also on the suspect to satisfy the court with their explanation of the circumstances. Those offenders who were thrice convicted were also subject to this legislation and could be sent to prison for a maximum of one year if they were found to be in 'suspicious circumstances'. This Act broadened the definition of rogues and vagabonds under the Vagrancy Act 1824 and extended the penalty for harbouring thieves. These definitions were further expanded by the Prevention of Crimes Act 1871 and subsequent legislation regarding the photographing of criminals.

In practice, the translation of this legislation into the surveillance, monitoring and identification of offenders was less straightforward. From this period onwards, the overriding problem that would beset legislation on habitual offending and ideas about preventive, incapacitating or indeterminate sentencing was the definition of the 'habitual criminal'; just what exactly did this mean? The petty recidivist serving multiple short sentences? The reoffending convict released from prison? (Radzinowicz and Hood, 1980). Stevenson (1986) has argued that the limited numbers of habitual criminals and variations in the labelling process across the country precludes the identification of a 'class' of offenders but also highlights the differing interpretations of the magistracy and the police in the implementation of the legislation.

The supervision of those identified as habitual offenders and the monitoring of those released on licence from penal servitude also posed significant issues for policing. The provisions of the legislation were wide and probably beyond the capacity and willingness of the police to enforce (Radzinowicz and Hood, 1980). The deficiencies of the provisions and instructions to the police aside, there were potentially huge numbers of people who could be subject to this legislation – over 2,080 in the first eighteen months and over 3,500 per year under seven years' supervision. It was eventually estimated that there would be more than 25,000 under police surveillance at any one time (ibid.). The Prevention of Crimes Act 1871 altered three main provisions. The burden of proof was changed to whether the court had reasonable grounds for believing in the innocence of the accused rather than whether the latter could prove it; released convicts were to report changes of address within 48 hours and to present themselves to the police each month; and whether or not habitual criminals were the subject of seven years' police supervision was to be at the discretion of the court (ibid.).

If we take the statistics at face value, then the number of 'known thieves and depredators' and the number of 'houses of bad character' did decline, and the gap between the criminal classes at large and those in prison was narrowing (Godfrey et al., 2010). The subsequent reduction in numbers committed for trial and the number of crimes reported to the police was also taken as evidence of the success of this legislation, yet 'all the evidence suggests that the attempt to convert the police into an effective agency of supervision failed from the very beginning' (Radzinowicz and Hood, 1980: 1345). Technically offenders were supposed to report to the chief officer of the police, though in practice this was not enforced. The Kimberley Commission changed the regulations in 1879 so offenders presented themselves to a constable or officer at a police station. The police were also widely accused of harassment; they would inform employers of an offender's ex-convict status, thus depriving them of a means to earn an honest living through gainful employment (see Chapter 3). Overall the Acts were stigmatising and had the potential to reproduce the very problem they were trying to control – repeat offending – and, as the whole system became increasingly unwieldy to manage, they began to fall into disuse (Godfrey et al., 2010). Petrow argues that the powers of the police were enhanced by the campaigning of moral reformers and the immediate threat of moral panics, but the authorities were not merely their instrument. Law enforcement responses were limited and favoured the practical policies of regulation; police 'policy was to remove the temptations to commit immoral behaviour by harassing the purveyors of immorality and by limiting their opportunities' (1994: 296). Thus, in bureaucratic terms, if these powers proved

> to be ineffective in practice, the Metropolitan Police and the Home Office sought more powers and gradually refined and supplemented the regulatory machinery … This shrewd use of discretion underlined state power: it rewarded those who conformed and stigmatised and marginalised those who did not. Once marginalised, recalcitrants were more easily controlled.
>
> (Ibid.)

Registering and identifying the habitual offender

The 'potential for the new juridical photographic realism was widely recognised in the 1840s' (Sekula, 1993: 344) though not widely used. From then, on across Europe, photography began to be used to document and identify; 'the "infallible" photographic camera seemed to solve the practical problems of recognising and recording delinquents' (Jager, 2001: 27), but practices varied within and across the various systems. Most early photography was employed by prisons rather than the police – often by governors with a keen interest in the new medium, such as at Bristol or at Carmarthen (see Ireland, 2002, 2007). After the establishment of the convict system, and certainly from the 1864 Penal Servitude Act onwards, the overwhelming majority of individual penal records (detailed case files of convicted prisoners) contain photographs. As Jager (2001) postulates, these images tend to be for identifying and recording the offender, gaining knowledge about the supposed 'criminal class' and those deemed a threat to society, rather than for use in the detection of individuals. Indeed, the photographs in the files of the National Archives (PCOM 3 and 4) were used as a means of identifying those who had been in prison before and those, released on licence or 'ticket of leave', who had breached their conditions. An accurate likeness to catch absconders and recidivists was the goal of prison authorities, and full-face shots were accompanied later by profiles and the subject's hands (Hamilton and Hargreaves, 2001), as missing digits and tattoos also proved a useful source of identification and were frequently used in court. These methods were employed after the arrest of a suspect, and were not therefore related to detecting offenders; this aspect of photography came in the latter decades of the century (Jager, 2001).

The police use of photography in England came most obviously in the legislation related to habitual offenders in the late 1860s and 1870s discussed above. Dealing with a mobile and large population was the main problem with regard to identification of criminals; legislation which required the accurate identification of a suspect's age or their number of previous convictions, for example, made this aspect of policing all the more important from the mid-century onwards. These problems were acute for the Metropolitan Police though difficult in all large urban areas (Stanford, 2009). Accurate knowledge about the criminal history of the offender was important both in sentencing and in classification in the prison, and the philosophies of punishment that lay behind the legislation rested on the reliability of this information. Jager (2001) argues that another intended effect was to encourage the offender to tell the truth about their criminal activities and to deter them in the future through the knowledge that the 'truth' of the photograph would identify them. This seems a strong possibility given the accuracy of the information contained in a proportion of the penal records in National Archives PCOM 3 and 4. There is a good degree of accuracy and completeness in the histories, multiple aliases and numerous court appearances across the country (Johnston and Godfrey, 2013a). This leads to the conclusion that some prisoners, once inside the convict system, may have 'told all' about their past, perhaps fearing that the authorities already knew all there was to know. A minority vigorously denied some crimes attributed to them, but in the main offences were admitted; some prisoners clearly thought that 'the system' knew far more about them than the mechanisms of the time could possibly have allowed (e.g., the large number of petty convictions from courts up and down the country so accurately recorded). But, once in the bureaucratic convict system and documented, an individual's penal record followed him or her through any subsequent sentences and made their previous criminal histories more difficult to deny.

The police also used photography but, in the early years, largely as a memory aid rather than as a means of detection or surveillance (Jager, 2001). The police relied for the identification of the criminal classes on other professionals, particularly prison officers, who were regularly called to court to identify the repeat offender. This exercise was largely about clarifying a person's identity. Records such as those in PCOM 3 and 4 demonstrate the range of 'aliases' that criminals used to try to evade the system, and these posed significant difficulties for the authorities (see Ireland, 2002). Nevertheless, examination of offenders' names and aliases also shows that often the records include names which document marriage or cohabitation, remarriage of a mother and the adoption of different surname, some of which may not have been related to any intention to deceive implied by the word 'alias'.

As it turned out, it would be the Metropolitan Police which would administer the photographic register after the Habitual Criminals Acts in 1869 and 1871 and not the prison system. The Habitual Criminal Office maintained in London required that all prisons send information on offenders to them. How effective this was in the monitoring of offenders and recidivists is much more difficult to ascertain. From the beginning of the system in 1870 to the summer of 1873, over 42,000 photographs were sent to the office. It was also noted that, between November 1871 and December 1872, more than 30,463 photographs had accumulated from prison governors, and this had resulted in the detection of 373 cases (*Photographs of Criminals*, PP, 1873), a paltry number for the volume of activity. It was probably impossible for the police to supervise the sheer volume of people, and the deficiencies in the system were immediately obvious. Subsequently, the register's reach was reduced. The Prevention of Crimes Act 1871 stated the conditions in which prisoners should be photographed; it was not to be used for all offenders. By 1877 there were further reductions, as the scheme was scaled down after it had become large and cumbersome (Petrow, 1994). In 1879, following the Kimberley Commission, the Convict Supervision Office was established, and plain-clothes officers were employed to work with discharged prisoners' aid societies. By 1888 there were over 37,000 licence holders or supervisees registered with the office (Annual Reports of the Commissioner of Police of the Metropolis, cited in Stanford, 2009: 61).

Photograph collections were unorganised (except by crime) and vast, so not useful aids to the police in any meaningful sense. Alphonse Bertillon created an alternative system to identify criminals which employed measurements of the adult body and offered both a means to identify people and a way to organise the thousands of photographs that had been collected. Bertillon took profile as well as full-face portraits and supplemented these with anthropometric data and, later, fingerprints (Jager, 2001). In Britain, the Home Office stopped the use of Bertillon system in 1902 and adopted fingerprinting instead; photographs were still used by the police and prisons locally but were not sent to central administration.

The residuum and the 'born' criminal

Some of the discussion from the mid-nineteenth century relating to the criminal class would also underpin later explanations on the notion of the 'born' criminal. Physical descriptions of the features of offenders, together with the association between generations of families committing crimes and the interest in the ideas of Charles Darwin, led some to believe that criminals were born rather than produced by the environment. In many of Mayhew's descriptions we can observe what would later be recognised as 'criminal traits' identified by the positivist school of criminology. Theorists across Europe developed the notion of the 'criminal man' as someone who was predisposed to crime from birth and who could be recognised by his physiognomy ('ape-like' features, shape of skull, sloping forehead, size of nose, etc.). Lombroso, Ferrero, Garofolo and others came to dominate the latter decades of the century with discussions of the degenerative criminal man and woman and biological explanations for their criminal behaviour. Identification photography is therefore also associated with these then prevailing ideas about race, degeneration and the hereditary nature of criminality. Though there were numerous commentators on the 'faces of the degeneration' (Pick, 1996; see also Wiener, 1994) across Europe and the United States (see Rafter, 1997), evidence as to how much this system actually influenced the penal system in England is sketchier. Many of the prison records do not suggest anything was done with the measurements of individual criminals beyond recording them, and this was perhaps more a reflection of the views of positivist criminology at the time (cf. Lombroso, 1876; Lombroso and Ferrero, 1895) than the realities of the operation of the English penal system. Indeed, Francis Galton, a leading eugenicist, biologist and cousin of Darwin, obtained photographs of criminals from Edmund Du Cane in 1877 in order to devise a new physiognomic record of common criminal features and to create a photographic mean and an image of a 'type'. But instead his results showed that 'the special villainous irregularities ... have disappeared, and the common humanity that underlies them has prevailed. They represent, not the criminal, but the man who is liable to fall into crime' (cited in Hamilton and Hargreaves, 2001: 97). This is precisely what they were – a collection of images of those who found themselves in the penal system. We will now turn to the case study of Annie Greenfield, who was just one of the types of offender at whom the raft of legislation in the latter decades of the nineteenth century was aimed – a persistent petty criminal who later found herself in the convict system and under the monitoring of the licence system.

Case study: Annie Greenfield (NA, PCOM 3, licence no. A38905/7205; A38905/7497; Convict Registry Office no. H.103; local/county prison register no. 3811)

Annie Greenfield, or Doyle, was born in County Dublin but lived in Liverpool. She was 5 feet 5 1/2 inches tall, had brown hair and grey eyes, and when committed into the convict system was married and had had one child, who had died. At the age of 32 Annie already had 48 summary convictions for petty offences; no doubt she had either paid the fines or served short periods in Walton prison as punishment meted out by the lower courts. But in 1881 she was convicted of stealing a purse and money on St Patrick's Day, sentenced to three months' imprisonment and removed to Walton prison. Unfortunately, by September she was back in court, this time on a charge of larceny from the person. Since she had a previous conviction for a felony, the court sentenced her to five years' penal servitude. Annie, described as having no occupation, pleaded guilty to stealing the money, 14 shillings, from a sailor, Thomas Griffiths.

Annie was sent from Liverpool prison down to Millbank convict prison, which she entered on 29 September. Her health was generally good with the exception of the syphilis she had suffered, which had left her with scars across her body. She had been vaccinated against smallpox and was of sound mind, but her lungs were described by the medical officer as weak. On reception at Millbank she was allowed to inform someone of her location, and she wrote to a Mrs Regan, of 9 Mansfield Court, Liverpool. This letter was subsequently suppressed by the authorities, as information from the Liverpool police stated that Mrs Regan was a 'low drunken woman and associate of thieves'. Annie was offered another form to send out but declined to do so. She was removed to the infirmary for treatment for syphilis and spent about six weeks there.

After about six months at Millbank, in March 1882 Annie was moved to Woking prison. The medical officer's report was that the syphilis had been treated but that she had been suffering from haemoptysis (coughing blood). She wrote a letter to Mrs Graham in Ben Johnson Street, Scotland Road, Liverpool, and found herself in trouble after breaking the pan lid in her cell; she was ordered to pay the value. A few months later Annie was admonished by the matron for violently shutting her cell door in a temper. She also hurt her hand on the pump while at work, though the medical officer described the injury as trivial. With apparently no reply from Mrs Graham, Annie wrote to another woman in Ben Johnson Street, a Mrs Rotch or Roach. This letter was also suppressed, as Ellen Rotch or Roach was described by the Liverpool police as keeping a 'brothel and thieves lodging house at 23 Ben Johnson St which is a very bad street'. The Scotland Road area of the city had a notorious reputation (Archer, 2011; Alker, 2014).

On 14 November 1882 Annie received three days' close confinement and 96 additional marks in third class (see Chapter 8) as punishment for going into Sarah Parker's cell and quarrelling and fighting with her. Three months later she was in trouble again, for making a noise during silent time, and received another day in close confinement as punishment. She also returned to the infirmary for treatment for syphilis. By September 1883 she had been charged with her fifth prison offence; this time she was removed from her place in the workroom after being in a bad temper, shouting, refusing to do her work and demanding to go back to her cell. Annie committed no more known offences inside Woking prison but spent the next eighteen months or so in the infirmary suffering from bronchitis and asthma. In April 1885 she was released from Woking (via Millbank) on a licence to be at large. She was discharged to the Royal Discharged Prisoners Aid Society, Charing Cross, and it is likely that they assisted her with her passage back to Liverpool. Annie had one year and five months of her five-year sentence still to serve and remained on licence for this period.

Given the small glimpses we have into Annie's life – numerous petty offences for drunkenness, disorderliness and theft; living in a poor and 'notorious' area of Liverpool; her association with brothel keepers and thieves; her lack of occupation – it is not surprising to learn that she broke the conditions of her licence. Perhaps because of her precarious social circumstances, she was again arrested for being drunk, behaving in an indecent manner and being a common prostitute. For this she was sentenced to seven days' imprisonment, as she was unable to pay the fine, and her licence was revoked. She was returned to Woking (via Strangeways) from Liverpool prison to finish the remaining part of her original five-year sentence. Immediately, she wrote to the Home Office about the revocation of the licence, but the response was that there were no grounds for her petition. Again, Annie suffered with her asthma while in prison, spending long periods in the infirmary. Five months later she was permitted to petition again and wrote to plead for the remission of the remainder of her sentence. She stated that she was returned to prison for being drunk and she did not have the 10 shillings to pay the fine. The medical officer reported to the Home Office that she was currently in hospital and had been under treatment for a long period. He noted that she had been in the infirmary frequently in the past six months as well as during her previous time in the prison, between 1881 and 1883, when she suffered from different forms of syphilis. Since 1883 she had also suffered from periodical attacks of asthma, some of which were very severe and endangered her life. The medical officer thought that her health would be better during the summer months but that she was unlikely ever to recover from the asthma. He did not, however, consider that her health was injured by her imprisonment; her petition was declined again as there were 'no grounds'.

Five months later, in July 1886, Annie was permitted to petition the Secretary of State again for the remission of the reminder of her sentence. On 17 August , noted as 'incapable' (due to her poor health), she was released on a special licence to be at large and headed back to Liverpool. In the end she was released only one month early, and, perhaps unsurprisingly, her movements after her return to Liverpool cannot be traced. Her interactions with the penal system and the system of licencing give an important insight into both the monitoring of offenders who were released under this mechanism and the bureaucratic arm of the criminal justice system that grew up across this period. Annie came from a poverty-stricken area of Liverpool that had a reputation for crime and criminality. While she was a frequent petty offender, a more serious crime drew her into the convict system; even though she was released early on licence, she was undone by drunkenness and her licence was revoked. Annie offended both outside and inside prison and from the evidence presented may well have continued to live a precarious lifestyle after records of her cease. Many convicts reoffended at some point during the rest of their lives, although only a much smaller proportion actually had their licences revoked for further offences or for breaches of monitoring rules and regulations (Johnston and Godfrey, 2013a).

3

POLICING ENGLAND, 1815–1880

This chapter will examine the changes in policing across the period 1815 to 1880, an important period in the development of the modern police force. By the end of the eighteenth century there had already been increased criticism of the old methods of policing, namely, the watchmen and the parish constables, as ineffective means of preventing crime (Emsley, 2010). By the early decades of the nineteenth century, legislative changes and frameworks for a 'new' police gradually began to be implemented. This chapter will briefly examine policing in the early nineteenth century before turned to the implementation of the Metropolitan Police Act 1829 and the subsequent legislation leading up to the County and Borough Police Act 1856.

Throughout the chapter, we will consider the implementation of the police and the degree to which the 'new' police were accepted by the communities in which they were active. It will draw together the changes in policing practice that occurred and summarise the debates about how these have been interpreted. The discussion will cover everyday policing and those who were the focus of police attention – those subject to police scrutiny or viewed as 'police property' (Reiner, 1992). This will be followed by a detailed case study of provincial policing which will examine the coming of the new police in nineteenth-century Shropshire; focusing on the early years of the force, it will provide insight into one of the first counties to move on these initiatives as well as how the magistrates there perceived the problem of crime and how to respond to it. Shropshire had long discussions about county policing and, 'in this sense, its magistrates appear to be the true authors of the County Police Acts 1839–40' (Philips and Storch, 1999: 106).

The development of policing across the nineteenth century can be viewed in two phases: the initial period, from the late eighteenth century to around the 1850s, sees the transition from what has been termed the 'old' methods of police to the 'new', while the second phase encompasses the professionalisation of policing and, into the twentieth century, what is often referred to as the golden age of policing (Godfrey and Lawrence, 2005). The discussion falls between these two phases and draws on wider explanations for transitions in criminal justice occurring from the mid-eighteenth to the mid- to late nineteenth century and how changes in policing have been interpreted in different ways by historians and criminologists.

As we have seen with other processes (see the Introduction), the traditional approach to these questions has been one explained by progress and reform. The rapidly expanding cities and towns were unable to cope with crime and disorder through existing policing controls, which were inadequate and inefficient, and so a 'new' police was required, with a new approach suitable to the demands of changing industrial society. As Emsley notes, this was the view of 'an old school of police historians, leaning heavily on the arguments of the early-nineteenth century police reformers' (2010: 227). There followed in 1829, through recognition of the problem by Sir Robert Peel, who was then Home Secretary, the establishment in London of the Metropolitan Police. These developments then spread to the boroughs and the counties through legislation and culminated in an obligatory new police for all local authorities from the mid-1850s onwards. A revised approach to this transition in policing was provided by the historians of the 1970s, who revisited the question with a more critical, often Marxist approach regarding the nature of the state power. They argued that the public order role of the new police was necessary for social control and the new requirements of capitalist society (Storch, 1976). It has also been argued that the perceived threat of urban communities and the 'criminal classes' was used by commentators in the early to mid-nineteenth century to their own ends; the 'moral entrepreneurs' Patrick Colquhoun, William Miles and Edwin Chadwick utilised and exaggerated concerns to reinforce their own campaigns for the reform of the police (Philips, 2003). Since then, there have been more nuanced accounts of the development of policing which acknowledge the continuities between the 'old' and the 'new' police, as well as exploring the earlier developments in policing which occurred in the eighteenth century (Emsley, 2010).

It is also necessary to reassert the importance of local governance in policing developments. As with local prisons (see Chapter 6), the decisions about policing in boroughs and counties across England for the majority of the nineteenth century were made by local authorities. The relationship between central government and the local authorities was key to policing developments throughout the period in question. As the nineteenth century progressed, the government sought to impose ideas of uniformity and methods of regulating the operation of policing across the country. This would increasingly involve a strong bureaucratic approach from the centre in some aspects of policing and the use of inspectors of constabulary to try to ensure the required degree of conformity. Though these issues were contested throughout the nineteenth century at parish and county level, control from the centre was more about exerting uniformity than through a notion of a national police force.

Policing before the 'police' and the Metropolitan Police Act 1829

The Metropolitan Police Act of 1829 is generally considered to have founded a recognisably 'modern' police force, at least in traditional accounts of the police, but discussion as to the role and nature of policing in England had begun long before this, and there were considerable developments in policing in the eighteenth century (see Emsley, 1996; Rawlings, 2002, 2003). Policing in the late eighteenth and early nineteenth century was carried out largely by parish constables and, in towns, by the night watch. Both of these were local initiatives. By this time, parish constables were remunerated through expenses or rewards for catching offenders, and members of the watch were paid a low but regular wage. Constables acted on information given to them by the communities in which they served; they could search premises, had powers of arrest and served warrants, but prosecutions were taken forward by the victims of crime and not by the police. Members of the night watch often had a beat that they patrolled at night or stood at a kiosk with staff and lantern and called out the time (Rawlings, 2003; Godfrey and Lawrence, 2005).

Advocates of police reform in the mid- to late eighteenth century – magistrates such as the Fielding brothers and commentators such as Patrick Colquhoun – were keen to abolish these old policing practices and the policing functions of the magistracy and instead proposed a uniformed and professional police force. They dismissed the practices of the constables and the watch as inadequate to deal with the rapidly changing urban and industrial environment. In some respects they were successful in their goals: professional constables such as the Bow Street Runners were created in the 1750s; from 1792 police officers on the same model were established across the suburbs of London, and in 1805 horse and foot patrols were set up in the Bow Street office (Godfrey and Lawrence, 2005; Cox, 2010; Paley, 1989). At this time, proposals on a larger scale were defeated in Parliament, as it was often considered that the new police duplicated existing services and were too expensive. Historical research in this area clearly demonstrates that these old mechanisms were not as 'inadequate, imperfect or wretched' as the reformers or traditional historians have suggested, and in many ways they met the needs of the communities they served (Paley, 1989; Emsley, 2010; Rawlings, 2002). Some constables, rather than being selected by the local community, gained considerable expertise as they remained in position for a number of years. It was also the case that, by the beginning of our period, many watches were uniformed, had organised beat systems and were more sophisticated than the negative stereotypes that prevailed (Beattie, 2002; Reynolds, 1998).

Although various proposals for developments in policing across London had failed to achieve the required support, this began to change in the 1820s. In 1822, Robert Peel was appointed Home Secretary, and later that year he established a day foot patrol out of the Bow Street Office. Peel had already been involved in policing and while Chief Secretary in Ireland had established the Royal Irish Constabulary. Once in office, Peel immediately established a Select Committee on the Police in

the Metropolis; though its report acknowledged the difficulties of parochial policing and the fragmented nature of policing across the city, it did not recommend a
unified system (Rawlings, 2002).

Peel persisted, and in 1828 was successful in getting a new parliamentary inquiry
into the police in London. The committee, presented with Peel's well-chosen criminal statistics and consisting of many who already shared his views on the state of the
police, recommended the creation of a centralised, uniformed, preventative police
for London (Philips, 1980; Emsley, 2010). Following these recommendations, Peel
guided the Metropolitan Police Act 1829 through Parliament, avoiding confrontation with the City of London by omitting the square mile from the jurisdiction of
the new force. The new uniformed constables began their patrols in London between
September 1829 and May 1830 (Emsley, 1996; Critchley, 1978; Taylor, 1997).

The traditional approach to understanding these changes is summed up by
Critchley, who maintains that '3,000 unarmed policemen, cautiously feeling their
way against a hostile public, brought peace and security to London in the place of
the turmoil and lawlessness of centuries' (1978: 55–6). Another approach, drawing
on our previous discussion, suggests that some parts of London were already ade-
quately policed. Criticism of the new police was rife in the 1830s; it was perceived
as costly, with fewer men on the streets, and there were fears over their 'military'
or political appearance (Williams, 2010). Immediate hostility was evident in 1833
during the Coldbath Fields disturbances, when people were shocked at the level of
brutality on the part of the police. This hostility, as well as criticism of the cost, presence and effectiveness of the Metropolitan Police, may have been replaced by more
tolerance in some quarters as the century progressed, but peace was still punctuated
with disturbances (Taylor, 1997). The degree of acceptance of the new police will
be returned to later in this chapter.

The borough police and the Rural Constabulary Act 1839

The Acts that followed the Metropolitan Police Act during the 1830s – the Municipal
Corporations Act 1835 and the Rural Constabulary Act 1839 – were intended to
spread the new police to the boroughs and the counties. The Municipal Corporations
Act 1835 required that all boroughs establish a watch committee, which in turn
would appoint the police force. As Hart notes, it is often presented that the

> new London police was so effective that after 1829 criminals migrated *en
> masse* to other parts of the country, with the result that the police in the bor-
> oughs was reformed in 1835; and, further, that the new watch committees
> in provincial towns were so active that a fresh migration took place to the
> rural areas, which in turn stimulated the reform of the rural police in 1839.
>
> (1955: 411; original emphasis)

Although it seems that many watch committees were set up quite quickly, the
resulting establishment of borough police forces was patchier, and many boroughs

were slack in fulfilling the statutory obligations. Of the 178 boroughs mentioned in the 1835 Act, only 100 could claim to have police forces by the beginning of 1838, and 15 years later at least six still had no force (Hart, 1955). On the other hand, some areas, such as Liverpool and Birmingham, were among the most strongly policed areas in the country (Godfrey *et al.* 2008).

The Constabulary Force Commissioners' report (PP, 1839) received a wealth of evidence from across the country on crime as it was perceived in rural districts. It was overwhelmingly the case that the many districts perceived the problem as one based largely on vagrancy; while acknowledging that they had their own local offenders, they believed that criminals travelled to these rural districts to commit crime and were 'outsiders'. Inhabitants of the towns and more urbanised areas were seen to make incursions into rural areas in order to commit crime, linking directly to the wider notions that the urban environment was the source of crime and criminality, as discussed in Chapter 2.

Typical was the position expressed by the magistrates of Droitwich, in Worcestershire, who noted:

> There are reasons to believe that the burglaries, horse stealing, and cattle stealing, whenever they occur, are committed by strangers; – that the burglars are supposed to come from Birmingham; the horse stealers still further off. The sheep stealer is generally a labourer resident in the parish where the offence is committed, or of an adjoining parish, and rarely escapes detection.
>
> (PP, 1839: 13)

This is representative of the kind of views expressed; smaller rural districts in the Midlands, such as Worcester, Evesham, Atherstone, Henley-in-Arden and Solihull, all saw their crime problem as emanating from Birmingham. Areas such as Hendon, Enfield, Chipping Barnet and Uxbridge thought crime in their area came largely from London. The unfortunate geography of the city of Chester ensured that 'most of the depredations have been committed by thieves coming from Liverpool, Manchester, Birmingham, London and other towns' (ibid.: 14). Travellers, fairs that moved from place to place, vagrants, and criminals from larger towns were seen as the predominant cause of crime in these rural districts. Such opinions are similarly expressed by the magistrates of Shropshire in the case study in this chapter, as well as in recent research on policing in Victorian Cumbria (Woolnough, 2013). The general thrust of the views expressed in the Constabulary Force Commissioners' report were that the existing police could cope with the petty thieves, poachers, sheep stealers and low-level criminals in their own areas, but the incursions of predators, urban criminals, organised gangs and roving thieves were simply too much for them to deal with. As noted earlier, the perceived migration of criminals from urban environments was used both to support and as a justification for the widespread adoption of borough and county police forces across the country (Hart, 1955).

Subsequently, the Rural Constabulary Act 1839 enabled the establishment of police forces in counties or parts of counties across England. Again, the translation of this legislation into county police forces was sporadic and emerged only slowly. Out of 54 provincial counties in England and Wales, only two-thirds had established constabularies by the mid-1850s; in nine, police forces were active only in one or two divisions or hundreds within the county (Emsley, 1996). However, it was not the case that these counties had no policing methods at all. Those that did not act directly on the provisions of the Rural Constabulary Act made use of alternative methods for local policing: they set up patrols using such legislation as the Lighting and Watching Act 1833 or reaffirmed the old system of parish constables and paid, superintending constables through the Parish Constables Act 1842. For some districts and divisions, these Acts offered a cheaper system of policing which was perceived as more suitable to their requirements and needs and also enabled control to remain in local hands (Emsley, 2010). Some areas campaigned for a smaller force on the basis of cost and value for money; people in rural districts claimed that they rarely saw a constable even though they had to pay for them. In Lancashire, for example, this resulted in a reduction in the county force from 502 to 355 men (Emsley, 1996, 2008).

By the mid-century, police reform as it existed across the whole of the country was slow in the classic model of progressive development; some forces looked to the London model for advice while others clung to what they perceived as their local needs, and therefore a variety of different policing models existed in the 1840s and 1850s (Emsley, 1996). Indeed, many of the officers were not 'new', as police forces at the county and borough level were often recruited from the 'old' police (Swift, 1988; Emsley, 1996). It would be inaccurate to see the coming of the new police as something that occurred directly as a result of the Metropolitan Police Act; across the whole country, the development of policing evolved in a much more protracted way than the traditional Whig Metropolitan-based model suggests. The County and Borough Police Act passed in 1856 further enforced the establishment of the police across England by making the provision obligatory to all local authorities. The Act laid down the legislative framework for the modern police, but of course its translation into effective policing was another matter (Taylor, 1997).

Enforcing change: the County and Borough Police Act 1856

After the passing of the County and Borough Police Act 1856, all local authorities were required to have a police force under its control – in this case, of the magistrates on the county bench. The Act also required boroughs that had not adopted a watch committee under the 1835 Act to do so (Emsley, 2008). Palmerston, the Home Secretary in 1853–4, had established a Select Committee in 1853 which urged the adoption of a uniform system of policing across the whole country and the amalgamation in county forces of smaller borough forces. The resulting Bill provoked considerable anger when it appeared. It took the earlier recommendations of the Select Committee even further by proposing amalgamations both between larger and smaller county forces and of all borough police in towns with populations of fewer than 20,000. The Bill had to be withdrawn and redrafted, and it was resubmitted, when Sir George Grey became Home Secretary in 1855, in a revised form; proposals for amalgamations were dropped but the use of a Treasury grant and a system of inspection was adopted. The government was unsuccessful in gaining support for a national uniform system of police, as local authorities clung to their powers; however, while the chief constables would be selected by the county magistrates as the appointing body, they had to be confirmed by the Home Secretary, which added an additional layer of control (Emsley, 2008; Taylor, 1997).

But the Act did implement basic standards, and it encouraged uniformity in certain policing practices, creating a national system of supervision through the establishment of three inspectors of constabulary. Teams of inspectors would inspect police forces and report annually on their efficiency. Keen to exert its influence over the development of policing across the country, the government tied standards and practices of uniformity to financial incentives for the local authorities through the Treasury grant. For example, a quarter of the cost of police pay and clothing in an area where the population exceeded 5,000 would be paid by central government if the police force was deemed 'efficient' by the inspectors. This was increased in 1874 to half, a considerable incentive for some forces (Emsley, 2008). This growing bureaucratic control of criminal justice by central government is similar to the approach taken with local prisons from 1835 onwards (see Chapter 6), though with policing the authorities clung to their local power, perhaps even more tightly than with local prisons, and the financial incentives formed a considerable carrot when it came to directions from the Home Office (Rawlings, 1999). This Act and previous legislation on policing between the 1830s and the mid-1850s coincided with a great deal of concern about Chartism, as well as the demobilisation of the army after the end of the Crimean War, but it was the virtual end of transportation to Australia and the problem of 'ticket of leave' men that pushed on the debates leading up to the 1856 Act (Rawlings, 1999; Taylor, 1997).

Policing everyday life

As we have seen in Chapter 1, the majority of offences processed by the criminal justice system were low-level crimes, crimes that occurred most often on the streets – offences such as drunkenness, disorderly behaviour, petty thefts, begging and vagrancy. Therefore, the activity of the police was in the poor and working-class districts, and attention fell especially on the lower strata, those dependent on the street economy or in irregular employment (Hopkins-Burke, 2003). The new police were to protect property and to keep the streets clear. While lone officers may have avoided conflict, the powers of the new police to move people on brought them into conflict with sections of the public (Williams, 2010). Those who affronted Victorian sensibilities through their immorality, vice or criminality and those with a precarious existence on the street were the subject of police attention. Policing focused overwhelmingly on what happened in public spaces, the types of offences encountered on the streets – vagrancy and related offences, people in the district or area who seemed 'out of place', those the worse for wear after too much alcohol or drink-fuelled fights, arguments and assaults and indecent behaviour, drunken women or those working as prostitutes, and offenders from the locality of whom the local force already had some knowledge. Certain communities received more attention than others, and in the nineteenth century this was often the Irish, who were denigrated for 'their poverty, squalid living conditions, their alien ways (which included the Gaelic language) and their lawlessness' (Swift, 1985: 182; Taylor, 2002; see also Chapter 1).

The surveillance of working-class communities fuelled hostility towards the police (Storch, 1976; Philips, 1977). How much weight can be put on the depth, length and intensity of this hostility and the degree of acceptance as the nineteenth century progressed is a matter of interpretation. As we have seen, traditional histories acknowledge the initial hostility towards the police in London – for example, the riots in Coldbath Fields in 1833 which resulted in the death of a police officer – but quickly move on to the view that, once the worth of the police was recognised, hostility evaporated, except of course in the minds of the criminals and the misguided (Critchley, 1978). Revisionist historians, on the other hand, notably Robert Storch (1975), argue that hostility towards the police was much more organised and long lasting than previously thought in the form of anti-police riots and disorder, particularly in northern England, against 'the plague of blue locusts'. He regarded the mission of the new police as 'an all-purpose lever of urban discipline' which 'brought the arm of municipal and state authority directly to bear upon the key institutions of daily life in working-class neighbourhoods, touching off a running battle with local custom and popular culture which lasted at least until the end of the century' (Storch, 1976: 481). Storch maintains that the police, understood as a complement to attempts by middle-class elites to moralise the working classes through religion, education, temperance and recreational reforms, or as 'domestic missionaries', were dispatched to mould these communities to the new discipline of work and leisure. 'Far from being sporadic, however, conflict was endemic and chronic, and it stemmed from the interventions of the police in the daily lives and recreational activities of the working classes, from their insertion into the heart of the working class neighbourhood' (ibid.).

The new 'policing was fundamentally concerned with the regulation of everyday life in the town and country', and as such the reception and impact of the police depended upon the environment they entered. However, opposition was not confined to the period in which they were first established, and, while middle-class opposition may have diminished over time, working-class opposition continued, if in a modified form (Taylor, 2002: 78). If rates of assaults against them in the second half of the nineteenth century can be seen as an indicator of the relationship between the police and the local community, then in some areas, at the very least, the police needed to be as hard or harder than the local hard man to survive (Emsley, 2009; Taylor, 2002; Archer, 2011).

The police were then part of a strategy to regulate and control street life and to moderate leisure and recreational activities in working-class communities and to impose order and respectability (Storch, 1976). Crime would be prevented through the moralisation of the poor, and the surveillance of deviant communities meant that, though they were 'watching St Giles and bad places in general', they were also watching more affluent areas such as St James's (Select Committee on the Police, 1834, cited in Rawlings, 1999: 77). So the police were not only to apprehend criminals, they were also to deter crime and immoral behaviour in general: 'to discourage antisocial choices and to provide an external restraint on impulse and self-will' (Wiener, 1994: 56). Longer term, the presence of the police would encourage people to be more self-disciplined and moral in their actions and more aware of the consequences if they were not (Wiener, 1994).

It is not simply that the working classes were repressed by the police. As they were most likely to be the victims of the routine crimes that were occurring, they benefited from the police presence, and the respectable or aspiring working class supported police actions, distinguishing themselves from the disreputable (Weinberger, 1981; Reiner, 1992; Hopkins-Burke, 2003). But, as Weinberger argues, the working class were the target of many police offensives; put simply, the police were 'interfering with people not previously interfered with', notably around drinking and licensing but also targeting leisure and pastimes, vagrants, youths, labourers and the Irish (1981: 75). Moreover, there is no doubting the reach of the police and the courts, as research from late nineteenth-century Sheffield demonstrates; at least one-third of the working-class men in the city had been arrested at least once (Williams, 2010).

Surveying and monitoring 'police property'

As we have seen in Chapter 2, the late 1860s and early 1870s saw the development of legislation relating to habitual offending, and the bureaucratic and surveillance role of the police was crucial in its implementation. Policing, as we have seen, was essentially about the monitoring and surveillance of 'suspect' members of the population. There was some disjuncture between the idea of monitoring and supervising habitual offenders and the actual realities of this for police work. There were potentially thousands of people subject to such legislation from the late 1860s onwards, and there was little chance that the police, given their resources and manpower, could regularly monitor all of them. Though the realities of the numbers of people under supervision may well have been fewer – estimated by Stevenson (1986) at 4,000 offenders per year – and, as we have seen, the 'criminal classes' were not distinguishable from the poor but honest working class, some offenders were targets for the police (Emsley, 2010).

Those offenders – habitual offenders or casual criminals – who were known to the police, either in urban or in rural areas, were 'police property' (Reiner, 1992). In general, the surveillance of offenders brought with it a number of issues both for suspects and for those previously convicted. In the 1870s, there was detailed discussion about the activities of the police and the manner in which they monitored offenders, those under police supervision and those released from prison. Many complained it was impossible to make a fresh start away from crime when the police would come along and inform their employers about their past record, which subsequently resulted in their dismissal. As early as 1857, the Earl of Carnarvon and Henry Mayhew met men on tickets of leave who discussed the difficulties of harassment by the police and finding employment (Emsley, 2010). These problems persisted at least until the end of our period, as recognised by the Kimberley Commission (1879). While it was acknowledged that some released prisoners did not report at their destination, or reported once and then went missing, most of the witnesses supported the system as 'a valuable means of controlling the criminal classes' (PP, 1879: 34). Evidence from the Royal Society for the Assistance of Discharged Prisoners suggested that individuals had lost employment as a result of the interference of the police; the Chief Commissioner of the Metropolitan Police said he took seriously complaints that were made in this regard but had found only two cases in which the police were culpable (also see Petrow, 1994). In Gloucestershire, in the interest of being 'open and honest', the police were ordered to inform all employers who had discharged prisoners in their service. The Kimberley Commission could not agree with this approach, fearing men would frequently lose their chances of employment and be driven back to crime. Instead, they recommend special police officers be employed (at least in London) to work with the discharged prisoners' aid societies. These recommendations were subsequently taken forward with the establishment of the Convict Supervision Office (see Chapter 2). Acknowledging the difficulties that police supervision presented, the Kimberley Commission thought that, 'if left in the hands of ordinary police constables …[, it] will tend more and more to become a matter of routine, harassing to the men who are subjected to it, and affording no real security to society against the criminal classes' (PP, 1879: 36). Towards the end of the nineteenth century most local prisons also had discharged prisoners' aid societies, but the difficulties of supervision persisted – in particular, the role of retired policemen as supervisory agents and the use of discharged prisoners as informants by the police. Reverend G. W. Reynolds, from Manchester, claimed that their 'Society was nearly ruined once by the employment of a very active ex-policeman' (cited in McConville, 1995: 322).

It was also the case that recidivists, prostitutes or younger offenders were pretty easy pickings for the police (Walkowitz and Walkowitz, 1974; Humphries, 1981; Weinberger, 1981); constables in urban districts knew the population and the haunts of those on the margins of society and regularly picked up the same offenders. This was particularly the case with recidivist drunkards, those who experienced the revolving door of imprisonment and lived their lives between the public house, the street and the prison. Indeed, the records of local prisons are peppered with incidents in which prisoners smashed up their cells, broke their cell pans, or shouted and screamed their frustrations at being arrested, once again, by the same police constable.

Most of the work discussed above with regard to the supervision of convicts was carried out by the detective section of the police. A small detective force had been formed in 1842 and was substantially increased in 1869. By the end of our period, in 1878, this was transformed into the Criminal Investigation Division (CID) (Petrow, 1994). The idea of detection, the potential for corruption and the methods of spying that such work implied had been a source of great suspicion and contempt in England – an invasion of freedom and individual liberty that smacked of the continent (Williams, 2010; Petrow, 1994). Indeed, Peel had argued in 1822 that England needed an efficient police system but not one based on a French model: 'God forbid that he should mean to countenance a system of espionage' (cited in Emsley, 1996: 25).

In the early years, a few detectives had been employed by the Metropolitan Police to observe known offenders and detect crime; in the 1860s, concerns about habitual offenders and the criminal classes allowed for a greater expansion. The detectives visited prisons to view those recently admitted and those about to be discharged, they monitored those on the registers (as discussed above), and divisional detectives could also patrol the streets and monitor the haunts of criminal activity (Petrow, 1994). As we have seen in Chapter 2, they also utilised photographs for identification and as a memory aid (Jager, 2001; Stanford, 2009).

By the early twentieth century, attitudes within the criminal justice system began to change and more emphasis was placed on mechanisms such as probation for petty or first offenders, as well as welfare provision and support (Garland, 1985; Wiener, 1994; Mair and Burke, 2012). The number of convicts placed under police supervision by this time was tiny; these changes marked out the difference between career criminals and those who could be helped: 'police supervision ... had been practically useless. It helped the police manufacture a criminal class, without really deterring criminals or diminishing crime' (Petrow, 1994: 82).

Case study: the establishment of the 'new' police in nineteenth-century Shropshire*

In the period before the 'new' police in Shropshire, the boroughs in the county were policed by parish constables and by the watch. The boroughs of Shrewsbury, Bridgnorth, Ludlow, Oswestry and Wenlock continued with the system of unpaid parish constables, who were appointed annually, and a watch which operated at night, some under the charge of a beadle. After the Municipal Corporations Act 1835, the borough of Shrewsbury, the county town, appointed a watch committee and 13 constables – four to act during the day and nine as night watchmen. Policing, as it existed, and lighting in the town were confined to the area within the bridges over the River Severn, and the Recorder of Shrewsbury was accordingly concerned about the suburbs:

> Frankwell and Coleman have usually been the main haunt and resort of the profligate gangs of juvenile offenders, and their still more wicked abettors, who infest the town, pilfering from the honest and heedless tradesmen – the hole-and-corner boroughs, if I may so express it, to which these noxious vermin run for refuge when pursued ... in Frankwell particularly, are whole

---

* Parts of this case study are adapted from Johnston, 2005b, with permission of Logaston Press.

rows of houses tenanted by shameless and wretched females, to which thieves and robbers have been frequently traced; or that the Castle-Foregate abounds with lodging-houses, in which a miserable class of vagabonds, without any apparent means of honest subsistence, are constantly housed.

(*Eddowes Salopian Journal*, 6 July 1836, cited in Elliott, 1984: 3)

Despite this concern, policing remained confined to the town centre until at least 1839, though during the day the number of constables declined to two. The other boroughs also moved on the Act; although evidence is patchy, in the early years most appointed a watch committee and, subsequently, constables and night watchmen. Larger areas had a constable and an office in each ward, and a house in Shrewsbury was converted to a police station. Some watch committees dismissed and then re-employed the 'old' constables; others tried not to employ local men. There continued to be a mixture between paid and unpaid constables, but most had uniforms and patrolled their respective areas during the day while the watch did so at night (Elliott, 1984).

Shropshire, along with Cheshire, was one of the first counties to act and initiate discussions for establishing a county constabulary. At first glance, this might be surprising for a county which, in comparison with others, developed relatively slowly during a period of rapid national social and economic change. The position of Shropshire, near to some of the most rapidly industrialising areas in the Black Country, on the route between the Midlands and the North and adjoining Wales, was the primary concern that seemed to drive the early development of county policing.

As Philips and Storch note, the Shropshire Quarter Sessions displayed a 'strong and continuing interest' in the reform of the police from the early 1830s, and the adoption of office constables was county policy from 1837: 'By 1839 every Shropshire Petty Sessions was a little Bow Street, each with its one (but lone) "runner"' (1999: 33). During the period 1820 to 1835, the need for a county constabulary responsible to the Quarter Sessions was discussed, and in 1829 neighbouring Cheshire Quarter Sessions requested an Act to enable them to create a county police force. Both of these developments showed that 'the local elites were moving on their own' (ibid.: 37) and that policing had become a major concern of the landed gentry.

One of the leading and most active magistrates in the county, Sir Baldwin Leighton, had already organised a subscription for the hundred of Ford and hired a London policeman, William Baxter, to work in the area. In a letter to Edwin Chadwick, Leighton wrote that the officer's work had showed

an extent of depredation of which none of us were before aware, for as tracing offenders occasioned formerly a great loss of time and ... often an expenditure of money, for the parish constable had to be paid, [farmers] seldom took any steps to find out the offender but quietly put up with their loss.

(HO 73/2/1, 27 February 1839, cited in
Philips and Storch, 1999: 49)

The long records of discussions about county policing at the Quarter Sessions show the main causes of concern to the magistracy. In 1831–2, these focused on striking coal miners from the neighbouring counties of Denbighshire and Flintshire, who were trying to bring out Shropshire colliers near Oswestry. The magistrates called on both regular troops and the county yeomanry and also swore in special constables. The confrontation at Chirk Bridge resulted in the reading of the Riot Act, and three miners were committed to the prison at Shrewsbury. This was not the first time the policing of large numbers of colliers had caused concern to the county magistracy. Ten years earlier, the Assize Court had sentenced a number of men to periods of imprisonment and others to death for their participation in a riot in the Wellington area; colliers had been protesting about reductions in their wages (see Chapter 4). The policing of large bodies of people was a challenge in rural areas across the country, and large-scale disturbances often had to be resolved by the introduction of the army.

The confrontation at Chirk led the county Quarter Sessions to resolve, in January 1831, 'that the formation of a Constabulary Force throughout the County ... with a view to the preservation of the Peace and security of property should be adopted, and that this Court strongly recommends the Magistrates ... to take immediate steps with a view to its organisation' (Philips and Storch, 1999: 106). This resolution lapsed, but a year later the magistrates faced a similar problem of striking colliers on the borders with Staffordshire and Worcestershire. This event led the court again to assert the desirability of a county police force, but, once more, the initiative lapsed.

In 1837, Leighton advocated the establishment of a committee to study the issue; he argued that his experiment with a paid professional policeman in the hundred of Ford had been particularly successful in reducing crime (Philips and Storch, 1999). The officer, Baxter, it was claimed, had detected and convicted a number of known offenders and recovered stolen property equal to his own salary; moreover, in the six months since his appointment, only five or six felonies had occurred, as opposed to sixty in the six months previous to that (Elliott, 1984).

The Shropshire justices were also in favour of a police force because of the problem of 'roving thieves'. As a Midlands county, they argued, Shropshire was particularly vulnerable; it had some industry and mining, bordered similar English and Welsh counties, and contained a number of major roads. They were concerned about 'bands of migratory thieves plundering the unprotected countryside', and Leighton maintained that these 'roving thieves' were 'inadequately contained by untrained annually rotating constables' (Philips and Storch, 1999: 108). As we have discussed above, these concerns were widespread in rural areas, where the threat was perceived as emanating from the more populous towns and cities (Constabulary Force Commissioners, PP, 1839), and anxieties were voiced about containing and monitoring 'outsiders' committing offences and roaming in areas such as Cumbria (Woolnough, 2013).

Similarly, another leading magistrate in the county, R. A. Slaney, favoured the reform of the police and the poor law to protect property and provide general safety. He noted: 'the position of Shropshire, almost on a direct line from Birmingham to Liverpool and Manchester (in which towns, with London, the most practiced thieves were reared) exposed the inhabitants to greater injuries from the characters than in more remote districts' (Philips and Storch, 1999: 108).

After discussions and correspondence with other counties, the Shropshire Quarter Sessions sent a petition to Parliament in January 1838:

> the Rural Police is at present totally inefficient for the prevention of crime, and ... the detection of it, as the former most important duty is not even attempted, and the latter is ... performed [in Shropshire] by ... office Constables attached to each Petty Sessions ... The passing of an Act to enable the Court of Quarter Sessions to appoint and pay out of the County Rate a body of Constables subject ... to the authority of the Magistrates but placed under the ... superintendence of a Chief Officer responsible to them for the arrangements and disposition of the force ... within the Shire would confer a most important benefit on Rural Districts inasmuch as such on Establishment would effectively provide for the prevention as well as the detection of Offences; for the security of Person and property and for the ... preservation of the Public Peace.
>
> (QSF/27/24, cited in Philips and Storch, 1999: 108–9)

Importantly, this particular petition 'contains the precise scheme for the crucial legislation of 1839, which became the framework for English provincial policing (outside the boroughs) into the twentieth century' (ibid.: 108). Shropshire therefore was one of the first counties to adopt the County Police Act 1839. There was no debate as to whether or not a force should be established; rather, the discussion concerned its size and the cost. Philips and Storch argue that the establishment of small locally paid policing initiatives in the early 1830s suggests that the landed gentry were no longer objecting to the principle of a paid force, as long as it remained under local control. As with the administration of prisons, the struggle for control over policing was a prominent feature in the discussions across many boroughs and counties of England.

In December 1838, the Shropshire Quarter Sessions adopted another resolution, known as the 'Salop Resolution', which read:

> That in consequence of the present inefficiency of the Constabulary Force, arising from the great increase in population and the extension of trade and commerce of the county, it is the opinion of this Court, that a body of constables appointed by the magistrates, paid out of the County Rate, and disposable at any point of the Shire where their services might be required, would be highly desirable, as providing in the most efficient manner for the prevention as well as the detection of offences, for the security of person and property, and for the constant preservation of the Public Peace.
>
> (Philips and Storch, 1999: 136)

John Russell (then Home Secretary) endorsed this particular resolution, having previously refused to commit to other proposals put to him by the county bench. This signalled his decision to work with the county government 'to employ a bona fide provincial initiative to attempt to foster a national consensus among the gentry via the justices of the peace' (ibid.). His comment also demonstrates that Russell recognised the local power of the magistracy and the need to gain acceptance of the proposals from this group.

The chairman, Thomas Kenyon, together with Slaney and Leighton, took the lead in pushing for the establishment of a county police force. In October 1839, the debate led by the aforementioned magistrates and a few other prominent county justices led to the unanimous adoption of the County Police Act. There had been a little disquiet in the crowded courtroom, but a substantial majority voted in favour (Philips and Storch, 1999; Elliott, 1984). By this time, the Act had already received royal assent, and the justices acted quickly to ask for advice on how to proceed. Perhaps a little tentative at first, they wanted to know more about the government's views on the number of officers, their salaries and hierarchy, and they requested copies of the rules and regulations in use by the Metropolitan Police. The Home Secretary, by this time the Marquess of Normanby, realised that he could not allow Shropshire, one of the leading counties, to waver or hesitate and responded swiftly, urging them to press on and asking for their suggestions (Elliott, 1984).

In December 1839, the Police Committee was established. It was intended to represent the whole of the county and thus had a large membership. The magistrates had toyed with the number of officers required. Leighton had suggested 12 or 14 in the initial discussions, but other magistrates were sceptical; J. A. Lloyd claimed they would need 200 constables for the population. Slaney stated that Hertfordshire, 'so near ... to the depredations of the London thieves', had thought one officer to 1,600 inhabitants sufficient. In the end, it was decided that the county police force would consist of a chief constable, six superintendents and 43 constables (Elliott, 1984: 17). Leighton was very critical of the administration and command of the Shropshire constabulary, and in the late 1850s he made the position of chief constable an uncomfortable one for the then incumbent, Captain Dawson Mayne. Leighton was particularly annoyed that Mayne, who had been involved in appointing the first chief constable, had married a cousin of Sir Rowland Hill, as he strongly disapproved of such personal connections (Elliott, 1984).

This discussion of the early county force in nineteenth-century Shropshire demonstrates the operation of local criminal justice and its evolution during this period. The authorities in the county did not seem to have questioned the necessity or desirability of a police force; the perceived problem of crime as they understood it – the roving thieves and vagrants, the vulnerable geography of the county – led instead to a discussion that focused on the size and cost of the new force. It is also interesting that Shropshire and neighbouring Cheshire were the first counties to move towards a new police (see also Tennant, 2014), even though neither experienced the rapid expansion in population, towns and industrialisation – or at least not to the same extent – that occurred in many urban environments.

4

CAPITAL AND CORPORAL PUNISHMENTS

From public to private

This chapter will examine the operation of the criminal justice system in relation to the ultimate punishment – execution – and the use of other types of public punishment. Two significant changes occurred in England across this period in the use of public punishments in general and of public execution in particular. The first was the decline in the use of execution and the subsequent rise of alternatives to the death sentence, such as transportation and imprisonment (discussed in the following chapters). The second change was a move from public to private executions, held behind prison walls, and, more broadly, a shift away from all forms of public punishments. The chapter will start with a discussion of public punishments then look at the operation of capital punishment, the decline of executions from the early nineteenth century, and the cessation of public executions in 1868. In the 120 years between 1750 and 1870, there was a significant change in the practices surrounding the execution of offenders and the use of public punishments (Foucault, 1991; Spierenburg, 1984; Pratt, 2002; Garland, 1990; Smith, 2008). This chapter will address how the criminal justice system and the law dealt with capital cases as well as the customs and public nature of the 'execution day'. The case study concerns public execution in nineteenth-century Shropshire. This will illuminate how changing sensibilities were experienced in provincial England. The final part of the chapter will examine how executions continued behind prison walls from 1868 onwards.

Public punishment: the decline of corporal punishment

Public punishments in general and public execution in particular played an important role in the criminal justice system throughout the eighteenth century. It was thought that the public nature of the infliction of pain and suffering meted out by the courts would deter others from committing crime as well as bringing shame or humiliation upon the convicted offender (Shoemaker, 2004). Punishment, an extension of state power, was 'seen to be done', and this applied to all forms of public punishment, from the whipping of offenders, placing them in stocks or the pillory, to carrying out the death sentence (Morgan and Rushton, 1998). All had an element of theatre and some participatory role for the audience.

While public punishment had played an important role, most kinds of corporal punishment carried out in public had declined and were removed from use by the early nineteenth century. Other punishments, such as branding, had already disappeared, though were not removed from the statute books until 1823; the branding of offenders – 'T' for thief, 'F' for felon, usually on the thumb – in order to recognise their previous crimes and past convictions ended at the end of the eighteenth century (Cox, 2014; Hitchcock and Shoemaker, 2010).

The use of the pillory had also largely ended by the second decade of the nineteenth century. The pillory was a wooden structure with holes for their head and arms in which the offender would be locked. They were then subject to the abuse of the crowd, who would often throw rotten fruit and vegetables, offal or animal blood, other waste, excrement, mud, or even stones or bricks at the offender, who was unable to protect him- or herself (Shoemaker, 2004). Frequently the pillory was used to punish those whose crimes provoked moral indignation – homosexuals, shopkeepers who used false weights, or those undercutting customers or speculating on the trade in grain. The crowd's participation, demonstrating their support of the sentence, reinforced the use of the pillory (Ignatieff, 1978; Beattie, 1986; Emsley, 2005). Their mood was also important: this type of punishment could, in the most severe cases, result in death or serious injury, but the crowd could sometimes be sympathetic to the offender. Pillories were often located near to marketplaces, main thoroughfares or similar spaces to maximise attendance and the visibility of the punishment, though on occasions they were placed at the location where an offence had taken place. The use of the pillory was abolished in 1837 but had already been restricted to perjury and related offences in 1816 (Cox, 2014). The stocks, a similar type of punishment where the offender was locked into the structure only by their ankles, continued to be used until the mid-nineteenth century.

Similarly, public whippings were organised to ensure the maximum deterrent effect through the location and timing of the punishment. Whippings often took place in marketplaces or on main streets and thoroughfares to attract the local population. The whipping itself was often inflicted by a parish or court officer, and the offender was tied by their hands either to a whipping post or, most commonly, to the back of a cart which was pulled by horse through the streets or to a public location. The offender would be stripped to the waist and was whipped as the cart travelled along the route, or 'until his back be bloody'. Attracting the largest possible crowd was the aim of the punishment, and the routes followed, and the day and time of the whipping, therefore became more precise in the late eighteenth century (Beattie, 1986). Whippings did also occur in private, and these were carried out inside gaols or houses of correction.

Beattie (1986) argues that, as a punishment, whippings must have varied considerably from case to case; the distances carts travelled differed, as did their pace, and those carrying out the whipping could be weak or strong, merciful or pitiless in their action. In court, those pronouncing sentence were not always clear about the number of stripes ordered, and 'until his back be bloody' was open to interpretation. But public whipping, like other public punishments, was not just about the pain or the damage to the body; it was also about the shame, degradation and humiliation of having such a punishment inflicted in front of family and local community, and so acted as a deterrent to minor criminality (Shoemaker, 2004; Beattie, 1986). Frequently such punishments were class based and inflicted on the poor and the working classes. Although it was perceived that such people had nothing to lose, this was not the case; the loss of reputation and character might well affect their chances of employment in the area or the community's views on the respectability of their families. Some petitioned against the sentence for these reasons, while others tried to get the punishment carried out in private to mitigate the harm done to their or their families' reputation (Beattie, 1986).

The public whipping of women was abolished in 1817, but men were publicly whipped until the mid-1830s; this punishment was not officially abolished until 1862 (Emsley, 2005, 2010). Whipping also continued to be inflicted inside prisons, often for disorderly offenders or juveniles, some of whom were sent to prison for short periods specifically to allow this to be carried out (see Chapter 9). Whipping was sometimes combined with other punishments, though across the period its imposition declined as a sentence. At various periods of anxiety or concern about certain offenders throughout the nineteenth century there were calls for the reintroduction of flogging. The Security Against Violence or 'Garrotters' Act 1863 introduced flogging for street robbery (see Chapter 2), and other offences were added to this list in subsequent decades, such as sexual offences and armed burglary (Emsley, 2005). Public whipping was removed for use by the courts in 1948 but continued to be employed inside local and convict prisons until 1967 to punish those who broke rules and regulations. However, as Emsley notes, the physical chastisement of children and young people persisted until 1987 in schools and had 'a much greater longevity in England than in many of the states with which the English generally liked to compare themselves' (2005: 164).

Capital punishment, the criminal law and the operation of the criminal justice system

By the end of the eighteenth century, the customary practice of public execution had already begun to diminish and the 'spectacle of suffering' had been curtailed. Public execution in England is most often discussed in relation to Tyburn, the main place of execution in London and the most frequently used site in the country (Hibbert, 1957; Linebaugh, 1975, 1993; Brooke and Brandon, 2004; Hitchcock and Shoemaker, 2010). The Triple Tree, the permanent scaffold at Tyburn, had been removed in 1759 and the procession there from Newgate gaol, about 2 miles through the crowded city streets, was ended in 1783. There had been a great deal of concern about the behaviour of the crowd at executions and whether or not such events conveyed the correct message of punishment. Social commentators feared that the gruesome displays of violence only hardened the brutal crowd, who thought nothing of the suffering of those on the gallows and neither sympathised with them nor feared a similar fate. The deterrent effect of punishment was called into question, as was the rowdy and unseemly behaviour of the crowd, which was seen as particularly distasteful (Linebaugh, 1975; Spierenburg, 1984; Laqueur, 1989; McGowen, 1987; Pratt, 2002; Devereaux, 2009).

On the statute books under the system known as the 'Bloody Code', there were a large number of capital offences, but in reality it was not quite as 'bloody' as the 250 or 260 crimes suggest; legislation was often minutely defined by a separate Act of Parliament and quite different to the criminal law in the early nineteenth century, when offences were consolidated into groups. That said, a large number of people were processed in the criminal justice system for offences that could warrant a capital sentence; while large numbers were sentenced to death, they were not necessarily all executed (Hay, 1975). Gatrell (1994) argues that, by the early nineteenth century, the increased numbers of prosecutions for capital crimes, resulting from both the larger population and more effective methods, meant that the number of people actually executed had to be curtailed. There were various ways during the criminal justice process by which a criminal or condemned person might be able to escape the noose, and many were pardoned or reprieved. For example, a jury might convict a criminal on a lesser charge, resulting in the avoidance of the gallows; a judge might strictly interpret the law to the same effect; and, even when sentenced to death, the condemned might be able to claim 'benefit of clergy' (reading a passage from the Bible, usually Psalm 51, the 'neck verse', could save them from the noose) to reduce the sentence to transportation or appeal to the monarch for royal mercy. Such variations, although alleviating the brutality of the system, caused concern about justice, fairness and equality before the law when it came to who did and who did not end up on the gallows and may have reduced executions to such a low level that the deterrent value of the punishment was lost (Gatrell, 1994). In addition, McGowen argues that what was 'in dispute was not how to secure the greater efficiency of the criminal justice system, but how to present a more pleasing image of justice' (1983: 96).

The consolidation of the criminal law at the beginning of the nineteenth century was not just about the rationality and humanitarianism that came with the period of 'reform'; it was also a response to a rapidly changing society and the perceived problems of the lower orders (Johnstone and Ward, 2010). The modernisation of the criminal law was not simply about reform and progress, similar to other developments in the criminal justice system at this time (see the Introduction). The narrative of progress has been challenged by those highlighting the nature of state power and the mechanisms by which the dominant powers in English society sought to control the lower orders and, by the nineteenth century, the development of new technologies of surveillance and power to discipline society (Hay, 1975; Foucault, 1991; Cohen, 1985; Garland, 1990). A wider theme within this book is the ways in which these developments translated into the everyday experiences of those who were drawn into the criminal justice system. As such it is important to note that the scope of the criminal law changed. It became a mechanism for dealing with people 'who had not been integrated in the disciplined, respectable and orderly working class', but it departed from classical jurisprudence principles even further when confronted not only with 'occasional offenders but with those whose whole way of life was at odds with the social norms which criminal law was now charged with upholding' (Johnstone and Ward, 2010: 59).

Public execution in the nineteenth century

Most of the customary practices of execution day, such as the last speeches of the condemned, the procession from Newgate to Tyburn and the dissection of bodies, had already ended by the beginning of the nineteenth century (Pratt, 2002). The main debates of the mid-nineteenth century were about whether or not the practice of *public* execution should continue and, more broadly, what crimes should lead to the death penalty.

In the period between the end of the eighteenth century and the 1860s there was a significant shift. Gatrell suggests that, while there were around 7,000 executions (on average around 115 per year) between 1770 and 1830, this figure declined to around 347 between 1837 and 1868 (1994: 7–10). Essentially there were two reasons for this: the first was that, across this period, the severity of the law was curtailed and the number of capital offences declined, but this cannot be disentangled from the second reason (perhaps a motor for the first), which was that the number of people who were reprieved or in other ways diverted from the gallows increased; overall this reflected the fact that views on capital punishment had changed.

The main debates surrounding the use of capital punishment concerned how execution was to be used in the criminal justice system – who was to be executed and for what crimes? Legal reformers in the late eighteenth and early nineteenth centuries, influenced by the Enlightenment, had already begun to consider questions of proportionality in the criminal law and had asked both whether the severity of the law was effective in deterring people from crime and what kind of message was sent out by the state when punishing its people.

From the mid-1820s and to the early 1830s, on average, just over 1,300 people per year were sentenced to death but only 56 per year were actually executed. This demonstrates the continued disparity between the numbers sentenced to death and those actually executed and the increased use transportation and, later, penal servitude as alternatives (*Report of the Capital Punishment Commission*, PP, 1866: 713). Substantial changes came in the 1830s and 1840s when a large number of crimes ceased to be capital offences. These included cattle, horse and sheep stealing and larceny in a dwelling house (to the value of 5 shillings) in 1832; housebreaking in 1833; returning from transportation in 1834; forgery, stealing in dwelling house, and cases of burglary, robbery, piracy and arson where there was no assault, wounding danger to life in 1837; and rape and the carnal abuse of infants in 1841 (ibid.: 712). In practice there were no executions other than those for murder from the 1840s. Between

1838 and 1852 there were 998 offenders sentenced to death of whom only 152 were actually executed – 148 for murder and four for attempted murder accompanied by dangerous injury to the victim. At this time, the bulk of those reprieved, 617 offenders, were transported for life (*Capital Convictions*, PP, 1852–3: 1; see also Chapter 5). Then in 1861 the Offences against the Person Act, which abolished the death penalty for all crimes except murder and treason (Emsley, 2010), essentially legitimised the system as it had already been operating for over twenty years.

The execution day

At the scaffold itself, the customary lengthy final speeches of the condemned had long gone, and the whole atmosphere of the public execution was reshaped to send a much more sombre message to the gathered crowds than the 'carnival' of the mid- to late eighteenth century (Pratt, 2002); the theatre of Tyburn had been recast (Devereaux, 2009). That said, the question still remained at the beginning of the nineteenth century as to whether the public nature of capital punishment was appropriate. What kind of message did public execution send out to the populace and should *public* executions continue? Other types of public punishment also declined; in particular, the public whipping of women was abolished in 1817. The displaying of corpses in chains or on the gibbet ended in 1834, so it might be argued that there was a growing distaste for all these kinds of public exhibitions. While this might have been the case among the middle classes, who complained about the gruesome spectacles, evidence suggests that the size of the crowds increased during the nineteenth century as executions became less frequent (Gatrell, 1994; Pratt, 2002; Crone, 2012). Infamous or noteworthy murderers whose cases had caught the public's eye or were widely discussed in the press drew thousands, even tens of thousands, of spectators. 'The levity, jokes, humour, rowdiness and apparent thirst for executions displayed by the lower orders provoked great concern among the higher classes, especially as growing numbers of the respectable lobbied for the abolition of public executions' (Crone, 2012: 81). The crowd's behaviour and willingness to view punishment, rather than the execution itself, became the focus of attention in commentary and print. The commercialisaton of the public execution, involving figurines of notable murderers and 'day trip' excursions to attend an execution, was also viewed as pretty unseemly (McGowen, 1994; Gatrell, 1994; Laqueur, 1989; Pratt, 2002). But by this time the hanging itself had already been curtailed: held early in the morning, it was completed within a matter of minutes, with only a brief address by the chaplain and the accused, the scaffold shrouded in black. Yet the crowd's behaviour persistently undermined the authorities' attempts to create a solemn event, and this would eventually be overcome only by a more appropriate and civilised setting (Pratt, 2002; Taylor, 1998).

By the mid-century, the use of capital punishment had declined, as had the frequency of executions, but there remained some persistent and pressing questions which the Royal Commission on Capital Punishment in 1866 sought to address. What was the deterrent effect of capital punishment? What about irrevocability of the death penalty? Is there a reluctance on the part of juries to convict in capital cases? Should the definition or classification of crimes such as murder be altered? What about cases of infanticide or murder cases using the insanity defence or other extenuating circumstances? Should the prerogative of mercy continue? Should appeals be allowed in capital cases? Should execution be in private or public? If there were no capital punishment, what alternative would be used? In the end, the commission did not recommend the eradication of capital punishment, and during the 1870s and 1880s there were continued unsuccessful calls in Parliament for its total abolition (Cooper, 1974). Instead it stated that wider questions of degree of responsibility, appeals and mercy were part of a larger discussion of the criminal law to be debated elsewhere. But it did recommend 'putting an end to public executions, and directing that sentences of death be carried out within the precincts of the prison, under such regulations as may be considered necessary to prevent abuse, and satisfy the public that the law has been complied with' (*Report of the Capital Punishment Commission*, PP, 1866: 51).

As a consequence of the Royal Commission, the Capital Punishment Amendment Act came into force in the May of 1868, and from then on all executions were held behind prison walls. The last public execution took place outside Newgate prison on 26 May, when the condemned was Michael Barrett, the Clerkenwell bomber (Pratt, 2002). By August of that year the first private execution had been carried out within Maidstone prison, and *The Times* observed: 'it is emphatically one of those reforms which are hard to realise before they are made, but which, once made, seem so simple and unobjectionable that they are treated almost as a matter of course' (14 August 1868, cited in McGowen, 1994: 257).

Most of the academic literature on public executions comes from material on London, since more executions occurred there, but public executions were carried out in many towns and cities across England. By the early nineteenth century they commonly took place at or near the local prison or in a large public space, where people from the surrounding areas could congregate for the event. Changes did not occur only in London; as Devereaux (2009) notes, a number of towns across England relocated their execution sites at the end of the eighteenth century. The following case study examines evidence of executions that were carried out in public in Shrewsbury, Shropshire, and illuminates the kind of problems that were encountered across provincial England.

Case study: executions in Shrewsbury, 1787 to 1868

In the early nineteenth century, public executions in the county of Shropshire were held at the front of Shrewsbury prison, 'on the flat roof of the northern lodge ... when all the culprits are drawn out into the area before it to behold the mournful scene' (Owen, [1808] 1972: 432). Between 1787 and 1868, 93 felons were executed in Shrewsbury. During the period 1787 to 1793, while the new prison was under construction (see Chapter 6), there were 27 executions held at the Old Heath.

From 1793 the site of public executions was at the front of the newly built prison. Reflecting the wider changes in criminal justice and punishment of the early to mid-nineteenth century, until the 1830s there were only one or two execution days a year held at the prison, although they may have involved more than one offender. Across the period, the death penalty was used increasingly only for the crime of murder, but in the earlier years it was handed down for stealing livestock and horses, killing cows, housebreaking, burglary and rioting. Only two women were publicly executed at Shrewbury at this time: Sarah Jones, aged 27, for the murder of her child in 1803, and Ann Harris, aged 50, for her part assisting in the 'Drayton murders' in 1828.

At the Shrewsbury Assizes in 1821, large numbers of colliers were charged with riot and related offences; all were protesting about a reduction in wages. The outbreak of protest and riot in the Wellington area had clearly caused a great deal of concern, and a number of colliers were sentenced by the courts to short periods of imprisonment. However, during the Assizes, 14 people were sentenced to death. Twelve of these men were reprieved even before the judges departed the town, but that left two – Thomas Palin and Samuel Hayward. Their crimes were regarded as very serious and, 'having assembled in a riotous and tumultuous manner, such as might indeed, but for the good Providence of God, have ended in the loss of many lives', they were both sentenced to death, with no hope of mercy. The pronouncing judge described them as 'infatuated individuals' who would pay with their lives and encouraged them to make use of the short time they had to seek redemption for their sins (*Chester Courant*, 3 April 1821). In the end Hayward's reprieve must have come in the days or hours before the appointed time, as only Palin was listed as executed on 7 April 1821.

During the 1830s, execution days at Shrewsbury were more sporadic, and until 1849 there were only six in total, sometimes involving a lone offender, and so numerous years when there were none at all. But in 1832 both Joseph Grindley and James Lea were hanged for arson, and in 1836 three offenders were all executed for highway robbery. In the 1850s and 1860s there were only one or two executions per decade, all involving men who had been convicted of murder (*Wattons News Cuttings*, 1837: 475).

The *Narrative of the Life of Thomas Williams*, published anonymously in 1815, documents the life of one such criminal sentenced to death and executed at Shrewsbury and provides particulars of the event. Thomas Williams, alias Cranberry, was 26 or 27 years old and had been sentenced to hang for housebreaking. He was not the only person to be executed that day, as Thomas Jesson, aged 25, was also hanged for burglary. The sentences were carried out on 8 April 1815, almost exactly one year after the last execution in the town (9 April 1814), when William Wheeler had been hanged, having been found guilty of an unnatural offence against a young child (SA, D34.6, 1815).

Thomas Williams had been in Shrewsbury gaol before, five years earlier, when 'his conduct was turbulent and riotous, and was the cause of constant trouble and uneasiness to the governor of the gaol and to all his servants, who had anything to do with him' (SA, D34.6, 1815: 13). Yet during his recent committal for housebreaking and subsequent sentence his conduct changed dramatically; now he was orderly and quiet and disapproved of his companions' vices. A crowd was waiting to view the execution, which took place on the right-hand bay of the prison entrance (Marsh, 1984: 106). 'From his cell he walked with a firm and steady step ... When he reached the platform, he requested the sheriff to grant him a quarter of an hour to address the multitude' (SA, D34.6, 1815: 15). The address which he made to the crowd and the other prisoners in the gaol had a similar basic structure to those given in the Ordinary of Newgate's Accounts recorded in the eighteenth century (Linebaugh, 1977; Rawlings, 1992). These final speeches were common across the country and encouraged the spread of the message of deterrence, often charting the demise of the individual through a life of crime and immorality and warning others of the perils that awaited those who choose a similar path:

> Williams admonished the crowd to take warning by his untimely fate, and to pray to God, that all might escape such a fate. Then, turning around to the prisoners, he attributed his untimely end to the wicked conduct of his step-mother, and to his transportation to the hulks at the early age of 13, which had made him a hardened wretch, fit for any diabolical act; and exhorted them all on their release from prison, to become faithful members of the Christian society, and so to become happy in their own minds, a thing which he never knew.
>
> (SA, D34.6, 1815: 15)

An execution in Shrewsbury a few years earlier, in 1811, provides a slightly different point of view, illustrating the brutal nature of the spectacle, which in some quarters was thought only to harden the feelings of the crowd and enable them to sympathise with the condemned. McGowen argues that the reformers who attacked hanging as a practice and proposed imprisonment as an alternative were two slightly different positions within the same movement for change. He maintains that the 'prison existed to save life and to serve life; its goal was to take the hardened offenders and by softening them render them good neighbours and citizens. Hanging on the other hand was seen as the counsel of despair' (1986: 326). Reformers found in the Quaker Elizabeth Fry a powerful symbol of their principles to oppose the gallows. They argued that her work among the female prisoners at Newgate demonstrated how sympathy could be used to create a link to the criminal and prepare the way for reform (McGowen, 1986).

This commentary on a multiple execution at Shrewsbury also highlights the severity of the criminal law and the seemingly random use of systems of reprieve such as royal mercy:

> At the last Shrewsbury Assizes, George Taylor, aged 43, William Turner, aged 33, Abraham Whitehouse, aged 23, James Baker, aged 19, and Isaac Hickman, aged 19, were convicted of burglariously breaking into a dwelling-house, and stealing some bank notes and other articles of value. They were *all left for death.* The three first were considered as old offenders. The two others, however,

were understood to have borne a good character; their parents were said to be respectable; the offence, as far as appeared, was the first they had committed; and they were *only nineteen*. A general persuasion therefore prevailed, that these unfortunate youths would be permitted to live. Under this impression, it seems, some kind-hearted person, a stranger to them, climbed to the top of the wall overlooking the press yard behind the Shire-hall, where the prisoners were waiting on the day of their condemnation, and cried out, 'You are all condemned, but only three of you will suffer.' The poor young fellows eagerly embraced the assurance. They knew how often mercy was extended to persons under the sentence of death, and could not suppose they should be selected as fit objects of peculiar severity.

(Anon, 1812: 206–7; original emphasis)

Although the young prisoners comforted themselves with the hope of a reprieve, it did not come.

they had but two days, – two days of consternation and despair, – to fit themselves for death and eternity. Those two days, the shortest they had ever known, were but too soon gone. The morning of execution came. On that day, the five prisoners, even the *two lads of nineteen*, were all hanged! The two poor fellows who were executed together, immediately as the drop fell from under them, caught hold of each other's hands, and expired in a mutual embrace! What a feeling has pervaded the county, among all who could feel, hardly need be described.

(Ibid.: 207)

The writer noted that

the extraordinary circumstance of five men being executed at once, for one offence, attracted vast multitudes of people, of the lower order, from all parts of the country. To see five of their fellow creatures hanged, was as good as a horse-race, a boxing-match, or a bull-baiting. If nothing was intended but to amuse the rabble, at a great loss of their time and a considerable expense, the design was undoubtedly effected. If a public entertainment was *not* the object, it may be asked, What benefit has a single individual derived from beholding the destruction of these miserable victims? Perhaps that question may be answered by stating, that many of the spectators immediately afterwards got intoxicated, and some cried out to their companions, with a significant gesture in allusion to the mode of punishment, 'It is but a ten minute job!' If such is the sentiment excited on the very spot, it cannot be supposed to be more salutary at a distance; and notwithstanding the sacrifice of these five men, the people of Shropshire must still fasten their doors.

(Ibid.)

However, if, in the future,

> a compassionate Shropshire jury should rather acquit some unhappy young
> culprit, when charged with a capital felony, and suffer him to go unpunished,
> rather than consign him to the executioner, – if house-breakers should learn
> to think lightly of human life, and adopt the precaution of committing a
> murder the next time they commit a robbery, since the danger of detection
> would be less, and the punishment no greater, – what will the inhabitants of
> the county have to thank for it, but this very spectacle! – a spectacle which
> cannot soften one heart, but may harden many; which confounds moral dis-
> tinctions, and draws away public indignation from the guilt of the offender,
> to turn it against the severity of the law.

> (Ibid.: 208)

The commentator, writing in *The Philanthropist* (a leading reform periodical of the
era), clearly reflects common concerns and debates of the time; he acknowledges
the arbitrary nature of the use of mercy and that execution was both a brutalising
public entertainment – only hardening those observing, many of whom have no
feelings (or at least not the desired response to the event) – and a practice which
allowed the crowd to sympathise with the offender and to criticise the severity of
the criminal law. The execution lacked any deterrent effect on the public, as the
people of Shropshire 'still have to lock their doors'.

The Lancaster Gazette reported the same execution in a more pragmatic fashion
than the writer in *The Philanthropist*, noting the downfall of the condemned and
reminding its audience of the perils of irreligion:

> On the fatal morning, they had very devoutly joined with the Chaplain in
> prayer, and received the Sacrament. – While they were upon the Scaffold,
> Baker and Hickman (each 19 years of age), fell to their knees, and, in an
> audible tone, engaged in prayer; Taylor and Turner spoke but a few words,
> in a very low tone, purporting that *Sabbath-breaking* was their first step to a
> vicious course of life; Whitehouse was silent during the whole time.

> (7 September, 1811: 4; original emphasis)

The last public execution at Shrewsbury prison was on Thursday 8 April 1868,
when John Mapp was hanged for murdering a young girl, Catherine Lewis, a few
days before Christmas 1867. Both the execution and the court case were reported
quite fully in the press. Mapp, it was later revealed, was not a first-time offender and
had in fact been convicted of the violent rape of a 60-year-old woman in Shropshire
in 1859. For that offence he had been sentenced to ten years' penal servitude, but
he had been released on a ticket of leave in 1866. The evidence presented also suggested that the murder of Catherine was sexually motivated (Cox, 2008).

The *Birmingham Journal* reported that, although he initially protested his innocence, after time spent in the condemned cell Mapp had admitted to the crime.

The gatehouse of the prison overlooked the town, and from seven o'clock in the morning as many as 5,000 or 6,000 observers were packed into the space in front of the prison, onto Howard Street, perching on the walls surrounding the railway station and on the tops of nearby buildings to gain a better view of the scaffold (*Shrewsbury Chronicle*, 9 April 1868, cited in Cox, 2008: 122). The *Birmingham Journal* reported that

> There were about the crowd none of the characteristics noticeable about similar assemblies at executions in large towns, they being for the most part respectably dressed, and, almost without exception, well behaved. The large number of decent-looking women present was remarkable, and some carried children in their arms.
>
> (11 April 1868: 3)

Concerning the execution itself, it was stated that the procession crossed the courtyard:

> The chaplain, in his gown, walked before him, repeating the burial service, but Mapp paid not the slightest attention to the solemn words, nor were his lips once observed to move in prayer. He walked steadily up the winding staircase leading to the tower on which the gallows was erected, and preserved his extraordinary firmness even while he stood upon the drop during the long moment that Calcraft [the executioner] was adjusting the rope. He said, 'Goodbye' when Calcraft shook hands with him, and as he left him turned his head as if about to speak, but at that moment the drop fell with electric suddenness, there was a cry from the crowd, and all was over.

As Mapp had turned his head, the rope was dislodged, and as a result the fall was not fatal; instead, 'he struggled desperately for fully half a minute before he died' (ibid.). Accounts of Mapp's death varied, but a number of reports suggested that he struggled at the end of the noose for ten minutes (Cox, 2008).

Executions behind prison walls

The Capital Punishment Amendment Act was passed in 1868, and the first execution behind prison walls took place later the same year at Maidstone gaol, where 18-year-old Thomas Wells was hanged for the murder of his boss at the railway station where they both worked (McGowen, 1994). Between the last public execution, in May 1868, and the end of 1880, there were 171 executions carried out in England and Wales, all in local prisons, usually in the county in which the Assizes had taken place. Following the case of John Mapp above, there was a gap of twenty years before the first private execution inside Shrewsbury prison. William Arrowsmith, aged 42, was executed on 28 March 1888 after being sentenced to death for murder.

The shift to private execution was also part of a broader shift in privacy in punishment; all forms of public punishment were now largely obsolete in this more 'civilised' age (Spierenburg, 1984; McGowen, 1994; Pratt, 2002), and the prison, as we shall discuss in Chapters 6 and 7, was to play a new and increasing role in severing criminals from the outside world. The respectable populace did not want to see punishment. This was one of the virtues of private executions, but it was also felt that 'an unseen punishment was juster for being freed of vindictive personal feeling' (Canetti, cited in McGowen, 1994: 282). Alternatively, the demise of public execution could be understood as a failure to communicate punishment on behalf of the state or as a crisis in its meaning (Smith, 2008).

Just over fifty years after the change, the report of the Prison System Enquiry Committee, *English Prisons To-day*, produced by Stephen Hobhouse and Fenner Brockway, argued that an execution had 'a demoralising effect upon the whole prison population, is degrading to every official concerned, and certainly ought to not take place in a prison' (1922: 250). Those sentenced to death were isolated from other prisoners, often placed in a condemned cell (health permitting), one larger than normal, where they would be under the constant observation of two prison officers. On the day of execution they would be moved to a cell close to the gallows for the final preparations and last ministrations by the prison chaplain, or else the condemned cell would be part of a cluster of cells used to house the condemned for all these purposes. It was the case, though, that other prisoners were aware of the impending execution. Depending on the layout of the prison, the condemned cell might be passed regularly by prisoners and staff on the wing, or the condemned might be observed in the exercise yard. The presence of a prisoner sentenced to death for the murder of the woman he loved, and the effects of this on the wider prison environment, were powerfully observed in Oscar Wilde's *The Ballad of Reading Gaol*, published in 1897:

> There is no chapel on the day
> On which they hang a man:
> The chaplain's heart is far too sick,
> Or his face is far too wan,
> Or there is that written in his eyes
> Which none should look upon.
>
> So they kept us close till nigh on noon,
> And then they rang the bell,
> And the warders with their jingling keys
> Opened each listening cell,
> And down the iron stair we tramped,
> Each from his separate hell.
>
> Out into God's sweet air we went,
> But not in a wonted way,
> For this man's face was white with fear,

And that man's face was grey,
And I never saw sad men who looked
So wistfully at the day.

(Wilde, [1898] 2002: 130)

As this extract demonstrates, it was not just the prisoners who were affected by executions but also the staff – chaplains, governors and officers. Forsythe (1990) notes that, while it is difficult to conceive of the impact of such events on those concerned, autobiographical and biographical accounts testify to the atmosphere and feelings of those who experienced the lead up to and the execution day itself. Prisoners were distressed and restless, watched from their cell windows or paced in silence; officers could not sleep and chaplains were torn between their duties to minister to the condemned and the morality of capital punishment. Hobhouse and Brockway echoed this view and pointed out that executions 'inevitably brutalise the already unhealthy atmosphere of the prison' (1922: 249).

Executions within Shrewsbury prison were similarly evoked in a poem by A. E. Housman in the collection *A Shropshire Lad*, originally published in 1896. Housman refers to earlier punishment practices of keeping flocks by moonlight – a colloquial phrase for 'hanging in chains' – and goes on to observe:

They hang us now in Shrewsbury jail:
The whistles blow forlorn,
And trains all night groan on the rail
To men that die at morn.

There sleeps in Shrewsbury jail to-night,
Or wakes, as may betide,
A better lad, if things went right,
Than most that sleep outside.

And naked to the hangman's noose
The morning clocks will ring
A neck God made for other use
Than strangling in a string.

(Housman, [1896] 1987: 15–16)

Prison officers were paid extra fees to attend before and to remove the body after an execution. Those condemned to death had to be constantly observed by two officers to prevent any attempts at suicide (Thomas, 1972). All those executed inside prisons were buried in unmarked graves within the prison walls. As McConville (1995) points out, although executions were the responsibility of the sheriff, the prison commissioners took *de facto* control after centralisation in 1878, and they were keen to avoid any whiff of scandal through 'botched' jobs. They also placed great emphasis on the need for decorum in all proceedings; the carnival atmosphere and drama of the public execution was to be sanitised, and silence would prevail (Pratt, 2002; McConville, 1995).

Despite the commissioners' efforts, there were problems in carrying out capital punishment inside prisons. It was difficult to find reliable hangmen: those involved were often drunk and courted the public in a manner viewed by the authorities as particularly distasteful. Problems also persisted with the length of the rope – where either the person was strangled and took a long time to die or near decapitation occurred – as did problems with the scaffold or the functioning of the trap door (McConville, 1995). The latter is exemplified by perhaps the most often quoted case, the attempted execution at Exeter prison in 1885 of John Lee, 'the man they could not hang'. Three attempts were made, but the trap door failed each time; Lee's sentence was commuted to life imprisonment.

Rowbotham (2010) notes that the performatory function of execution was also played out in the hangmen. Where once they had been the hooded villains of the piece, by the end of the nineteenth century the then 'national' hangman, William Marwood, was discussed in the press as more professional than his predecessors. Visible, uniformed in black with a large ring and chain as he arrived at executions, he was celebrated in a popular rhyme: 'If Pa killed Ma, who'd kill Pa? – Marwood!' (cited ibid.: 193). Though Marwood and his predecessor, William Calcraft, both courted the media and the public, Marwood had a makeshift museum which included some personal effects of those he had executed; encouraged by drink, he would tell stories of the events he had experienced (Smith, 2004). Marwood gave the impression that he was the state's 'public executioner' (he preferred this term to 'hangman'), though no such post existed. On his death in 1883 the Home Office and the authorities in London and Middlesex were inundated with over 1,000 applications to take up the role as England's 'willing executioner'. What this also reveals is a more complex relationship between the public and execution and that perhaps the death penalty had wider support than has been thought. Concerns about its use were class-based but, certainly, 'there was no shortage of willing executioners among her majesty's civilised subjects' (ibid.: 304).

After 1868 the theatre of execution no longer existed, and the fact that an execution had taken place within a prison was marked by the raising of a prominently positioned black flag and the tolling of prison bells for 15 minutes both before and after the actual deed. Yet, as Pratt (2002) notes, by the early twentieth century even these elements came to be seen as excessive or melodramatic; black flags were revoked in 1902, prison bells tolled only after an execution, and by 1925 the press were also excluded and a death notice was posted at the prison gate.

5

TRANSPORTATION

Convicts to the colonies

This chapter will consider the use of transportation – a process used by the British government from the seventeenth century onwards. In particular it will look at the use of transportation to Australia, which had begun at the end of the eighteenth century, through to its peak employment and then decline in operation. While the banishment of offenders overseas had occurred from the seventeenth century, the Transportation Act 1718 had established its use more fully in the criminal justice system. After the American War of Independence and the cessation of transportation to America in the 1770s, Australia became the new destination for what is thought to be over 160,000 convicts (Hughes, 1996; Shaw, 1998; Godfrey and Cox, 2008). During the 1830s, when the system was at its height, approximately 5,000 people per year were sentenced to transportation and departed for what was, on average, a four-month journey. The use, operation and then decline of this system will be examined until the last ships sailed in the late 1860s. While transportation was in decline, the convict prison system was being established. During this time, and after the eventual end of transportation, convicts were sentenced to long periods of imprisonment known as penal servitude and were held in the government-run convict prisons in England (see Chapter 7). The chapter will close with the case study of George Pobjoy, just one of the many thousands of convicts who found himself transported to the Antipodes.

By the early nineteenth century, transportation to Australia had been under way for three decades. This first section will examine the process and administration of transportation between 1815 and the final journeys in the late 1860s. In Britain, the process of removing criminals out of the country and putting them to labour in remote locations had existed for hundreds of years (for transportation to America, see, for example, Beattie, 1986, 2002; Morgan and Rushton, 2004; Cox, 2014). By the early nineteenth century the primary locations used were Australia (1787–1868), Bermuda (1823–63) and Gibraltar (1842–74).

While I focus here on those who were sent from England, it is important to note that many people were transported from or between British colonies across the world, be they in the Caribbean, Canada, the Cape, India, Hong Kong, Mauritius, Australia, New Zealand or British penal settlements across the Indian Ocean (Maxwell-Stewart, 2010; see Anderson, 2000, 2012). Transportation had already been established as an alternative to the death penalty; Beattie argues that, by the mid-eighteenth century, it had 'introduced stability and flexibility into the administration of the law … It had provided not only a secondary punishment that the courts plainly sought … it also made the discretionary application of the increasing capital statutes tolerable' (1986: 519). After the Transportation Act 1718, transportation could be employed when defendants were permitted 'benefit of clergy' (see Chapter 4), and convicts were branded on the thumb (to ensure the sentence was carried out only once). By the late eighteenth century it was providing an intermediate sentence; a lengthy period of banishment of seven years' minimum was expected to have a deterrent value (Beattie 1986; Maxwell-Stewart, 2010).

In America, transported convicts had worked in exchange for their keep and were often released early in order to keep costs down, but convicts returning to Britain after transportation had been a continual problem for the system. As Australia was a long way away and geographically isolated, the possibility of returning to Britain was slight; 'banishment there, even for those on a seven-year sentence, would for all intents and purposes be for life … construed as a punishment the poor would fear' (Maxwell-Stewart, 2010: 1228). The numbers of convicts sent to Australia in the early years was a little sporadic on account of the Napoleonic Wars, but after 1815 the colonies developed more quickly as increasing numbers of convicts were sent out.

By the early decades of the nineteenth century, transportation was firmly established as an alternative option for the judiciary when sentencing. Since it allowed for an intermediate penalty for the courts to apply to those who deserved more than a short period of imprisonment or a fine, it became a sentence in its own right. Emsley (2010) notes that during this period around one-third of those convicted at Quarter Sessions or Assizes were sentenced, or had their death sentence commuted, to transportation. In the 1830s, the Select Committee on Secondary Punishments considered it to be 'a most valuable ingredient in the system' for this very reason:

> Unless there existed some such mode of disposing of criminals whose offences do not merit the penalty of death, but whose morals are so depraved that their reformation can hardly be expected, no alternative would remain between perpetual imprisonment and the constant infusion into society of malefactors, who, after the term of their punishment had arrived, would again be thrown as outcasts on the world, without friends, without character, and without the means of gaining an honest livelihood.

(PP, 1831–2: 16)

Transportation also offered the potential for reform, and the organisation and development of the sentence as served in Australia was designed to assist with that process. Before boarding the ships that would take them to Australia, convicts were held in England in decommissioned war ships known as hulks.

The hulks

Conditions on board the hulks were often overcrowded and damp, and prisoners spent much of their time in irons. The hulks had been a temporary measure after the outbreak of the American War of Independence, but they continued to be used to some extent until the 1850s. Despite the criticism of the hulks, there has been surprisingly little written about them, except that they were mostly in an appalling state – a largely universal comment made on the conditions that convicts endured. Indeed, mortality rates on board were high; as many as one in four of those committed to the hulks never got beyond them, especially in the early years (Ignatieff, 1978). However, it is also important to note that some convicts were invalided out of the system at this point, served so long on the hulks that they were sent on to prison in England, or were released through gaining a pardon.

In the early part of our period, hulks were located on the River Thames and the River Medway and in harbours on the South Coast. In 1815, for example, there were five hulks: the *Justitia* docked at Woolwich, the *Retribution* at Sheerness, the *Captivity* and the *Laurel* at Portsmouth Harbour, and the *Portland* at Langston Harbour. Together these vessels held just over 2,000 inmates; the largest was the *Justitia*, with 500 prisoners, the smallest the *Laurel*, with just over 250. The overwhelming majority of those confined on the hulks were men, but 5 to 10 per cent – nearer 10 per cent on the smaller vessels – were boys aged between 11 and 19 (*Papers relating to Convict Hulks*, PP, 1814–15: 1–2; Branch Johnson, 1957). Other evidence suggests children as young as eight were held on the hulks (HO 9 Convict Prison Hulks: Quarterly Register of Hulks, Oct–Dec 1825).

The Select Committee on Secondary Punishments viewed transportation as a necessary part of the penal system, albeit one requiring improvement, but it was highly critical of the use of the hulks. While significant changes had occurred in local prisons (see Chapter 6) in terms of the organisation of prisoners, who were classified with a view to preventing the corruption of the young or the first offender by more hardened criminals, none of these principles were operating on the hulks. Neither, thought the committee members, were the hulks operating with a 'severity of punishment sufficient to make it an object of terror to the evil-doer' (PP, 1831–2: 12). Their report noted that the capacity of the hulks varied between 80 to around 800 prisoners, often held in wards of between 12 and 30. Inmates were put to labour during the day but at other times associated freely within the wards. The committee lamented the lack of religious or moral instruction, association with friends from outside and generally defective rules. Witnesses testified that, although contrary to the rules of the hulks, prisoners were

permitted the use of musical instruments; that flash songs, dancing, fighting and gaming take place; that that old offenders are in the habit of robbing the new comers; that newspapers and improper books are clandestinely introduced; a communication is frequently kept up with their old associates on shore; and that occasionally spirits are introduced on board.

(Ibid.: 12–13)

The hulks represented a throwback to the vice and corruption of the unreformed gaols and houses of correction of the eighteenth century, seemingly uninfluenced by the new philosophies of punishment and penological methods of the early nineteenth century.

The Committee on Secondary Punishments also criticised the labour undertaken on the hulks; prisoners worked in the dockyards and the Arsenal, but the hours were claimed to be shorter than the those for the average free labourer and the work was declared less severe (evoking the concept of 'less eligibility'; see Chapter 1). The hulks needed more order, more silence and the separation of convicts, in a manner similar to that used under the separate system (see Chapter 6), and communication with visitors and the outside world in general should be strictly limited. The committee proposed that the government use prisons rather than hulks to house convicts before transport, suggesting a new penitentiary be built or the use of Dartmoor prison. These proposals were not taken up, even though it was already the case that a proportion of those sentenced to transportation were being sent to the new government penitentiary at Millbank. The government would later also use Pentonville model prison to hold individuals under separate confinement before their removal overseas (see Chapter 7).

Nevertheless the hulks were an important part of the system and, as McConville (1981) notes, even by the 1840s they still held over 70 per cent of the home-based convicts. This changed only when the new penitentiaries of Millbank and Pentonville were used more extensively from 1843 onwards. As these two prisons were then used either for separate confinement or as a depot for convicts to be assessed, and a few years later Portland convict prison became available for those on public works, the composition of the prison population sent to the hulks changed. Fewer were sent to the hulks, but those who ended up there were classified as old or infirm or those who, because of poor health, could not undergo either separate confinement or labour on public works.

The hulks were exposed again in the late 1840s, when allegations of ill-treatment were made by T. Duncombe, MP. At this time, hulks were still moored at Portsmouth and Devonport, but it was the *Justitia* and the *Warrior*, both moored at Woolwich, that drew Duncombe's concern, particularly on account of the poor health and mortality rates of the convicts held there. In calling for a select committee inquiry, Duncombe

attributed this result to the excessive cruelty of the discipline, to the brutality of the medical officers, to the oppressive manner in which men were treated while alive, and to the reckless manner to which they were cast aside when dead – circumstances which required and ought to undergo immediate revision.

(*The Times*, 29 January 1847: 5; see also Branch Johnson, 1957)

The subsequent inquiry, led by William J. Williams, one of the inspectors of the hulks at Woolwich, revealed that the cleanliness in the hospital ships was 'most disgraceful and discreditable' (cited in McConville, 1981: 200). He also reported the neglect of lunatic prisoners, trafficking among inmates, laxness in authority on the part of the officers, and poor religious and moral education. Although this led to the reorganisation of the hulks and to the Directorate of Convict Prisons recommending their abolition, they remained in use, though in reduced capacity. After 1852 only two survived: the *Warrior* was decaying and rotten and was broken up after Chatham convict prison had been completed in 1856, and a fire destroyed the *Defence* in the summer of 1857 (McConville, 1981).

After the hulks were finally abandoned, temporary incarceration in a government penitentiary was the fate of all convicts awaiting transportation (see Chapter 7 for the establishment of Millbank and Pentonville). But many prisoners were held on hulks overseas – particularly in Bermuda and Gibraltar, where they were used until the 1860s and 1870s. Labour carried out by convicts at these establishments remained very important to the Admiralty and Ordnance departments of the government at home, but this was especially the case in the colonies. The hulks overseas continued to be viewed as a corrupting or contaminating influence for the spread of criminality (Brown and Maxwell, 2003), and they stood out in a system which, in England at least, had shifted towards the use of prison regimes based on separation and silence, order and discipline, designed to prevent the transmission of crime and immorality. Those convicts in Bermuda were shipped back to prisons in England in the 1850s and 1860s, and found that the regimes they had experienced overseas were in stark contrast to that of the newly established convict prison system (Brown and Maxwell, 2003; McConville, 1981).

The journey

For the majority of the period when transportation to Australia took place, between two-thirds and three-quarters of those sentenced were actually dispatched overseas (Emsley, 2010; Shaw, 1998). For these convicts, beyond the hulks lay a difficult and hazardous journey of around four months to the other side of the world. Ships transporting convicts and free settlers were often lost at sea, and the worst disaster happened in 1842, when the convict ship *Waterloo* broke up off the Cape coast. Accounts vary slightly, but the *South African Commercial Advertiser* (3 September 1842) reported that 190 people had lost their lives; of the estimated 330 persons on board, 143 were convicts (3rd September, 1842). But most of the deaths on the convict ships occurred as a result of disease. Some of these issues had also been of concern with transportation to America, but conditions improved when remuneration to contractors was related to the numbers landing safely in Australia rather than numbers boarding ship in England. Prisoners did die on the convict ships, and in the earlier period at higher rates, but administrative changes which ensured better screening of those ill or diseased and cleaner, more hygienic and sanitary ships after 1814 reduced the mortality rates. This was especially the case after the introduction of surgeon-superintendents who accompanied the ship, at least from 1818 onwards (McDonald and Shlomowitz, 1989).

Those transported to Australia were largely young people sentenced for property offences, but people were sent to the colony for all types of offences, including serious sexual and violent crimes. By the early nineteenth century, the sentence was firmly established as an alternative to the death penalty. There is some evidence of unremittingly harsh penalties meted out to children. For example, Thomas Bailey, aged 11 and described in the record as a 'notorious rogue', was sentenced to seven years' transportation for stealing a halfpenny; Hannah Hambleton was ten years old when she was transported for seven years for stealing a handkerchief, a net collar and a ribbon from a shop (Briggs et al., 1996). But cases such as these were in the minority, and most transportees were aged between 16 and 29 and were drawn from the working classes (Maxwell-Stewart, 2010), reflecting those who were drawn into the criminal justice system more widely.

Convict life in Australia

In the early years in Australia, the governor, Captain Arthur Phillip, who had led the first fleet to Botany Bay, was presented with difficulties relating to both the establishment and the organisation of the new colony and the environment. Overseers – later the establishment of a police force – and people with expertise in construction and building, as well as the necessities of medicine and law, all had to be found from among the convicts. The cultivation of land, the growing of crops necessary for the colony to be self-sufficient in food, was challenging in a climate and terrain very different to England but also with a workforce who may have had little or no experience in agricultural work (Hirst, 1998).

The debate about the use of transportation and the penal colony at this time was largely about the deterrent effect of the sentence. Jeremy Bentham criticised its use as an uncertain punishment; it could be severe or it could inflict very little pain. These opinions changed as the colony grew and became more prosperous. The deterrent capacity in the eyes of some observers in England was greatly diminished by this, and letters from a few convicts who had made decent lives for themselves were frequently cited as evidence. In New South Wales, the case against transportation became intertwined by the 1830s with the principles relating to the debate and subsequent end of slavery. It was not just that the unfortunate in the colony were corrupted or undone by the evil and the depraved, but that the system itself was tainted (Hirst, 2008).

At that point, the peak of transportation to Australia, the 'assignment' system had been developed. Free settlers were encouraged to move to the colonies and have convicts 'assigned' to them; the employer would clothe, feed and accommodate them in exchange for their labour. Often convicts were allocated according to their skills; demand was higher for more skilled workers and trades. Any physical punishments were not to be meted out by the settler but by the state. The benefit of the assignment system to the convict was that 'good conduct' ensured release on licence, or what was called a 'ticket of leave'; the benefit to the government was that it was cheap. Those who continued to offend would find themselves punished by the courts in the colony and could be flogged or sent to road parties, chain gangs or penal stations; female would be confined in factories (Maxwell-Stewart, 2010).

The idea behind transportation was that making the labour of the able-bodied available to the new colonies was more important than punishing them in revenge for vices displayed in the mother country. But, back home, disquiet about the operation of transportation continued. As had been the case with the earlier system of transportation to America, concerns were raised about the deterrent effect of the punishment. This satire of the sentence of transportation, written in 1826, epitomised the sentiments voiced:

> Because you have committed this offence the sentence of the court is that you shall no longer be burdened with the support of your wife and family. You shall be immediately removed from a very bad climate and a country over burdened with people to one of the finest regions of the earth, where the demand for human labour is increasing every hour, and where it is highly probable that you may ultimately gain your character and improve your future. The court have been induced to pass this sentence upon you in consequence of the many aggravating circumstances of your case, and they hope that your fate will be a warning to others.
>
> (Cited in Emsley, 2010: 284)

Such was the view of the potential for a better life in the colony that the newspapers claimed men were committing crimes simply to be sentenced to transportation.

In Britain, the increasing numbers of hostile voices surrounding the use of transportation culminated in the established of the Select Committee on Transportation, known as the Molesworth Committee, which reported in 1837 and 1838. It rightly pointed out that the penal colonies were so far away that people in England were unaware of the severity of life, and consequently the deterrent effect of such a punishment was lost. The committee acknowledged the contrasting and various experiences that convicts might endure in the colony: simple contracted employment as a servant or worker; a status similar to slavery; arduous penal work in a chain gang; or the 'gates of Hell' at Norfolk Island (see Maxwell-Stewart, 2008; Causer, 2011). But it also acknowledged the futility of trying to convey this to the population of Britain. Convicts in Australia could gain employment, wealth and status and build a prosperous life for themselves and their families, but they could also find themselves in a world of desperation and despair. On the efficacy of transportation the committee reported:

> It is proved, beyond a doubt, by the testimony of every witness best acquainted with the actual conditions of convicts, and likewise by numerous facts ... that most persons in this country [Britain], whether belonging to the criminal population, or connected with the administration of justice, are ignorant of the real amount of suffering inflicted upon a transported felon, and underrate the severity of the punishment.
>
> (PP, 1838: 19)

Despite the recommendations of the Molesworth Committee against the use of transportation, described by Hirst as an 'official, public indictment of the convict system in New South Wales' (2008: 27), the government ploughed on with the system. But by 1840 transportation to New South Wales had ceased and, under the newly developed probationary system, convicts were sent to Van Diemen's Land. Instead of being assigned to settlers, they would be put to probationary labour on the roads; after completion of their sentence they could then be 'hired' by a settler for a nominal wage. This system did not work as expected. A global recession hit. Britain continued to send convicts, but the new arrivals and those looking to complete probation could not find work and quickly filled the depots. 'In this climate, many colonists joined the clamour of voices from the British Isles calling for an end to transportation ... Transportation was increasingly seen as a morally polluting institution that had to be abolished on order to protect the reputation of the colony' (Maxwell-Stewart, 2010: 1233). The stage system was adapted so convicts spent part of their sentence in penitentiaries in Britain; some therefore arrived already having gained a ticket of leave. However, the final nail in transportation to Eastern Australia was a 'gold rush' (Maxwell-Stewart, 2010).

At the height of the system, in 1833, 7,000 convicts were transported to Australia, and in the 1830s as a whole around 5,000 per year were sent out. It is estimated that, of the total of 160,000 convicts, just under 25,000 were female. In the early years, the government wanted to encourage marriage, but the system was a lottery, open to prostitution and to violence and sexual exploitation. Later the system was tightened up, and from the 1840s women were sent to solely to Van Diemen's Land. The assignment system for women frequently meant 'imprisonment' in domestic service or confinement in 'female factories', where they were put to labour and subject to severe penal regimes (Hirst, 1998; D'Cruze and Jackson, 2009).

The last ship sailed to Van Diemen's Land (renamed Tasmania in 1856) in 1853, as the island refused to receive any more convicts from England. However, Western Australia continued to take them – indeed, colonists petitioned for convicts to be sent, as labour was short in the region. Transportation as a judicial sentence was abolished in 1857. From then on, all classes of convicts were sentenced to penal servitude, though for some this could still be overseas, and therefore the system remained until 1867. Across the eighteen years that Western Australia continued to accept male convicts, just over 9,600 individuals were sent out, two full ships per year (Shaw, 1998; Gibbs, 2001; Godfrey and Cox, 2008). There were still voices of dissent regarding the danger to the colony of moral corruption, but the area desperately needed labour. The economy of the region was stimulated by the presence both of the convicts and of the free migrants who accompanied them. Those who were sent from England had been selected on the basis of their behaviour and, although they were temporarily housed in the early years, as the colony grew, prisons were built at Fremantle and then at Perth. At these institutions convicts underwent separate confinement and then undertook public works, largely on the roads and building country depots (Shaw, 1998).

Transportation of juvenile offenders

It was common in the late eighteenth and early nineteenth century for juvenile offenders to be punished by transportation after commutation of a capital sentence. Like adults, they would be sent to the hulks to await removal to Australia or New Zealand. The first separate establishments for juvenile criminals were the *Bellerophon*, used initially from 1824, and then the *Euryalus*, which was adapted for juveniles from 1825 and moored at Chatham. Many juvenile offenders spent their whole sentences in the hulks. Despite the separate provision for youngsters, the conditions were deplorable: they suffered long hours locked up below deck, a meagre diet, harsh discipline, and extensive hours of labour. Although the hulks were increasing seen as 'nurseries for vice', especially when it came to the treatment of juvenile criminals, the *Euryalus* was not closed down until 1843 (Shore, 2002b; Radzinowicz and Hood, 1990; for more on the *Euryalus*, see Select Committee on Gaols and Houses of Correction, 1835, PP, Vol. XI, 258–66).

Many of the problems and concerns with transportation more generally also applied to young offenders. However, it was often voiced that juveniles would have the opportunity of a new start overseas; those who had had their lives interrupted by crime could reinvent and rebuild them after completing their sentence (Shore, 2002b). Transportation was not just about punishing youngsters by banishing them to the other side of the world, nor was it just about deterrence. It was widely held that young offenders would be unable to break their connections with the criminal class should they remain in England. But the reality of the opportunities of transportation was quite different to the assumptions of many of these commentators back in England (Radzinowicz and Hood, 1990).

Separate provisions for juveniles also gradually appeared in Australia; accommodation for young offenders was established at the Hyde Park Barracks in Sydney, and by the 1830s policies were designed in New South Wales so that convict boys would be assigned to masters to learn a trade or be apprenticed in exchange for board and learning. The 'worst' types were sent to a boys' school at Port Arthur in Van Diemen's Land, and in 1834 a special penal colony was opened at Point Puer (Radzinowicz and Hood, 1990). Point Puer took over 1,200 young males from convict ships in the 1830s and 1840s, though it is estimated that between 10,000 and 13,000 individuals under the age of 18 were sent to Van Diemen's Land as a whole across the period 1803 to 1853 (Humphrey, cited in Shore, 2002a: 135). Drawing on the principles in prisons mooted in England, Point Puer operated a regime of separation and silence as well as discipline and labour and took over from the juvenile barracks at Sydney, which were closed in 1833 (Shore, 2002a). Point Puer, which closed in 1849, operated a more punitive model. The boys held there were usually all under 16 and, 'despite the rhetoric', the aim of the institution was to 'shape the juvenile convicts into more useful colonial workers' ... 'The unyielding and unskilled juvenile delinquents, Britain and Ireland's flotsam and jetsam, were to be remade into compliant, skilled workers' (ibid.: 93). The regime was underpinned by the use of the lash, although in England the feeling of reformers at this time was generally against the use of such severe penalties when it came to the treatment of young offenders (see Chapter 9). Evidence suggests that some boys at Point Puer could and did adopt strategies of survival; they were not mere cogs in a machine or helplessly at the mercy of the grinding institution but challenged authority, disobeying and misbehaving, swearing, refusing to work, pilfering rations and destroying government property (Shore, 2002b).

Conditions in many of these establishments were degrading; punishments such as flogging held sway and abuse was rife. Though the system of transportation was coming to an end by the 1850s and 1860s, it was still the case that placing young offenders overseas, through 'voluntary' emigration or colonial apprenticeships, continued to be viewed as an opportunity for a new life for young people. This perspective had a long legacy. Similar policies existed well into the mid-twentieth century and demonstrate the extent to which they were used to relocate a wide range of children and young people who were 'in need', not just those who were 'encouraged' through contact with the law to leave (Constantine, 2008; Bean and Melville, 1989).

The demise of transportation to Australia

Fear regarding the end of transportation was widespread in England. As we have seen in Chapter 2, the identification of a criminal class and a panic about violent street crime thought to be committed by those released early from prison on licence fuelled concerns that the country would be invaded and overrun by convicts. The author of *What is to be Done with our Criminals?* wrote:

> The 5,000 criminals hitherto annually sent to our penal colonies, where they have so corrupted society, that feelings of justice and decency compel the Legislature to abolish transportation, are henceforth to remain, corrupting and increasing the swelling mass of criminals at home. Already there are upwards of 20,000 working out their sentences, and an equal number annually turned on society, without an easy means of obtaining subsistence, their minds filled with a sense of injustice, and their hearts influenced with hatred and revenge. All that sweltering venom is henceforth to be confined here ... There is ground for fear ... 'lest England herself become a penal settlement.
>
> (1847: 835, cited in Radzinowicz and Hood, 1980: 1310)

There is no doubt that the end of transportation had a profound effect on penal policy in England at this time (Smith, 1982; Bartrip, 1981).

The attitude of the British government towards transportation also began to change; after the mid-1850s transportation was increasingly costly, and it was cheaper to keep criminals imprisoned in England (Shaw, 1998). The Select Committee on Transportation in 1861 wanted to maintain the status quo and continue to send convicts to Western Australia. Though the numbers in the colony were quite small, as at June 1860 there were 2,432 convict men in the district, of whom 774 were maintained by the government and 1,658 were on tickets of leave. The committee acknowledged that the Australian colony was against transportation to any area of the country and that regions had passed laws to prevent any convicts entering their boundaries, but concluded that transportation 'may still be available, to the limited extent to which it is now reduced, as a mode of ultimate discharge or disposal of prisoners; or even as a final stage of progressive alleviation of a punishment' (Select Committee on Transportation, PP, 1861: 5).

The Royal Commission on Transportation and Penal Servitude two years later, in 1863, went further, calling for the extension of the use of transportation to Western Australia for as many convicts who were fit to be sent out. Transportation, they thought, could be properly regulated and convicts sent

> where they may be removed from their former temptations, where they can be sure of having a means of maintaining themselves by their industry, if inclined to do so, and where facilities exist for keeping them under more effective control than is practicable in this country, with its great cities, and large population. This mode of disposing of convicts affords by far the best chance of making them useful members of society.
>
> (PP, 1863: 34)

The then Home Secretary, Sir George Grey, had already pledged that the government was against the resumption of transportation and so, despite both of these committees' recommendations, he held firm. Even in the face of the perception of increasing crime rates, Grey maintained that the prison authorities favoured the expansion of the prison system in England (Smith, 1982).

The aforementioned committees came before the Carnarvon Committee inquiry into prison discipline in 1863. This Select Committee advocated a penal policy based on deterrence and, despite the criticism of the separate system, wished to continue its use as a central part of the disciplinary regime without the reformatory goals (Smith, 1982; Johnston, 2013). In the mid-1860s two Acts were passed – the Penal Servitude Act of 1864 (which applied to convict prisons; see Chapter 7) and the Prisons Act 1865 (which applied to local prisons; see Chapter 6). Both Acts implemented the philosophy favoured by the prison authorities at the time: harsher regimes based on long hours of hard labour, meagre living conditions and minimal diet.

In the end, 'transportation failed, partly because it was misunderstood at home, partly because it is hopeless to rely solely on deterrence to get rid of crime' (Shaw,

1998: 359). Even though transportation and the assignment system had the potential to offer a new environment in which people could, if circumstances allowed, find the opportunity to reform, the mood in mid-century England was against such a view. Transportation as a means of disposing of offenders across the British Empire, though, continued to be used in and between various British settlements, into the twentieth century (Maxwell-Stewart, 2010; Anderson, 2012).

Convict reform and reintegration in the colonies

The last fleet set sail from London to Western Australia in October 1867, arriving at the port of Fremantle in January 1868 (Godfrey and Cox, 2008). After serving time working for the colony in a depot (building bridges and public buildings, for example) the convicts could receive a 'ticket of leave'. In this system they remained under police supervision; they had to adhere to strict regulations and were subject to a nightly curfew and prohibited alcohol. Ultimately, individuals were trying to progress towards a conditional pardon; when the period of the original sentence had expired, they could obtain a 'certificate of freedom'. But any infraction of any of the rules or further law-breaking would set them back a stage (Braithwaite, 2001; Godfrey and Cox, 2008).

Braithwaite (2001) has argued that former convicts in the colony were able to integrate, and the life chances available to them in Australia allowed them to lead useful lives in a society that was more accepting of previous mistakes. He contends that the colony needed labour to grow and that the ex-convicts (freed or pardoned) had a stake in this future; free settlers therefore had a more restorative view of punishment in which people were given a second chance, and as a result the former penal colonies had lower crime rates.

More recently, Godfrey and Cox (2008) reconstructed the lives of over 200 men who were transported on the 'last fleet', aboard the convict ship the *Hougoumont*, to understand the extent to which individuals were aided in their reformation or further damaged by their removal overseas. They found that, while many convicts continued to offend in Australia, they were committing largely minor crimes – drunkenness, fighting, low-level public order and regulatory offences – similar to those in the lower courts in England and not the felonies for which they had been transported. The employment opportunities the colony offered and potential for forming new relationships did allow for the possibility of settling into colonial life, and there were success stories. However, for most of these men, 'emancipation from convict status still left them facing a hard struggle to survive and prosper' (ibid.: 254). This low-level offending offered contemporary commentators proof of the 'convict stain' on Australian society, but there is no evidence of hereditary criminality (Godfrey and Cox, 2008; Godfrey *et al.*, 2007; see also Chapter 2). Further research by Godfrey (2011) also demonstrates that, while some were able to desist from criminal behaviour, others were unable to establish the positive links – employment and family relationships – that criminological literature associates with a movement away from crime (Farrall and Calverley, 2006).

Case study: George Pobjoy (NA, PCOM 3, licence no. 405; Australian Convict Register nos. 3489, 338, 20329, 4734)

George Pobjoy was born and brought up in the Bath area of Somerset. His first appearance in court was in 1836, aged about 19, when he was charged with larceny from a dwelling house but was found not guilty. In his early to mid- twenties he had a relationship with Harriet Vennell, who was around five years his junior, and this produced two children, George and Mary Ann, though the couple remained unmarried. Harriet also found herself in trouble with the law when she was sentenced to three months' imprisonment for stealing a shawl and a coral necklace. George, it appears from the census data, continued to live with his parents and brother, William, in the Monkton Coombe area and worked as a labourer in a local quarry.

In 1849, George was sentenced to four months' imprisonment for stealing leather. This was followed one year later by another conviction for larceny, this time of a bridle rein, for which Wells Sessions court sentenced him to seven years' transportation. George was described in his penal record as a stonemason, as 'honest and industrious'. Although imperfect with reading, he was 'not wanting in intelligence and slightly informed in religious subjects'. George was taken from the local prison at Taunton to London, where he spent twelve days in separate confinement at Millbank before being moved to Pentonville prison to serve a further twelve months and fourteen days in separate confinement. At this time, both Millbank and Pentonville were being used by the government to hold convicts before they were transported overseas (see Chapter 7). On 17 December 1851, George was moved to the convict hulk the *Stirling Castle*. However, he did not get transported but was instead sent to Portsmouth convict prison, where he served a further two years. His conduct in all of the prisons was described as good, and he does not appear to have committed any breaches of rules or regulations while inside. In March 1854 he was released on licence. By this time he had served three years and six months of his seven-year sentence, and his destination after leaving the convict system is recorded as his brother's house in Coombe Down. During the period of George's imprisonment his family had been finding life difficult; his son George had being living in Bath Union Workhouse, his father had passed away and his mother was destitute.

Unfortunately, George's experience in the convict system did not end with his return to Somerset, and in 1856 he was back in court, this time at the Assizes charged with robbery. *The Times* reported the case on 1 May 1856 with the headline 'Highway Robbery by a Ticket-of-Leave Man'. It stated that George, still on licence from his previous sentence of transportation, a woman, Harriet Trueman, with whom he was co-habiting (Harriet Vennell, reportedly the mother of George's children, had married one John Truman in the mid-1840s), and one other, had been charged by Bath magistrates with assaulting and robbing William Harding. Harding was a medical gentleman who had been returning from Bath to Coombe Down late one Monday evening. On a lonely part of the road he was overtaken by the accused, who must have followed him from the city, and Harriet pushed him against the wall, holding him forcibly by his throat and threatening him to keep quiet, while the two men stood behind her. The victim was rendered insensible through the pressure on his throat and begged the woman not to kill him. She then took his gold watch and chain and rifled his pockets of their rest of the contents. The method of attack – the pressure on the victim's throat leaving him unable to defend himself – bears similarities to those in incidents described as 'garrottings' that occurred in urban areas across the country in the mid-1850s and the early 1860s, and violent crimes carried out by repeat offenders were exactly those that raised public fears and anxieties about safety (see Chapter 2).

Having recovered from the attack, William Harding returned to Bath to call for the police. Three officers returned to the site of the robbery at around two o'clock in the morning and found the accused searching the road by candlelight. The latter were therefore unable to avoid apprehension by the police, who found some of Harding's property in Harriet's pockets. More was discovered when they searched George's house, but the watch and chain were not found. The accused were all remanded in custody, and at the Assizes in Wells on 1 August 1856 the court noted George's two previous convictions for felony and sentenced him to ten years' penal servitude overseas. Harriet was sentenced to eight years' penal servitude, and but their co-accused, Thomas Hodges, who pleaded not guilty to the crime, was acquitted of the charges.

On 18 September 1857, as convict no. 4734, George was sent to Western Australia aboard the convict ship *Nile*, which arrived in Perth on 1 January 1858. The convict database registers of Fremantle prison indicate his occupation as a 'mason' but describe him as 'illiterate' (www.fremantleprison.com.au/Pages/Convict.aspx). Just over three years later, in February 1861, George gained his ticket of leave in Australia and began working as woodsman on his own account. The ticket of leave conditions prohibited the drinking of alcohol and ensured that men remained under police supervision; they were also subject to a curfew at 10.00 p.m., needed permission to change employment and were prevented from taking certain jobs and from sitting on a jury (Godfrey and Cox, 2008). George continued as a woodsman until New Year's Day 1863, when Perth Magistrates Court withdrew his permission to work 'on his own account', as he had been found drunk on St George's Terrace. After employment as a labourer under the ticket of leave system in the Fremantle area, he received his conditional pardon in June 1864.

Like many others, George stayed in Western Australia for the rest of his life, though there is little evidence to indicate what kind of relationships he had been able to establish. By the 1880s he was in his sixties. He worked as a cook and then as a groom and an overseer. Life was obviously hard and his health may have been failing, as he was committed several times for vagrancy and admitted to the Mount Elizabeth invalid depot. He had another brush with the law in 1885, when he was fined 5 shillings by Perth magistrates for being drunk on Bazaar Terrace. By 1893 he was an inmate of the Waterside depot in Perth. In the early years, both of these depots appear to have been places where settlers could go to hire labour and where ticket of leave men without employment could be allocated to public works or where they were returned when ill or misbehaving (Gibbs, 2001). The administration of these depots reverted to the colonial government after the end of transportation. George died the same year, aged about 76; his body was found floating in the Swan River by the William Street jetty on 19 June 1893, and the coroner returned an open verdict. In many ways his story is one typical of men who appear (from the evidence available) to have been unable to establish the necessary links to embed themselves in Australian society. He is perhaps one example among a group of convicts who could not overcome their circumstances, ending up in 'a washed up life, alcoholism, and drifting both through the colony and life' (Godfrey, 2011: 103; Godfrey and Cox, 2008).

6

LOCAL PRISONS

Diversity, discipline, centralisation

Local prisons, or gaols, and houses of correction, as they were then known, were a diverse range of places of detention in the early nineteenth century, and until 1878 they were run by local authorities. They became known collectively as 'local prisons' after the Prison Act 1865, and this term will be used for ease here as well as to distinguish these prisons from the government-run establishments at Millbank and Pentonville and the convict prison system (see Chapter 7). There are three important aspects that will be addressed: first, how imprisonment developed (or, perhaps more accurately, redeveloped) as a sentence of punishment in its own right; second, how the experience of imprisonment varied across the country; and, third, how the government became increasingly involved and concerned with the policy and practice of imprisonment.

In the early nineteenth century, local prisons were incredibly diverse in their size, use and form – ranging from gatehouses with two or three holding cells or tiny lock-ups to larger arcaded buildings with courtyards surrounded by sleeping cells and, from the 1830s, the newly built large Victorian institutions with imposing architectural facades that held hundreds of people in row upon row of identical cells. It is this diversity in the size, shape and experience of the local prison that is significant in this period and which, together with the local administration, led to a considerable degree of innovation and advanced thinking about the use of imprisonment in some parts of the country. However, it also allowed for laxity, abuse and irregularity in others – and these practices were not mutually exclusive. Newly emerging ideas were frequently put into practice in local prisons before any implementation or instruction by government. The 'reform' of prisons at the end of the eighteenth and into the nineteenth century was something that was carried out largely in local prisons but received national attention due to campaigns for change by key figures such as John Howard and Elizabeth Fry. The extent to which prison 'reform' was implemented across the country is demonstrated by evidence which shows that at least 45 local prisons were built or designed in the last quarter of the eighteenth century (Evans, 1982), before the government really had any involvement. The case study at the end of this chapter examines one provincial local prison – Shrewsbury – between the end of the eighteenth century and the centralisation of local prisons through the Prison Act 1877. This prison was just one of the 45 reconstructed in the last quarter of the century, and its development demonstrates the protracted change and evolution of practices across the period.

Prison reforms in the early nineteenth century

By the early nineteenth century, the period of prison 'reform' was already under way. John Howard (1777) investigated many prisons across England and Wales, and later in Europe, and reported on their condition in the 1770s and 1780s. His campaign was supported by other influential figures, and he gained considerable support and interest from some magistrates who were involved in the running the local prisons (through the Quarter Sessions Court) in their area. Howard exposed the poor health of inmates and the unsanitary conditions in prisons, and a major part of this crusade was to improve hygiene and control the spread of disease. This was probably the most successful aspect of his campaign, and many local magistrates embraced Howard's model of sanitary, healthy prisons. Yet he was frustrated that they had scarcely touched upon 'that still more important object, the reformation of morals in our prisons' (Howard, cited in Forsythe, 1987: 16).

As we will discuss in Chapter 7, the Penitentiary Act 1779 proposed a 'penitentiary' prison set down some early principles regarding the moral and religious transformation of the prisoner which reflected wider discussions on the philosophies of punishment at this time. Reformers such as John Howard and Elizabeth Fry had reported and campaigned nationally regarding the poor conditions in local prisons; both were active and engaged with similar-minded religious philanthropists (Ignatieff, 1978). They were not alone: Sarah Martin was a Christian prison visitor who ministered to the inmates in Great Yarmouth gaol, though she did not widely publicise her activities (Rogers, 2009). Although the intended penitentiary was never built – Australia providing the immediate solution to the transportation of convicts overseas – a large number of local prisons were remodelled at the end of the eighteenth and into the nineteenth century, some decades before the government began constructing prisons.

The Gaol Fees Abolition Act of 1815 was a particular success for John Howard and the 'reform' campaign. One of Howard's key proposals had been the abolition of 'gaol fees'. Before this Act, a prisoner committed to a local prison had to pay for all aspects of their living – for admittance to the gaol, for straw or bedding, for meals, for water or the 'tap' (alcohol), and even a fee to be released once they had completed their sentence. Howard's study *The State of the Prisons in England and Wales*, published in 1777, found that many inmates were still confined in prisons despite having completed their sentence, as they did not have enough money to pay the discharge fee. The Gaol Fees Abolition Act was therefore a small but significant step, as it abolished all fees and gratuities and directed that salaries for gaolers or servants be paid by the county rates or equivalent authority rather than prisons being run as profit-making business.

Other elements that had concerned Howard and figures such as Elizabeth Fry was the degree of unrestricted or free association between the different sexes in prisons and between those seen as frequent or 'hardened' criminals and those who were young or first-time offenders. Fry had begun visiting female prisoners in Newgate in the first quarter of the nineteenth century (also see Chapter 8). Concerns regarding the mixture and association of prisoners were addressed, at least in theory, by the Gaols Act 1823. Probably the most significant Act in the first half of the nineteenth century, it gave local authorities much stricter instructions about how to administer the prisons under their charge. It ordered that prisoners be held in 'classified association' – divided up into different classes according to their sex, their status in the criminal justice system and their offence. This resulted in a range of different classes: those awaiting trial or sentence; those awaiting removal for transportation or the death penalty; those sentenced to a period of imprisonment for serious or less serious offences – known as felons or misdemeanants; and those who were vagrants or civil prisoners detained for debts.

The Gaols Act also directed that the gaoler or keeper of the prison should be employed solely to this duty, that every prison should have both a chaplain and a matron, to maintain the female side of the prison, and that a surgeon should examine all prisoners on entry. Inmates should be put to work or hard labour (depending on their sentence), receive instruction in reading and writing, attend religious services on Sundays and be permitted air and exercise. The local authority would pay for the maintenance of prisoners; as such, prisoners should receive 'plain and wholesome' food, though the prison 'tap' was abolished. The Act also required that a committee of justices be appointed to the visit the prisons on a regular basis and report their findings.

Despite the instructions in the Act, it was difficult for some prisons to put such classifications into practice, primarily because of the size of buildings or the small numbers of prisoners. For example, in theory, Abingdon County Bridewell in Berkshire was to accommodate five classes of both male and female prisoners, but, in practice, there were only two wards or rooms for each of the sexes – those on remand and those who were convicted. They were also yet to appoint a female officer (*Gaols: Copies of all Reports*, PP, 1824). There remained considerable diversity in the local prisons across the country; cities and towns had larger prisons – for example, the New Bailey prison, Salford, or Newgate gaol or Westminster house of correction in London – but there were many small prisons in market towns and rural districts. Only 23 and 16 prisoners, respectively, were committed during the year to October 1823 to Lichfield city gaol and house of correction and Launceston gaol in Cornwall. In some counties there were a larger number of small prisons, but in others – Staffordshire, Shropshire and Worcestershire, for example –they had been amalgamated on one site during the 'reform' period (ibid.).

The large number of prisoner classifications in the Gaols Act also highlights the considerable diversity in the prison population. Many were being held securely for only a short sentence or until another punishment (transportation, death) was carried out. Although prisons had been used to detain and to punish people since at least the eleventh century (Harding *et al.*, 1985), the nineteenth century brought with it a new focus on imprisonment and a new goal, as it was increasingly seen as an opportunity to affect people's behaviour. The origins of the ideas about changing, altering or reforming people's behaviour are rooted in the late eighteenth century and exemplified in the proposals for the Penitentiary Act 1779. But they are perhaps most obvious in the discussions between two competing philosophies of punishment, known as the separate system and the silent system, which emerged in early part of the nineteenth century. Under such regimes, prisoners would not just be detained but would be encouraged through isolation, silence, religious instruction or hard labour to change their behaviour. It was in this period that many Western societies came to believe that a prison sentence could be used to transform or alter criminals and potentially return them to society as law-abiding citizens.

The separate system and the silent system – transforming the offender

Both the separate and the silent system were disciplinary regimes that had originated in America and were thought to offer new insights into how to reform prisoners' behaviour. The separate system was used in the state of Pennsylvania and the silent system in the state of New York. Both focused on the individual prisoner and how to generate a change in their behaviour: while the former isolated prisoners in cells and saw religion as a potent and influential factor, the latter relied on associated labour but prevented all communication between inmates. The overriding objective of both systems was to prevent communication between or the moral 'contamination' of prisoners. These goals would reduce the corrupting influence that hardened or repeat offenders had on first-time or young criminals and allow for personal reflection on their own behaviour.

The separate system operated by keeping prisoners apart from on another at all times. Inmates were held in isolation in individual cells, where they would work, sleep and eat. They were permitted to leave their cells only for exercise – even then they would remain alone, often in a separate yard which prevented them seeing other prisoners – or to go to chapel, during which they would wear masks or caps covering their faces to prevent them recognising one another. Experiments in penal discipline had begun at the Walnut Street prison in Philadelphia in the late eighteenth century, but it was the Eastern Penitentiary, which opened in 1829, which implemented the separate system to its fullest. This was thought not only to deter the criminal but to also to offer the potential for moral reform.

As noted earlier, across the nineteenth century the influence of central government on local prisons was also growing. One significant way in which this was felt was through the introduction of prison inspectors as directed in the Prisons Act 1835. The Gaols Act 1823 had introduced a range of regulations which began the process to ensure more uniformity in prisons across the country. The Prisons Act

1835 extended this by instructing that all rules and regulations had to be approved by the Secretary of State and that inspectors would visit all prisons (see also Stockdale, 1983). The Act had followed a Select Committee on Prison Discipline which had reasserted the importance of hard labour, religious instruction and the separation of prisoners to prevent 'moral' contamination between inmates.

Two of the first prison inspectors for the Home District, William Crawford and Reverend Whitworth Russell, would prove to be quite influential in the development of prisons in England in the following decades. William Crawford went to the United States in the early 1830s to examine the operation of different regimes. In comparing the separate system and the silent system, he reported that:

> the discipline of Auburn is of a physical, that of Philadelphia of a moral character. The whip inflicts immediate pain, but solitude inspires permanent terror. The former degrades while it humiliates; the latter subdues, but it does not debase. At Auburn the convict is uniformly treated with harshness, at Philadelphia with civility; the one contributes to harden, the other to soften the affections. Auburn stimulates vindictive feelings; Philadelphia induces habitual submission. The Auburn prisoner, when liberated, conscious that he is known to past associates, and that the public eye has gazed upon him, sees an accuser in everyman he meets. The Philadelphia convict quits his cell, secure from recognition and exempt from reproach.
>
> (*Penitentiaries*, PP, 1834: 19)

As this quote demonstrates, Crawford's preference was for the separate system. While the two American systems did not translate exactly across the Atlantic, both were put into operation in modified ways in different parts of England.

There was considerable debate in England in the 1820s and 1830s about the benefits of the two systems. Reformatory endeavours were underpinned by ideas of evangelicalism and of association theory, and until the 1860s all such practices were based upon one or the other or an integration of these views (Forsythe, 1987). Evangelicals saw Christianity as central to the reform of prisoners and as a key feature of prison life. The main objectives were to correct inmates' moral and spiritual defects and to provide them with skills to live a dutiful and industrious life on release (Forsythe, 2001; Rogers, 2009). Pain and personal suffering through isolation, it was believed, would make the criminal more open to Christ and to repairing their sin; but pain, purely for deterrence, would only harden the offender. Spiritual revival was to be achieved through separation, allowing the individual to recognise sin and enable them to be open to 'reform' (Forsythe, 1987), and therefore prison chaplains played a central role. Reverend John Clay, chaplain at Preston house of correction, spent time conversing and instructing prisoners; he believed that, through 'the process of self-examination which a prisoner, capable of exercising it, must undergo in his cell, he is encouraged to review his past life, and to trace to their source his faults and sufferings' (Clay, 1846: 13).

The silent system, on the other hand, drew more on association theory, advocating a process of pain and reward to encourage deterrence. Prisoners worked together in large workrooms, but communication was strictly forbidden and tightly monitored by staff. The silence would allow prisoners to reflect on their previous conduct. Those who worked hard were rewarded and encouraged into new skills; those who defied the system were punished swiftly and with increasing severity. George Laval Chesterton was a notable supporter of the silent system and operated the regime as governor of Coldbath Fields house of correction in Middlesex. In practice, the silent system was cheaper to operate; while larger numbers of staff were needed to control the prisoners, no structural changes were required to prison buildings (Forsythe, 1987).

In the end, Crawford and Whitworth Russell's advocacy of the separate system proved to be influential, and a new Bill was drafted; the Prisons Act 1839 ordered that all prisons should use the separate system. All separate cells that were constructed had to conform to strict regulations and were to be certified by one of the prison inspectors. Not only did the use of the separate system confirm the belief that the prison could alter people's behaviour, but architecture and space became an important aspect of imprisonment – the cell became the space in which the prisoner would be transformed (Johnston, 2013).

Despite the Prisons Act 1839, the shift to the use of the separate system was in practice a protracted one; many prisons lagged behind in its adoption but, perhaps more importantly, there were already increasing concerns about its use and legitimacy. The national penitentiaries of Millbank and Pentonville will be discussed more fully in Chapter 7, but here it is sufficient to say that the problems in the operation of these government-run prisons drew increasing attention to the use of the separate system and its effect on those confined under it. Criticism emerged on two central but conflicting issues. The first was the extent to which prisoners were being driven insane by the long periods of isolation; the second involved conflicting ideas that separation was not absolute, that prisoners were able to communicate with one another, or that they duped chaplains into believing they had reformed when they had not. Other commentators argued that some groups of prisoners were so hardened in crime and depravity that reform was impossible and they instead needed to be deterred (Henriques, 1972; Johnston, 2006).

Local prisons at mid-century

In terms of 'reform', local prisons were very different places by the mid-nineteenth century; many aspects of prison life as we would recognise them in the twenty-first century had been implemented – prisoners were classified, placed into uniforms, subject to a range of rules and regulations within the timetabled schedule of the daily regime, put to work or hard labour, and given basic educational and religious instruction (McGowen, 1998). Nevertheless there still remained considerable diversity across England.

The Select Committee on Prison Discipline in 1850, known as the Grey Committee, examined evidence from many local prisons and noted that, while large sums of money had been spent on altering or rebuilding many prisons since

1835, there were still several in a 'very unsatisfactory condition, and that proper punishment, separation, or reformation in them is nearly impossible' (PP, 1850: iv). The committee examined a huge amount of evidence but largely reasserted views similar to those predominant in the previous two decades. Variety in prison construction and discipline in local prisons was regarded as a 'great evil' that should be tackled by increased powers from a central authority. It stressed that

> entire separation, except during the hours of labour and of religious worship and instruction, is absolutely necessary for preventing contamination, and for securing a proper system of prison discipline; and … every prison ought to contain such a number of cells as would enable each prisoner to be kept separate, by day as well as by night, both before and after trial.
>
> (Ibid.)

It recommended provision for hard labour in all prisons and that the diet be kept as minimal as possible without impairing health, and expressed concerns at how the separate system was implemented in some prisons. Unable to ignore the widespread discussions on the use, effects and potential abuses of the system, it said that, while the evidence was conflicting, 'the great preponderance of Evidence … is highly favourable to it, and … if conducted under proper regulations and control separate confinement is more efficient than any other system which has yet been tried, both in deterring from crime and promoting reformation' (ibid.: v).

As this indicates, deterrence as well as reform was increasingly foregrounding the direction that penal philosophy would take in subsequent decades, and problems with uniformity in prison practice were seen more and more as an issue that could be overcome only by central government intervention. Difficulties relating to the uniformity in prisons continued to cause concern, and this was only confirmed by two 'scandals' in the early 1850s involving the gaols in Birmingham and Leicester.

What became clear during the investigations of events at Birmingham and at Leicester local prisons in 1854 was not only that magistrates were implementing the separate system in a variety of ways but that magistrates or governors and other staff were exceeding their powers and misusing the system (Henriques, 1972; Webbs, 1963; Roberts, 1986). The severity of practices at Birmingham was revealed after the suicide of a 15-year-old prisoner, Edward Andrews. Andrews's death sparked an investigation which uncovered his was the third known suicide in the recent period (there had been 11 other suicide attempts in the preceding 16 months and a total of 17 since the prison had opened in October 1849), and the coroner's inquest and subsequent inquiry detailed the excesses of the regime. Andrews had been sentenced to two months' hard labour for stealing 4 pounds of beef, and this was his third offence. The inquiry revealed that straitjackets were used illegally for minor breaches of the rules and for prolonged periods of time. Prisoners were deprived of proper food and given only bread and water and yet were still expected to turn the crank 10,000 revolutions per day (2,000 times before breakfast, 4,000 times before dinner and 4,000 times before supper). The crank was pointless device – 'a wheel set against cogs that exercised a resisting pressure, and turned by a handle weighted at will to fix the amount of effort required to make a revolution' (Griffiths, cited in Priestley, 1999: 129).

Cranks were used widely in local prisons to serve as as hard labour as they were relatively cheap and easy to install. The accumulative effect of this system at Birmingham was that, although 10,000 revolutions was not unduly severe, the cranks were incorrectly weighted and prisoners received only bread and water and had their beds held back for two hours for not completing the task. They found themselves in a cycle of severe punishment and meagre diet from which they were unable to escape (Roberts, 1986). This scandal received widespread attention in the press and later formed the basis for a novel by Charles Reade entitled *It's Never Too Late to Mend* (1856; see also Anderson, 2005).

Similarly, at Leicester prison, inmates' meals were withheld as punishment when they were unable to complete the required amount of hard labour. The level of resistance of the crank could be set by prison warders through turning or tightening of a screw set outside of the cell – this seems to be the origin of the term 'screw' to refer to a prison officer. At Leicester, the regime required prisoners to turn the crank 14,400 revolutions in stages across the day. During the investigation, the prisoners argued that the weight to which the cranks were set was arbitrary and that the warder 'had been in the habit, wantonly and cruelly, of increasing the hardness of the cranks, and gave utterance to expressions of bitter resentment against him for his supposed cruelty in doing so' (*Report of the Commissioners … Leicester County Gaol*, PP, 1854: 13). The minutes of evidence expose the ways in which prisoners were affected by the combination of hard labour, withdrawal of meals and corporal punishment. For example, the following is an extract from the daily report and punishment books under discussion during the investigation concerning prisoner no. 2405, who had been placed in cell C.3.7 on 18 September:

> (Captain Williams) He was reported the day before 8,000 bad [deficient revolutions], and therefore, of course, they kept his dinner and supper away. 'Dinner and supper kept back, and reported idle, third report; 6400 bad.' 21st, 'his food kept back.' 23d, 'absent from school, had Friday's dinner at 1 p.m. and supper at 6 p.m.'

> (Mr Welsby) That was Monday; Sunday was the 22d.

> (Captain Williams) 25th, 'supper kept back and reported idle; fifth report; 6200 bad.' The 26th, 'had yesterday's supper at 1 p.m., breakfast at 6 p.m.; reported idle; sixth report, 2700 bad.' 27th, 'had yesterday's dinner at half past 10 a.m., supper at half past 3, and today's breakfast at 6 p.m.' The 28th, 'reported idle; seventh report; 4500 bad.' 29th, 'removed to refractory cell, at 8.30 a.m.; gave him his bed at quarter to 9 p.m.' The 30th, 'released from refractory cell at 6 a.m.; supper kept; reported idle; eighth report; 13,400 bad.' October the 1st, 'his food kept back (i.e. four meals); reported idle; ninth report; 13,500 bad.' 2d, 'dinner at 1 p.m. by order of the governor,

whipped at 2.30 p.m.; supper at 6 p.m.; reported idle this forenoon; tenth report; 6900 bad.'

(Dr Baly) The surgeon 'witnessed the punishment of C. 3.7, 2405, who received two dozen lashes.'

(Ibid., minutes of evidence: 87)

The evidence highlights not only the different ways in which local prisons might implement individual regimes but also the wide use of discretionary administrative powers. Conditions at Leicester had resulted in an excessive use of corporal punishment, but in the end the magistrates were merely admonished for not getting approval for the use of such a system.

By mid-century, the problems of variations in prison practice continued to be evident (DeLacy, 1981, 1986), but the separate system itself had begun to fall out of favour and there were increased calls for more severity. Criticisms of the separate system in the print media presented conflicting accounts that swayed between claims of severity, which resulted in prisoners' insanity, and accounts which argued the system could be subverted by prisoners, who were able to recognise and communicate with one another or who faked religious conversion (Henriques, 1972; Johnston, 2006; see also Chapter 7). Opposition also came from those advocating more deterrence, but there was the added problem that the bulk of prisoners in local prisons were serving only short sentences, and it was thought that reformatory practices needed time to take effect (Johnston and Godfrey, 2013b). The power of the reformatory project had been increasingly called into question, and what emerged was an approach that saw more deterrence.

Deterrence, centralisation and the Prison Commission

By the late 1850s, disillusion with the ideas of reform and the potential of regimes such as the separate system resulted in a more deterrence-based approach. The changes need to be considered in light of wider aspects of the criminal justice system: the perceived threat of the 'criminal class' or habitual offender, the garrotting panics of the 1850s and 1860s (see Chapter 2), the decline in the use of transportation, and the imprisonment and release of convicts in England (see Chapters 5 and 7).

The Carnarvon Committee examined prison discipline in 1863, and the subsequent legislation was based on its recommendations; the resulting changes affected both local prisons and convict prisons (see Chapter 7). What emerged was a system of prison discipline based on 'hard labour, hard board, hard fare'. Deterrence would operate through the use of long hours of hard labour, strict separation and harsh living conditions and aimed to outweigh the potential benefits of committing crime (McConville, 1998a, 1998b). This philosophy of punishment would dominate the regime in prisons until at least 1895. Separate cells were still used, but the transformative element – the cell as a space or place for moral or religious conversion – was replaced by isolation to deter the offender (Johnston, 2013).

The Prison Act 1865 instigated the new regime, which stipulated hard labour for between six and ten hours a day. Hard labour of the first class was bodily labour such as the treadwheel, the shot drill, the crank, the capstan, or stone-breaking. The shot drill consisted of 'stooping down (without bending the knees) and picking up a thirty-two pounder round shot, bringing it up slowly until it is on the level with the chest, and then taking two steps to the right and replacing it on the ground' or a variation of this ('One-Who-Has-Tried-Them', cited in Priestley, 1999: 130–31). Oakum-picking, mat-making, repairing clogs, tailoring, washing, and making and mending clothes were considered hard labour of the second class.

The pressure for uniformity culminated in the centralisation of local prisons in 1878. The Prisons Act 1877 enabled this process, and local prisons came under the control of the Prison Commission alongside convict prisons. The government closed down smaller prisons across the country, and by July 1878 the closure of 38 gaols has already been pushed through (*Report of the Commissioners of Prisons (RCP)*, PP, 1878, 1879). Those chosen for closure highlight the continued local diversity, even by the late 1870s. For example, in Devon, both Exeter and Plymouth prisons were retained, but the smaller establishments at Tiverton, Barnstable Borough and Devonport were shut down. Some large counties, such as Middlesex and Lancashire, together with those that had amalgamated their prisons earlier in the century or during the period of reform – for example, Bedfordshire, Buckinghamshire and Durham – experienced no closures at all.

The control and administration of the entire local prison system was now the responsibility of the Prison Commission. All staff, from assistant warders to the chaplains, medical officers and governors, became civil servants, new pay scales and grade structures were issued – some dependent on the size of the prison – all local variations were abolished, and the staff system assumed a pyramidal structure (*RCP*, PP, 1878; Thomas, 1972). The staff who lived inside the prison walls – required of the governors, matrons and female staff, but not necessarily of male warders, as this depended on location – were provided with rent-free quarters as well as a uniform, and some were given a water, light and fuel allowance and could receive medical attendance and medicines. Staff accommodation varied considerably, and those in local prisons were not paid on the same scales as those in the convict prison system until the early twentieth century (*RCP*, PP, 1878; also Johnston, 2008b, 2014).

Centralisation gave the Prison Commission the opportunity to iron out any variations in practice across the system; uniformity would be the policy from now on. From 1878, all local prisons would operate under the same regime, the same weekly timetable and the same diet and hours of hard labour, and all would be administered under the same rules, regulations and procedures. Discipline would operate through a system of marks and progressive stages, which was already in use in the convict prison system. The commissioners claimed that a prisoner would to some extent have the 'rigour of discipline' in their own hands. Having started the regime with the

most severe discipline and the hardest and most uninteresting labour, he
may pass through four stages, on attaining each of which he secures certain
advantages or the remission of certain penal discipline, but each of these
stages is attained only after the performance of a certain amount of labour,
and misconduct may delay his promotion, or cause his degradation.

(*RCP*, PP, 1878: 8)

Prisoners would earn six, seven or eight marks per day for labour except on
Sundays, when marks would be matched to their performance in the preceding
days. For example, prisoners were required to earn a total of 224 marks across the
first 28 days in prison, when the most severe conditions were to be endured: hard
labour in strict separation for ten hours per day, of which between six and eight
hours should be hard labour of the first class (crank, treadwheel or similar) with
only a plank bed and no mattress to sleep on; no earnings or gratuities could be
gained. Conditions would ameliorate a little during the following stages, with a
change to hard labour of the second class, the opportunity to obtain a small amount
of earnings, school instruction and books, and exercise on a Sunday.

The amount of food, as in the preceding decades, would be measured exactly:
a simple and economic diet that 'furnishes sufficient, and not more than sufficient,
amount of food' (*RCP*, PP, 1878: 10). This was divided into four classes according to
the length of sentence being served. All prisoners would receive the Class 1 diet for
the first seven days. This consisted of 8 ounces of bread for breakfast, a pint and a half
of 'stirabout' for dinner and 8 ounces of bread for supper. Stirabout was a very thin
type of porridge, and a pint and a half consisted of two and half pints of water, boiled,
to which was added half an ounce of sugar, 3 ounces of Indian meal and 3 ounces of
oatmeal, all stirred continuously until it had reduced to the requisite amount (ibid.: 44).
The diet improved slightly with the length of sentence and was dependent on whether
hard labour was included or not, as well as the sex and age of the prisoner.

By the time prisoners reached the fourth stage they would be eligible to be
employed in a position of trust, have a mattress to sleep on, receive education and be
permitted library books in their cell, enjoy exercise on Sundays, and be able to earn a
gratuity to a maximum of 2 shillings. They would be permitted to write and receive
one letter and to have a visit of 20 minutes; thereafter they were allowed to write
and receive a letter every three months and have a half-hour visit. However, this
stage could be reached only after at least four months in a local prison, and therein
lay the problem. As McConville (1995) has pointed out, the overwhelming majority of those in local prisons were serving a short sentence of less than one month
and therefore experienced the most severe conditions; because of the length of their
sentence it was impossible for them to gain any benefits. No matter how hard they
worked or how well behaved they were, they could not improve their situation.

Recidivism was of great concern at the end of the nineteenth century, and levels
were very high in the local prison system. It was frequently the case that individuals
were convicted more than once during a year – especially in cases of drunkenness.
Most who committed minor offences were often incarcerated for a short period

of one or two weeks and so would experience this severe regime repeatedly over a year, apparently to little effect in terms of reducing their reoffending. Despite, then, the aims of the Prison Commissioners in 1878 to place some degree of responsibility on prisoners for their own conditions, this was in fact an exercise in futility for the overwhelming majority (*RCP*, PP, 1878; McConville, 1995, 1998b).

Centralisation allowed the diversity and inconsistent practices in local prisons to be overcome but replaced these with a highly bureaucratic and closed-off administration. Edmund Du Cane, then the chairman of the Prison Commission, proceeded with policies aimed at uniformity and economy in the local prison system. In subsequent years this administration would increasingly be called into question for its austere regime, high rates of recidivism, problems with groups of prisoners to whom such severity could not be applied (the young, women, those with babies, the mentally ill, for example) and the lack of accountability of the chairman. However, this regime would remain in place at least until the recommendations of the Gladstone Committee investigation into prisons in 1895 (see also Harding, 1988; Forsythe, 1990; McConville, 1995; Pratt, 2002, 2004).

Case study: Shrewsbury prison, 1823–1877

In the eighteenth century, there were a number of small prisons in Shrewsbury. During the period of nationwide reform, the magistrates of Shropshire were keen to develop the prison and agreed to construct a new establishment in the Dana (now Howard Street) in the town; this opened in 1793. The new prison brought

FIGURE 6.1   Bust of the prison reformer John Howard above the gatehouse of Shrewsbury prison (author's image)

together the former small buildings, amalgamating what had been the county and borough gaols and houses of correction onto one larger prison site. The magistrates in Shropshire were clearly influenced by the views of John Howard, particularly as regards location, and a bust of the reformer was placed over the gatehouse to the new prison, which was designed and built by William Blackburn and a local architect, John Haycock. Blackburn was an influential architect who built numerous local prisons during this period (Evans, 1982; Jewkes and Johnston, 2007), and was described as 'the only man capable of delineating on paper his [Howard's] ideas of what a prison should be' (cited in Tomlinson, 1978a: 61).

Shrewsbury prison was therefore constructed, with Howard's principles of classification in mind, in such a way as to separate prisoners into different courtyards according to their gender and their crime – subsequently a requirement of the Gaols Act 1823. How the different classifications translated into the architecture of the prison can be seen in figure 6.2. Between 1836 and 1877 the prison held around 120 to 160 prisoners per day, of whom around 20 were women. Prisoners were received from Petty Sessions courts across the county as well as those convicted or committed by the Quarter Sessions, which met regularly in the county town. Most were serving short periods for summary offences and turnover was high. The majority were released having completed their sentence, with only a few

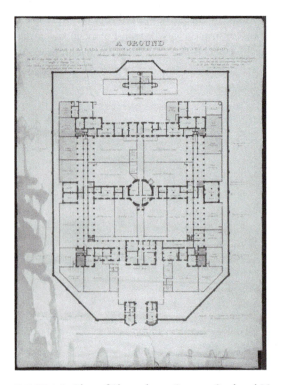

FIGURE 6.2 Plan of Shrewsbury County Gaol and House of Correction, 1797 (1831) (SA 6007/70 with permission of Shropshire Archives)

being sent down to the convict system, transferred to juvenile reformatories or lunatic asylums, or being executed (Johnston, 2004, 2005a).

Most of the prisoners were men aged between 15 and 40 and residents in or from the county of Shropshire, larger numbers being committed from the more populous market towns of Shrewsbury, Wellington, Oswestry and Ludlow (Johnston, 2004). Evidence from chaplains' reports in the 1840s and from Home Office returns in the 1860s (NA, HO 24/20-24/29) suggests that the overwhelming majority were working class, often unskilled or manual workers. Most were labourers, domestic or farm servants, colliers or miners, reflecting the agricultural nature of the local labour market and the cyclical and seasonal nature of these occupations. Most prisoners were also recorded as members of the Church of England and were baptised, although did not regularly attend church. The chaplain claimed many lacked any religious knowledge, but a number had been schooled in some form, often at church or national Sunday schools or charity schools or while previously in prison (Johnston, 2004, 2005a).

The separate system at Shrewsbury

By the 1830s, discussions of the separate and silent systems also drew the attention of the magistrates in Shropshire. Keen to keep pace with current penal developments, they embarked on a small-scale experiment with the separate system in 1837, even before its use was regularised by the Prisons Act 1839. In 1836, the visiting justices stated that 'perfect discipline, such as may afford a reasonable hope of effecting, if not the reformation, at least the amendment of a prisoner, cannot be maintained without the means of enforcing complete silence and separation by day as well as night' (SA, QA 2/1/1, Visiting Justices Reports (VJR): 128). At first the justices were reluctant initiate the system without Home Office direction but, having received no communication, they decided to set their own system in motion (ibid.: 131).

In 1837 the experiment started with a small number of cells for a few months and was then extended to a larger number of prisoners. By this time the government was urging the adoption of the separate system, and the justices further expanded the number of cells, but they were unable to convert the whole prison because of the cost. However, prisoners confined in the separate system experiment regarded this as an additional punishment to which many of their fellows were not subjected (SA, QA 2/1/1, VJR: 146–7), and the justices therefore recommended the separate system be applied to a whole class of prisoners – those summarily convicted. The inspectors of prisons, however, disagreed, stating that untried prisoners should be the first class to be separated. The magistrates agreed that the 'least depraved' criminals should be separated, to ensure that, if not reformed, at least they would not be contaminated by their imprisonment. But they thought prisoners summarily convicted were less hardened in crime than those committed for felonies; although an innocent person could be found among the untried prisoners, in general they had several previous convictions.

Subsequently, the justices approved a plan from the county surveyor to convert the wing occupied by debtors and misdemeanants into further separate cells (SA, QA 2/1/1, VJR: 147–9). The inspectors Captain Jebb and Reverend Whitworth Russell were sent to Shrewsbury by Lord Russell and approved the plan. The county surveyor was also sent to London to inspect the separate cells at Millbank penitentiary (ibid.: 149). In 1838 the new separate cells were completed at a cost of £1,150. Some months later the chaplain reported that the prisoners were discontented and restless; they were aware that such confinement was not part of their sentencing but seen as an additional punishment. The prisoners frequently tried to get the chaplain to obtain permission from the governor for them to return to the normal courts, but the chaplain thought that keeping them in the separate cells for the whole of their sentence 'would be a means of reconciling them with their present punishment and of making their minds more open to receive instruction' than was previously the case (ibid.: 27).

However, despite the initial enthusiasm for adopting the separate system, the complete conversion of the prison was slow. The primary reason was cost: the separate cells needed to be constructed, sufficiently large, and well ventilated. In 1839 Reverend Whitworth Russell made an inspection visit but refused to certify the new cells, as two provisions of the Act had not been met. The Prisons Act 1839 had stipulated that all separate cells had to have means by which prisoners could communicate with an officer and provision for them to take air and exercise. The justices altered two yards for air and exercise and directed that bells be installed in the cells so that inmates could call officers if necessary. Russell also refused to certify one of the cells as it was damp. By the end of the year the alterations had been completed and the cells were certified as fit for use (SA, QA 2/1/2, VJR: 31, 110; NA, HO 20/8, Miscellaneous Documents, 1839).

The adoption of the separate system at Shrewsbury prison proceeded gradually during the 1840s and 1850s as various wings and sections were converted, but it was not until the mid-1860s that the whole prison had been adapted. In the early 1840s the separate cells had been constantly occupied, on average for three-month periods, but the longest stay was for ten months. All the officers of the prison were unanimous in support of their use. The chaplain thought that the prisoners in the separate cells were more favourable to education and religious and moral improvement, and that the separation in no way affected their minds injuriously. The surgeon thought the health of those confined separately was better than that of those held in the common courts. Out of eight cases of typhus fever in the previous six months, only two had occurred in the separate cells. In addition, the governor argued that those in the separate cells were more orderly, less tempted to break the rules, and 'less obnoxious to punishment'. He remarked that 'the comparatively innocent were not liable to be annoyed or corrupted, by communication with more hardened offenders, and that the latter had ample and uninterrupted opportunities for reflecting on their past lives, and a chance therefore, for reformation' (SA, QA, 2/1/2, VJR: 110). With such sentiments being regularly expressed, the visiting justices continued in their aim to convert the whole prison.

At various times the building work was thwarted by a lack of bricklayers and builders in the prison, or the separate system was undermined by the need to place three prisoners in a cell at night because of overcrowding, but the justices continued in the belief that it was effective and claimed that those who had been in the separate cells were less likely to be recommitted to the prison. It is difficult to ascertain whether the high rates of insanity experienced at Millbank and Pentonville were also a problem at Shrewsbury. The chaplain and surgeon claimed that the system was not injurious to the health of the prisoners, although they did not provide much supporting evidence. It may be that the short sentences in local prisons meant that those inmates who were subjected to the separate system experienced the regime for only a short period of time, and so it may not have had the severe implications for mental health that was the case in the national penitentiaries. By the 1860s, the final phase of developments took place, and on completion there were 171 separate cells for males and 23 for females – a total of 194 – plus an additional three punishment cells (SA, QA, 2/1/4, VJR: 154). However, by this time, as we have seen, the use of the separate system as a disciplinary regime had fallen out of favour, the reformatory aims had been lost, and the separate cell became part of a prison regime based on deterrence.

Hard labour and diet at Shrewsbury prison

In the early decades of the nineteenth century, prisoners worked on a variety of tasks. They operated a treadmill which ground corn and pulled water and took part in the usual work in the prison – cooking, baking, bricklaying and building. The magistrates had also tried out various other types of employment that might generate revenue. But, from around the mid-century onwards, government preference was for hard unproductive labour.

The provisions of the Prison Act 1865 demanded greater severity and deterrence, and at Shrewsbury this exposed the limited nature of hard labour at the prison. During the year 1865, 24 prisoners were employed on the shot drill and 763 prisoners on the crank; both activities were hard labour of the first class. However, the prisoners were employed at these activities for only about three hours a day; the remainder of time they worked in their cells on hard labour of the second class (NA, HO 24/25). In comparison to the Prison Act 1865, which stipulated hard labour for between six and ten hours, this was a comparatively short time. The then inspector of prisons, John Perry, was highly critical of this, stating that hard labour at the prison was 'not more than what would be considered healthy constitutional exercise' (SA, QA, 2/1/4, VJR: 108). The justices at Shrewsbury, in a similar manner to many magistrates across the country, attempted to adapt the regime to their needs and facilities and the views they held on punishment. This brought them into conflict with the inspectors, who wanted to ensure that all prisons operated in the same way.

While the justices were unable or unwilling to expand hard labour of the first class at Shrewsbury, they placed a greater significance on the prison diet. The inspectors, though, did not agree with this course of action either. As had been demonstrated, local prisons were subject to growing intervention by the government with the aim of unifying practices. By the 1860s there were nine different classes of diet in use, as directed by the Home Office. However, the visiting magistrates at Shrewsbury wanted to give only bread and water to those prisoners sentenced to seven days or less. They argued that, for short terms, the allocated diet was 'no punishment at all' and unlikely to deter offenders. Perry strongly objected to this policy, pointing out that prisoners would have an interest in committing acts of insubordination as the punishment regime was less severe. However, the justices stuck with their plan, which was subsequently sanctioned by the Secretary of State. Perry was also critical of the diet given to prisoners sentenced to hard labour. He argued that alterations would not be necessary if hard labour at the prison were more satisfactory. The justices acknowledged the limited nature of hard labour but believed this was the case in a great majority of prisons. Less than a year later, in 1864, the government issued instructions for a new prison diet which Shropshire Quarter Sessions approved. However, it was maintained that no ill effects had resulted from the bread and water regime for prisoners sentenced to less than seven days, and the magistrates wanted to maintain the status quo in those cases (SA, QA, 2/1/4, VJR: 102-9, 125).

The discussion of dietary regulations and hard labour demonstrates the conflicting viewpoints of the visiting justices and the inspectors concerning the management of the prison. The the inspectors were highly critical of the moderate hours at hard labour of the first class at Shrewsbury. But the justices were concerned about the cost of buying more cranks and the potential impact an outdoor treadwheel might have on the prisoners' health during the colder months of the year. They were, however, prepared to be more stringent in use of diet as punishment. The short terms of imprisonment and the high turnover of population was viewed as an impediment, as there was little time for the regime to have any impact on inmates. During the ten years 1860 to 1869, the average total number of those committed to Shrewsbury prison was 1,475.1, the average number of those removed, discharged or bailed was 1,474.6, and the average remaining in the prison at the end of the year was 144.4 (NA, HO 24/20–24/29). As deterrence could not be achieved through long hours of hard labour, a more meagre prison diet was necessary to increase the effect of short-term sentences. Despite criticism from the inspectors, the justices maintained their position and continued with their bread and water regime for short-term prisoners even after the new government prison diet was implemented. This is just one example of the tussle between the local interest and autonomy of the magistrates and the growing influence of the government in administering prisons.

The case study of Shrewsbury prison presented here and the small body of work published on local prisons in different parts of the country (Brown, 2003; DeLacy, 1986; Forsythe, 1983; Saunders, 1986; Southerton, 1993; Zedner, 1994; for Wales, see Ireland, 2007) have highlighted the considerable diversity in regimes and provided the local context in which prison reform developed from the late eighteenth century onwards (Stockdale, 1977; Whiting, 1975). They have allowed much greater insight into how policies of uniformity and centralisation translated into the practices of the mass of local prisons across the country. Research on local prisons has provided us with a window into the experiences of those who were confined and those who worked in such institutions. Although there is a great deal of emphasis placed on the national 'model' penitentiaries, particularly Millbank and Pentonville, it was the local prisons that held the overwhelming majority of inmates. In the year 1877, the average daily local prison population was 20,361 but this disguises the huge number of committals to the system; over 157,700 people were sent to local prisons, most for summary convictions, compared to just over 1,600 sentenced to penal servitude in a convict prison (*Report of the Commissioners of Prisons*, PP, 1879). Although the early government experiments were important – and we shall move on to an examination of these in the next chapter – from the nineteenth century onwards the local prison provided the most common experience for those sentenced by the courts, and many of these institutions have remained the backbone of our prison system in the twenty-first century (Jewkes and Johnston, 2007).

7

CONVICT PRISONS

Experiencing penal servitude

This chapter will document the shift to the use of long-term imprisonment in England and Wales. It will examine the establishment of the first national penitentiaries, Millbank and Pentonville, and the development of the convict prison system from the mid-nineteenth century onwards. This was the beginning of a tighter grip on the regulation and administration of prisons, which culminated in 1878 in both local and convict prisons being brought under central government control.

As was discussed in Chapter 6 on local prisons, the period from the early nineteenth century to the 1880s was one in which local authorities and the increasing bureaucratic and centralised administration in London tussled for control of local criminal justice agencies and institutions. This had begun with the appointment of prison inspectors and had continued through legislation and financial incentives which encouraged uniformity in practice across the country. But the situation was also influenced by the increasing role that central government played in the administration of prisons. Before this time, it had had limited involvement, as the transportation of convicts overseas had been subcontracted; the operation of the hulks, however, had remained the responsibility of the government (see Chapter 5). The early nineteenth century would bring the first government-controlled prisons – Millbank and Pentonville. Both were used initially to accommodate those awaiting transportation to Australia, and both would end up functioning as part of the convict prison system. The convict prison system developed from the 1850s; instead of transportation, prisoners would undergo a sentence of penal servitude – a period of long-term imprisonment. This chapter will outline and analyse the development and operation of the convict prison system. The case study in this chapter will illustrate the life of John Baines, who was sentenced to five years' penal servitude and, once inside the convict system, categorised as 'star class'. Star class, introduced in the 1870s, and was used to classify and identify those who had no previous convictions and, as far as the authorities could ascertain, no proven contact with others who had.

Two interrelated factors were central to the development of the convict prison system at this time. Firstly, this was a government-controlled system – there was restricted participation of other groups, such as magistrates, in the way there was in the local prison system. Secondly, because of the government's increasing involvement, particularly after 1878, a highly bureaucratic centralised system was created which imposed on both prisoners and staff an internal regime of regulation, monitoring and control. The huge raft of standing orders, rules and regulations which came into being lasted into well into the twentieth century.

Early government penitentiaries: Millbank and Pentonville

While the government had been involved in the detention of prisoners in the hulks, (see Chapter 5) the first notable step in the direction of a government-run prison had been the proposal contained in the Penitentiary Act 1779. In the end, the penitentiary was not constructed, but the Act did lay down some principles which influenced the expansion of prison building at the end of the eighteenth century. The development of local prisons during the 'reform' period has been touched upon in Chapter 6, but the Act was also an early template for a large government project – the first national penitentiary, Millbank, which opened in London in 1816. One key feature of both Millbank and the second government prison, Pentonville, was that they were originally designed for prisoners who had been sentenced to and were awaiting transportation to Australia.

Despite the failure to construct a prison following the Penitentiary Act 1779, just over two decades later a similar proposal was back under discussion. As McConville (1981) points out, this was not simply a reiteration of the reform arguments of the late eighteenth century but reflected broader arguments from legal and penal campaigners, who were keen to curtail the use of capital punishment (see Chapter 4) and to increase the availability of secondary punishments. There were also fears that transportation was losing its deterrent effect (see Chapter 5). As such, the Holford Committee, which reported in 1811, recommended the construction of what they termed a 'penitentiary house' for the counties of London and Middlesex. The committee examined a range of evidence from local prisons, predominantly from Gloucester, where Sir George O. Paul had erected a penitentiary in 1791, and Southwell house of correction in Nottinghamshire, which operated a slightly different regime (see Chapter 6 on local prisons; see also Whiting, 1975; Ignatieff, 1978, on Gloucestershire). It also took evidence from Jeremy Bentham, who was keen to reassert his modified ideas for the construction of his Panopticon. The Panopticon design, consisting of six floors in a circular structure, was based on principles of surveillance, observation and inspection; each floor of the prison would have cells around the circumference, all facing an observation tower in the centre of the structure. Prisoners in their cells were therefore observable at all times from the central guard tower, their conformity induced by the fact that they could not tell at any one moment whether or not they were being observed. Bentham had originally put forward the design for the tender invited under the Penitentiary Act 1779 and had spent considerable time since then lobbying the government to adopt it. However, his plans for management and labour were not to the taste of the Holford Committee either (Holford Committee, PP, 1811; see also Semple, 1993; Fiddler, 2008; Devereaux, 1999).

In the end, the penitentiary built was Millbank; it opened in 1816 and by the time it was finished had cost a considerable sum of money. Millbank was to be supervised by a committee made up of MPs and prison reformers. The new penitentiary and its regime would not just detain prisoners but would extend to 'the reformation and improvement of the mind, and operating by seclusion, employment and religious instruction' (Holford Committee, PP, 1811: 4). However, the project did not work out as the government had hoped. In the following decades there were a variety of problems that brought the prison into the public eye and signalled its demise. Millbank never accommodated as many prisoners as it had been designed for; it was built on poor marshland on the banks of the Thames, which had contributed to its enormous financial cost. There were outbreaks of disease and illness, allegations of staff shortages and corruption, revolts and disturbances as prisoners endeavoured to get transferred, and claims that the solitude and isolation was having a serious effect on the mental health of the inmates (McConville, 1981; Ignatieff, 1978; Wilson, 2002).

In the early years, George Holford, who had taken up the role of chairman of the Millbank Committee, tried to respond to criticism in the press of a weak administration and charges that the prison was a 'fattening house' for convicts. He withdrew reading material, cut visiting times, and ordered closer observation of the inmates, and in 1822 the diet was cut back. This resulted in an outbreak of typhus, dysentery and scurvy and the deaths of over 30 prisoners, the illness of hundreds and, subsequently, the temporary abandonment of the prison (Ignatieff, 1978; McConville, 1981; Sim, 1990). In the latter years, a new governor-chaplain, Reverend Daniel Nihill, reasserted a reformatory regime of religious zeal and strict separation. After a short period of apparent success, the situation declined rapidly, as the number of cases of insanity in prisoners increased and deaths occurred. Initially, Nihill refused to alter his rules: 'Health is certainly a great consideration ... but are morals less?' By this time, though, Millbank already had a reputation as an unhealthy prison because of its site and construction, and this further confirmed the view of *Punch* magazine, which described the penitentiary as 'a capital substitute for capital punishment' (cited in Collins, 1962: 151). The committee intervened, and periods of association for prisoners were introduced. From 1843, Millbank became a convict depot: prisoners were sent there for up to nine months during which time they were assessed, and adults went on to either to Pentonville or the hulks and juveniles to Parkhurst prison (McConville, 1981); Millbank was later integrated into the convict prison system. The contested nature of prison development at this time is exemplified by the Millbank experience and, as Wilson (2002, 2014) argues, while the penitentiary is often dismissed quickly as a failure, the discussions reveal the lack of legitimacy of prison in eyes of the public, the staff and the inmates.

By the early 1840s there was already the prospect of a second government prison, one that would fully embrace the separate system and would be a 'model' for other prisons across the country. As we have seen in Chapter 6, two of the prison inspectors, William Crawford and Reverend Whitworth Russell, placed considerable emphasis on the separate system as a reformatory method and were keen to implement it in prisons across the country. As Tomlinson has noted, for some commentators, separation was the panacea for increasing crime; the ultimate in classification, it 'reached its apogee in separate confinement as it protected everybody from everybody else' (1978b: 62).

The first experiment had been at Parkhurst prison, where, from 1838, juvenile prisoners had been held under the separate system (see Chapter 9). Crawford and the administrators then turned their attention to an adult prison, and in 1842 Pentonville 'model' prison, designed by Joshua Jebb, then the Surveyor-General of Convict Prisons, was opened. Pentonville was designed to hold 520 adult inmates under the strict application of the separate system, initially for periods of 18 months. The idea was that convicts sentenced to transportation would be sent first to Pentonville to spend a period of time under the separate system. It was thought that this experience would allow them to be more open to reform and better prepared for the colonies than the hardened and corrupt offenders from the hulks. As Sir John Graham wrote to the Pentonville Commissioners in 1842:

> The chain of former habits would be broken; his early associations would be altered, a new scene would open to his view, where skilled labour is in great demand; where the earnings of industry rapidly accumulate … This is the prospect which will revive hope in the bosom of the prisoners, which will confirm his good resolutions, and which will stimulate him to energy and virtue.
>
> (Cited in Tomlinson, 1978b: 64)

Even before the prison opened the proposed regime came in for criticism. Robert Ferguson, writing in the *Quarterly Review*, outlined the regime behind the walls:

> They are fed at the same moment, rest at the same hour, are out in masses in the open air. They are catechized in the school, and respond in the chapel – yet no man knows not man. There is contiguity, but no neighbourhood; and the very names of the prisoners are lost in the mechanisms which assigns *numbers* in their stead.
>
> (1847: 183; original emphasis)

The four large wings of the prison radiated out from a central hub from which all of the cell doors could be observed; each cell was identical and separation was absolute. As McGowen notes, 'Pentonville represented the apotheosis of the idea that a totally controlled environment could produce a reformed and autonomous individual' (1998: 92). 'Standing on a huge six-acre site, behind twenty-five-foot-high walls, it loomed over the workers' quarters around it, a massive three-pronged fortress of the law' (Ignatieff, 1978: 3).

Unfortunately, the exacting regime of separation at Pentonville resulted in high numbers of cases of insanity in prisoners during the first few years. The convict's day began at 5.45 a.m. and finished with lights out at 9.00 p.m. The meticulous timetable was punctuated by the ringing of bells, indicating inspection, labour, meals, chapel and exercise, and all this centred on confinement in a separate cell, measuring 13½ feet from window to door, 7½ feet across and 9 feet from floor to ceiling (Ignatieff, 1978). Subsequent investigations led to a reduction in the period of separation from 18 to 12 months and then finally down to nine months. Social commentators and the press had all called the system into question. Even before the new prison opened, *The Times* called the proposed regime 'unnecessarily cruel' and claimed that 'if the system be carried to far, madness will seize those whom death has for the present spared' (20 May 1841, cited in Johnston, 2006: 107). During the inquest into the death of a prisoner in 1843, the coroner summed up the mood in relation to Pentonville when he commented: 'Out of doors there is strong feeling against this place, and some persons can hardly find terms vehement enough to use in speaking of it' (*The Times*, 12 December 1843).

By the late 1840s, the tide of feeling was against Pentonville and the separate system more generally (Henriques, 1972). Criticism of the prison continued in relation to the rates of insanity, but there were also growing censure in the other direction – that the system was not severe enough. Evidence was presented that the regime was too soft and that the living conditions were better, or the diet more plentiful, than those experienced by the honest free labouring population; views about prison regimes in the nineteenth century oscillated between these extremes, all underpinned by notions of 'less eligibility' (see Chapter 1). Just one example of this criticism is that of the author and critic Thomas Carlyle, whose essay 'Model Prisons' launched a scathing attack on Pentonville:

> what a beautiful Establishment here fitted up for the accommodation of the scoundrel-world, male and female! As I said, no Duke in England is, for all rational purposes which a human being can or ought to aim at, lodged, fed, tended, taken care of, with such perfection. Of poor craftsmen that pay rates and taxes from their day's wages, of the dim millions that toil and moil continually under the sun, we know what is the lodging and the tending ... lodged in their squalid garrets; working often enough amid famine, darkness, tumult, dust and desolation, what work they have to do: – of these as of 'spiritual back-woodsmen,' understood to be pre-appointed to such a life, and like the pigs to killing, 'quite used to it,' I say nothing. But of Dukes, which Duke, I could ask, has cocoa, soup, meat, and food in general made ready, so fit for keeping him in health, in ability to do and to enjoy? Which Duke has a house so thoroughly clean, pure and airy; lives in an element so wholesome, and perfectly adapted to the uses of soul and body as this same, which is provided here for the Devil's regiments of the line? No Duke that I have ever known.

> (Carlyle, [1850] 2008)

Observers also claimed that separation was not absolute, that the prisoners were able to recognise and to communicate with one another other, and that they deceived the administrators with their fraudulent claims of reform and religious conversion. Representations of a number of these criticisms can be found in the latter part of Charles Dickens's *David Copperfield*. Heep, the villainous clerk in the book, sentenced to transportation for fraud, forgery and conspiracy, is confined in the 'model prison' under the separate system. Heep and another villain, Littimer, are presented to Copperfield by the magistrate as 'model prisoners' during a visit to the penitentiary. Yet Copperfield sees them as 'perfectly consistent and unchanged; ... exactly what they were then, they had always been' ([1849–50] 1994: 699), aware as they were of the importance of a 'good character' for life in the colonies (see also Johnston, 2006).

Similarly, Ormsby, writing in the *Cornhill Magazine*, thought that the exertions of the criminal classes were owed to the

> stately and substantial palaces which adorn some of our unsightly districts, such as Millbank and Pentonville. For these, in their natural state believing nothing, and fearing the devil only when we appears in the form of a police-man, their country maintains an infinite variety of chaplains – Protestant, Catholic, Wesleyan, Mahomedan, Mormon, so nice do their religious scruples become after conviction; and for these – albeit when they live at their own charges they live on fried fish and gin – it is necessary to provide strengthening meats and nourishing soups lest that muscle, which they never employ but for the good of their species, should be wasted.
>
> (1864: 634)

It is not simply the case that views had turned against the reformatory project; indeed, the goal and methods of such practices, as well as the expense of providing the new prisons, had been contested since at least the early nineteenth century. On the one hand, those who built the new prisons held them up as architectural manifestations of their benevolence, philanthropy and civilisation (Evans, 1982; Pratt, 2002; Jewkes and Johnston, 2007). On the other, these 'prison palaces' were castigated for their luxurious diets and modern facilities, which compared favour-ably to the conditions in the homes of the labouring poor and the workhouse, providing for 'Bill Sikes and his friends ... well aired and ventilated, clean, tidy, winter-warmed, snug and cheerfully lighted places of abode' (Anon, 1869, cited in Tomlinson, 1978b: 65; Ignatieff, 1978; Pratt, 2002, 2004).

Convicts at mid-century and the establishment of penal servitude

By mid-century, Millbank and Pentonville were both operating as depots for the classification and further allocation of those sentenced to transportation. By this time, some convicts were also confined at Portland, undertaking labour on public works, and at a former barracks at Shorncliffe in Kent; the government rented additional cells in a number of local prisons across the country. In 1850, the Directorate of Convict Prisons was established, administrative processes were all regularised, and the first appointed officials, Joshua Jebb, Captain D. O'Brien and Herbert P. Voules, took office. In the following years these men – particularly Jebb, who was chairman of the directors until 1863 – were to have considerable influence over policy in the convict system (McConville, 1981).

As we have seen, despite the high number of convicts being sent to Australia and other places in the 1830s, at the peak of the use of transportation the system was already under threat. After the end of transportation (see Chapter 5) a new type of sentence was established based on a system of long-term imprisonment. This became the convict prison system, and the sentence undergone was known as penal servitude. Under the first Penal Servitude Act in 1853, long-term imprisonment was introduced alongside transportation. Seven to ten years' transportation became four to six years' penal servitude and ten to fourteen years' transportation became six to eight years' penal servitude, but those sentenced to more than fourteen years' transportation were still sent abroad (Tomlinson, 1981). At this time there was no remission from a sentence of penal servitude, but those sentenced to transportation and who were still in the penal system were able to gain a reduction in the time served.

In this early stage of the system, four years was the minimum sentence, consisting of one year of separate confinement and three years on public works. Millbank and Pentonville (and Perth in Scotland) were used for separate confinement, and all had been utilised as convict depots in the preceding years following the failed attempts to instigate the reformatory system. Public works prisons, on the other hand, had to be constructed, and over the following decades a number were built or adapted, including those at Brixton, Chatham, Chattenden, Parkhurst, Portsmouth, Portland, Dartmoor, Borstal and Woking. Brixton and Parkhurst were used for women in the early years, but by the time the system was more established, after the period of separation at Millbank, female convicts were sent either to Fulham Refuge (although called a refuge, it was a convict prison) or Woking (for more on female convict system, see Chapter 8).

The second Penal Servitude Act in 1857 altered sentencing and removed the distinction between transportation and penal servitude. From then on, penal servitude comprised three stages: the first was a period of separation, the second a period on public works and, finally, if a period of remission had been earned, release on licence. The minimum sentence was also reduced to three years; this, it was believed, would allow for penal servitude to become a more effective secondary punishment.

At Chatham, these changes in the system contributed in 1861 to one of the largest riots in English prison history. Over 800 male convicts were involved, and order was restored only after the intervention of the military. There had been complaints about the severity of the regime and allegations of staff corruption. Further, there was a sense of injustice at the disparity between the two groups of convicts at the prison: one group held under the Penal Servitude Act 1853, who had no possibility of remission on their sentence, and the other held under the 1857 Act, who did (Brown, 2008, 2003; Tomlinson, 1981).

As we have seen, in the late 1850s and the 1860s, growing fears about the criminal classes and habitual offenders, panics about convicts on licence committing violent street crimes, and increasing disillusion with the reformatory prison project drew calls for greater severity in all aspects of punishment and criminal justice. This resulted in the establishment in 1863 of the Penal Servitude Acts Commission and the Carnarvon Committee, whose recommendations led to further legislation. The Penal Servitude Act in 1864 reflected the overall change in penal philosophy and, in parallel to the Prison Act 1865, which applied to the local prison system, set about implementing a more severe prison regime based on deterrence.

The Penal Servitude Act 1864 increased the minimum sentence of penal servitude to five years. Although the commission had actually recommended seven years, this was not followed through when the Bill went to Parliament. The commission had been holding out for the continuation of transportation to Western Australia for those prisoners not physically or otherwise unfit, and had included a provision for those sentenced to penal servitude to be sent abroad; however, as we have seen, no convicts were sent there after 1867 (the convict establishment at Gibraltar was also recommended for closure, but it was not shut down fully until 1875). But the Act did set a minimum term of seven years for those offenders who had previously served a sentence of penal servitude. Reflecting the mood of the time, in 1878 the Kimberley Commission believed that the system of penal servitude was not operating as a means to deter people from crime: it was 'not sufficiently dreaded either by those who had undergone it, or by the criminal classes generally' (PP, 1878: 9). This, it was felt, was on account of the shortness of the sentence and, to a lesser degree, defects in the disciplinary regime.

The convict prison regime: experienced penal servitude

For most of the remainder of the nineteenth century, the convict prison system operated largely under the regulations of the Penal Servitude Act 1864 and the changes in the regime it had recommended. The three stages of penal servitude – a period of separate confinement, a period on public works and then, if earned, a period under release on licence – continued, but various aspects of the regime were tightened up in order to increase its deterrent effect.

Experience in the preceding decades perhaps influenced the decision to set the term of separate confinement at nine months, and convicts continued to serve this stage at Millbank or Pentonville – although Millbank was later discontinued and replaced by Wormwood Scrubs. Under separation, convicts worked in their cells at tailoring, hammock, bag, mat or shoe making, weaving, or oakum picking; they were out of their cells only for daily attendance at chapel and for exercise – one hour per day, during which they were in silent association. Female convicts were employed in their cells at needlework and knitting. A system which had been constructed for reform thus shifted to one based on deterrence, and the fact this 'did not result in any significant alteration of the regime ... casts a revealing light on earlier efforts' (McGowen, 1998: 93). The cell, once integral to the transformative powers of the reformatory separate system, now became pivotal in a regime of deterrence and isolation (Johnston, 2013).

During the public works stage of the sentence, while convicts slept and ate their meals in separate cells, labour was undertaking in association, although all communication beyond what was necessary for work was prevented. Inmates passed through progressive stages where they earned marks. They undertook excavations and building work, built sea defences and docks at Borstal, Brixton, Chatham, Portland and Portsmouth, as well as making bricks for the Admiralty and the War Office. At Dartmoor they reclaimed moorland, and those unfit for the rigours of such full labour worked on farming supplies there and at Parkhurst and Woking (the latter two establishments had provision to hold those classified as 'invalid' or 'weak-minded'). Other trades were also undertaken at all of these prisons; 'superior jobs' working as tailors, shoemakers, carpenters and blacksmiths, or in the bakery, were used as an incentive to good behaviour.

There were five stages in the classification of convicts: probation, third, second, first and special. Promotion through the system was based on good conduct and industry, although the first three stages also required that a minimum period of time had been served. (This differed slightly for female convicts; see Chapter 8.) No convict was allowed first-class status unless they could read and write. Special class could be granted only through exemplary conduct in the first class and was permitted only within 12 months of discharge. Prisoners' uniforms differed slightly by stage, but all male convicts' clothing was marked with the 'broad arrow' or 'crow's foot' which denoted the property of Her Majesty's Prison system. Privileges such as letters, visits, exercise and gratuities all increased as prisoners progressed through the system.

In the early to mid-nineteenth century, most of the memoirs or chronicles of prison life came from staff, often prison chaplains or governors – for example, *Female Life in Prison* (1862) and *Prison Characters* (1866), both by 'A Prison Matron' (a pseudonym for Frederick W. Robinson), and Arthur Griffiths's *Memorials of Millbank* (1875) – and commentators such as Henry Mayhew and John Binny, whose *The Criminal Prisons of London* was published in 1862. But in the late nineteenth century more biographies and memoirs appeared that documented the prison experience from the prisoner's point of view, the overwhelming majority of which emanated from the convict system (for discussion, see Anderson and Pratt, 2008; Brown, 2003; Brown and Clare, 2005; Priestley, 1989, 1999). The official discourse of the prison authorities was then contested by a range of voices from inmates who offered a different truth (Pratt, 2002, 2004). Often these memoirs were from particular groups of offenders – those who were more literate and of a higher class than the majority, fraudsters, embezzlers, those convicted for their political beliefs (Irish Republican prisoners), and others protesting their innocence. Frank Henderson's *Six Years in the Prisons of England* (1869) and *Five Years' Penal Servitude by One Who Endured It* (1877), attributed to Edward Callow, are just two examples. These texts often focus on the day-to-day deprivations of imprisonment; one significant feature in many such memoirs is food.

TABLE 7.1 Diet schedule for male convict prisoners at hard labour on public works

Day	Breakfast	Dinner	Supper	Daily bread allowance
Sunday	$\frac{3}{4}$ pint of cocoa	4 oz cheese	1 pint of gruel	30 oz of bread
Monday and Saturday	$\frac{3}{4}$ pint of cocoa	5 oz beef and 1 lb potatoes	1 pint of gruel	23 oz of bread
Tuesday and Friday	$\frac{3}{4}$ pint of cocoa	1 pint of soup and 1 lb potatoes	1 pint of gruel	23 oz of bread
Wednesday	$\frac{3}{4}$ pint of cocoa	5 oz mutton and 1 lb potatoes	1 pint of gruel	23 oz of bread
Thursday	$\frac{3}{4}$ pint of cocoa	1 lb suet pudding and 1 lb potatoes	1 pint of gruel	23 oz of bread

Source: *Convict Prison Dietaries* (PP, 1864: 7).

In the 1860s and 1870s there was no additional food as prisoners progressed through the stages; in general the diet was sparse and had been meticulously calculated to be the minimum that convicts needed in order to endure the long hours of hard labour, as can be seen in Table 7.1.

As we have seen in the discussions of Millbank and Pentonville, diet was an important area of the prison regime. Indeed, committees of doctors and medical experts met to assess the exact amount of food that could be given to prisoners to ensure maximum deterrence but allow prisoners to endure long hours of hard labour without affecting their health. Ensuring the principle of 'less eligibility', no one should be encouraged to seek a prison sentence by the thought of a plentiful diet, though by this time the inspectors pressed the view that food should not itself be an 'instrument of punishment' (Tomlinson, 1978a). Discussions about diet across the local prisons were rife as the quantities varied so much across the country, and comparisons with local workhouses were frequently made (see Chapter 6). In the convict system in the 1860s, the general discontent with punishment and fear of the 'criminal class' was fuelled by claims that convicts were given 39 ounces of meat per week and cocoa sweetened with molasses (Tomlinson, 1978a; *Convict Prison Dietaries*, PP, 1864). Though disquiet was apparent, the directors were firm in their belief that adequate food was needed to undergo labour on public works.

By the late 1870s the diet was again standardised, and 'stirabout' (see Chapter 6) was introduced. Inmates' memoirs continue to testified to the monotony, scarcity and deficiency of prison food: 'searching for the bacon among the beans is like looking for the needle in a bundle of hay. And when it is found, it is not a tempting morsel. It is very fat bacon, suitable for greasing engine wheels' (Nicholl, 1897, cited in Anderson and Pratt, 2008: 186; Pratt, 2002). The Kimberley Commission also received evidence of convicts who resorted to eating candles but dismissed this as arising 'from a desire … to eat more fat than the dietary affords, and not from any deficiency in the quantity or quality of the diet'. Similarly, it was thought that the eating of refuse, of various kinds, occurred among those who were depraved or 'weak minded', thus not 'affording any reason for objecting' to the diet (PP, 1879: 38).

Through the progressive stages, convicts were to earn between six and eight marks per day. Eight were rewarded for steady hard labour, seven for a lesser degree of effort, and only six for a fair or moderate day's work. Marks were no longer awarded at the separate confinement stage, and remission would not be granted automatically but would be a reward, earned through good conduct and industry. This says nothing of the consequences of breaking the rules and regulations and the subsequent punishments for such offences – for example, forfeiting remission marks, being put back a stage or to probation, and being given only bread and water, time in what was termed 'close confinement' (basically solitary confinement) or, in some cases, a flogging. As John Pratt has neatly summarised it, if, 'at this time, prisons were spoken of, then it was as a terrible punishment the authorities now intended it to be' (2002: 86).

At Chatham, extreme cases of self-injury or self-mutilation among prisoners were evident in the early 1870s. The authorities claimed that these prisoners were 'malingerers' who would resort to any means to escape hard labour. They did not interpret it as evidence of the severity of the regime. Convicts had placed their limbs under the moving wheels of trucks and engines while at hard labour and, as a result, in 1871 the medical officer performed 33 amputations (Brown, 2003). Frank Henderson's account states that one convict who had been transferred from Chatham said it was '"the worst station out ... they are starved and worked to death" ... The "screws" there are – tyrants, and if they don't mind what they are about some of them will get murdered' ([1869] 2007: 122–3). The authorities continued to fear that convicts evaded work by feigning illness and attempting suicide, or they self-harmed simply to obtain the better conditions of the hospital wing. This view might have influenced the decision to allow only six marks per day to be gained during a stay in the hospital wing, and therefore not enough to count towards remission of a sentence.

In this apparently unremitting regime, the only hope for convicts was release on licence, and this was, at least, a realistic prospect. As has been touched upon, remission of a sentence and release on licence or 'ticket of leave' had been part of the system of transportation in Australia, and this continued after the Penal Servitude Act 1857. It was consistently the case that the prospect of remission was seen as an important element of convict penal policy, if in practice it was acknowledged as a difficult and sensitive issue for public opinion, as was revealed during the 'garrotting panics'. Despite this episode, though, the majority of the members of the Penal Servitude Acts Commission in 1863 agreed that earning remission supplied 'the *most powerful* incentive to good conduct and industry which could be brought to bear on the minds of prisoners' (Kimberley Commission, PP, 1879: ix; emphasis added). Instead they tightened up the conditions of licences and the penalties by which these were forfeited. After the 1864 Act, male convicts could earn between one-sixth and one-third remission, depending on the length of their sentence (unless it was for life). Female convicts could earn marks during separate confinement and up to one-third remission of sentence, but women could be released on a conditional licence which meant confinement in a refuge for up to nine months (see Chapter 8).

Kimberley Commission, 1878–9

By the close of the period under discussion here, the convict system was fully developed. The Kimberley Commission examined the operation of the Penal Servitude Acts in 1878 and produced a substantial document of over 1,400 pages with evidence. It reported that 'the system of penal servitude, as present administered, is on the whole satisfactory; that it is effective as a punishment and, it is free from serious abuses' (Kimberley Commission, PP, 1879: 26). The commissioners recognised that

> a certain number of criminals, especially those that had undergone more than one sentence, become accustomed to prison life, and lose much of the dread that is felt by those not hardened in crime. But this is necessarily incidental to all systems of punishment, and we believe that a sentence of penal servitude is now generally an object of dread to the criminal population.
>
> (Ibid.)

They thought that the stricter regime that had been brought in by the 1864 Act had had the desired effect. However, while they recommended that the minimum sentence of seven years for reconvicted convicts should be abolished, the minimum term of five years should be retained. Penal servitude would not be used for offenders under the age of 16, and treason-felony convicts would be placed in a separate class.

Another significant change that was advocated by this commission was the introduction of the 'star class'. While the members felt the overall regime offered sufficient deterrence, it failed to reform, and in the case of less hardened or first-time offenders it produced a 'deteriorating effect from the indiscriminate association in all classes of convicts' (Kimberley Commission , PP, 1879: 27). The perennial problem of what to do with first-time offenders in order to prevent the evils of moral contamination would be dealt with by the new administrative category of 'star class'. This distinct category was for those who had no previous convictions whatsoever and was concerned purely with the prevention of contamination; in all other ways the punishment would remain the same. Some prisoners would be unfit for such a status, the commission thought – the receivers of stolen goods who had escaped conviction during a long criminal career, men guilty of unnatural crimes or indecency – but as much as possible they wanted to separate 'habitual criminals, such as notorious thieves, burglars, … men who have made crime their profession, and are eager to initiate others in the mysteries of their nefarious craft' from others (ibid.: 30). Subsequently, the administrative arm of the convict system went to considerable lengths to investigate whether or not an offender should be given the status of star class.

The regime was adapted to some extent. During the separation and public works stages convicts continued to earn marks. Each stage had a set of privileges and a uniform; privileges included the number of visits allowed, the number of letters permitted, and the time and frequency of exercise. Plank beds and gruel in the first stage could be replaced by a mattress and tea and bread. Marks could be taken away at any time, and inmates could be demoted or put back a stage for infractions or breaches of the prison rules. As previously, remission could be earned through the marks system and good conduct on public works, leading to release on licence.

In the wider criminal justice system there was no other mechanism to deal with first-time offenders who were found guilty; this would come with the passing in 1887 of the Probation of First Offenders Act, which allowed for the diversion of some offenders. At this stage, however, it applied only to those who, if convicted, would serve a maximum of two years' imprisonment, and, in practice, it was often thought to apply to young offenders. More substantial changes would not come until the early twentieth century (McWilliams, 1983; Mair and Burke, 2012).

'Star class' case study: John Baines (NA, PCOM 3, licence no. A35749/45239; Convict Registry Office no. J.447; Local/County Prison Register no. 312)

John Baines, or John Bell Allen, was just the kind of offender who, at least on the face of it, had the background to obtain 'star class' within the convict system. As noted earlier, the administrators were loath to classify too many people in the star class, and evidence suggests that any contact or association with anyone who had committed or been suspected of committing an offence or living a disorderly life was enough to prevent such a status being accorded, even if the record indicated that it was a first offence (Johnston and Godfrey, 2013a). John was about 29 years old in 1883 when he was found guilty of fraud and forgery at Manchester Assizes and sentenced to five years' penal servitude. He had been charged with seven indictments relating to forging and uttering deeds relating to property, forging and uttering credit orders and falsifying accounts, all of which involved large sums of money. These offences took place in the course of his employment as a bank clerk at the Barrow in Furness branch of the Lancaster Banking Company, where he had worked for over ten years. John's downfall had been gambling by speculating in stocks and shares. This had led to large losses, which entailed either transferring credit to people he owed or falsifying accounts, and had allegedly occurred over a period of around four years.

John had started work at the bank in 1871. He came from what appeared to be a stable middle-class background, he was a Roman Catholic and he could read and write well. He was born and lived in Borwick, Lancashire, with his parents and five siblings. His father was a registrar and respected farmer (of 52 acres) and ran a grocery shop; he had been 'very well brought up, and enjoyed a very high character'. By 1881, John was living with his sister and brother in a house in Barrow in Furness; they were all single. John worked at the bank, his brother Henry was an auctioneer's assistant, his sister Jane, a housekeeper, and they employed one female domestic servant. By the time of the criminal charges against him, John was living in Warton, near Carnforth, and his brother Thomas, then an articled clerk, was lodging with him. John was declared bankrupt, and in the criminal proceedings against him he pleaded guilty to some of the charges – not, as his defence counsel outlined, through legal advice but through 'his own better feeling'. According to the Judge, he had yielded

> to the terrible temptation which gambling in any form presented to men – particularly young men like the prisoner, perhaps greedy to become rich, and perhaps led on and encouraged by others to believe that by engaging in these reckless and wanton speculations he would achieve speedy wealth … A bank clerk who betrayed his trust could not be treated as an ordinary offender.
>
> (*Lancaster Gazette*, 7 July 1883)

Taking into consideration John's good background, and that this was a first offence, the judge passed a sentence of five years' penal servitude.

While the factories and workplaces of the working classes were increasingly coming under surveillance through the use of overseers, foremen and private policing methods (Godfrey and Cox, 2013; Godfrey *et al.*, 2008), from the mid-century onwards there was also concern about fraud and white-collar crime committed by 'respectable' offenders. The largest financial crimes drew the attention of the news media, but frauds and embezzlement by a range of middle-class (and lower-middle-class) offenders meant that the respectable criminal did not go unnoticed. Their increasing numbers before the courts during this period challenged prevailing assumptions and discourses about the commission of crime (Locker, 2004, 2005, 2008; see also Wilson, 2010).

Unsurprisingly, John Baines was a good prisoner, and his penal record consists largely of information relating to the letters he wrote and the people who visited him during his confinement. He was initially committed to Strangeways prison in Manchester and spent his time picking oakum. About four months later he was moved down to the convict system and on 6 June 1883 entered Pentonville prison. After three days he was allocated to Wormwood Scrubs, where he was put to work as a tailor. Once he was inside the convict system, the administrators started enquiring about his character. The local police completed the questions in the standard forms regarding the possible status of 'star class' and reported positively. John had been known to them for over twenty years, and he was an 'honest, industrious, sober and respectably connected up to the time of his imprisonment'. Having been awarded star class, he spent about six months under separate confinement at the Scrubs and then in January 1884 was moved to Chatham, where he worked as a labourer. For few periods here and there he received light labour, suggesting a health-related issue, though it is not clear what this was.

John's record shows the regular contact, both in frequent letters and in visits, he had with his family and with his solicitor. During his time at Wormwood Scrubs, his father was declared bankrupt, and John was taken several times from prison to the bankruptcy court as a witness. There is more than a suggestion in the newspaper accounts of this case that his father had colluded in John's activities and at the very least had had knowledge of his fraudulent transactions. During his time in Chatham, John requested and was granted extended visiting time (30 rather than 20 minutes), and in February 1885 he also appeared as a witness in the defence of George Nelson at a trial at St George's Hall in Liverpool. As he progressed through the stages his visits were permitted more regularly, and from September 1885 he received visitors every four months, some for as long as an hour.

In February 1887 John was visited by two of his brothers, and two days later he wrote to tell the family he would be released on licence on 21 March. He had 13 months left to serve of his five-year sentence. He did not breach the conditions of his licence. In the latter part of 1889, at Barrow in Furness, he married Elizabeth Slater, whom he had known before his conviction; she had visited him in prison at various times from 1885 onwards.

John resumed his business activities after his release from Chatham and worked as a commission agent. In early 1890 he was declared bankrupt under the name John Bell Allen, though during the proceedings he initially denied his previous bankruptcy and said he had never been to Barrow in Furness. He also tried to avoid giving his wife's maiden name to prevent her being 'dragged through the public press' (*Lancaster Gazette*, 18 March 1891). By the 1891 census John and Elizabeth had two children and were living in Camberwell, London, with John's parents, his sister Mary, his brothers William and James, and Elizabeth's sister Mary. We lose track of John Baines after 1911, but at that time the family was living in West Derby, Lancashire. John was described as an 'inventor and director of limited company'; he had two sons – John, then a shipping clerk, and Francis, a student – and a daughter, Elizabeth, who was then 11 years old.

John Baines had no further criminal convictions following his imprisonment. The authorities were probably correct at the time in categorising him in the 'star class', but his business activities seemed in the early years after his release to have the potential to undermine his progress. While his employment suggests a degree of superiority or social status had been achieved by 1911, his son John was also declared bankrupt in 1921. His other son, Francis, died of gangrene poisoning during the First World War.

8

WOMEN, CRIME AND CUSTODY

This chapter will examine the perceived causes of and dominant views about female crime and criminality in the nineteenth century. It will discuss the ways in which women were dealt with by the criminal justice system but will focus in particular upon women in the penal system. While the wider social controls experienced by all women – views about feminine conduct, family structure and motherhood, the double burden of work in and outside the home – meant that the majority did not come into contact with the criminal justice system, those who did were often seen in distinct ways (Heidensohn, 1985). Women's crimes were gendered, as were the responses to their infractions. Women committed all types of crime but were overrepresented in certain categories of offending: theft and offences under the Pawnbrokers' Acts; being drunk and disorderly; lower-level assaults and public disorder; and offences relating to prostitution. There were concerns about their involvement both in these crimes and in others such as poisoning, baby farming and infanticide (Zedner, 1994; D'Cruze and Jackson, 2009; Godfrey et al., 2005).

This chapter will also look at the responses to these crimes and examine the ways in which women were dealt with by the penal system. Many women, like men, experienced the revolving door of the local prison, and a smaller proportion were sentenced to transportation (see Chapter 5) or, from mid-century on, committed to the convict system. A much smaller number were executed. As we have seen in Chapter 4, the number of people executed declined across the period 1815 to 1880, and those who reached the gallows after the 1840s were overwhelmingly those convicted for murder. Throughout the period under study there were a range of semi-penal institutions – homes, refuges, retreats, and the like – that were used after or instead of imprisonment for either criminal or deviant women, some of whom were admitted 'voluntarily'.

Female crime and its causes

Overall women commit less crime than men. Research that has examined this issue across in all periods, from the fourteenth to the twentieth century, demonstrates that women are a minority of those were are prosecuted (Beattie, 1975; Kermode and Walker, 1994; Heidensohn, 1985; D'Cruze and Jackson, 2009). Women made up 20 to 25 per cent of those prosecuted by the courts in nineteenth-century England. Then, as today, women committed all types of crime but were overrepresented within certain categories.

Women committed mostly low-level or minor offences. The summary convictions data for the period 1857 to 1892 shows that they accounted for around 17 per cent of all summary convictions. The largest single category of offence was drunkenness (or drunk and disorderly; this increased as a proportion of female offending across the period), which was also the largest category for male offenders. The next largest category was common assault, where women made up about 20 per cent of those convicted, followed by larceny (Zedner, 1994). Both assaults and thefts were declining across the nineteenth century (Gatrell, 1980), and those taking a longer-term view have argued that, from the late seventeenth century onwards, the number of women brought before the courts for these offences had been 'vanishing' (Feeley and Little, 1991). Others have contested this view, and, indeed, an increase in women's participation in summary offences can be observed in the latter half of the century, though the figures are also affected by the reorganisation of summary jurisdiction (D'Cruze and Jackson, 2009). In addition, women were convicted for such offences as breaches of the peace, begging, and breaking local by-laws or Acts – offences public in nature but also poverty related. Women outnumbered men in only one category of offence: those relating to the Pawnbrokers' Act. Charges were brought against domestic servants, seamstresses and other home-workers who pledged goods to obtain money quickly and then were unable to redeem them in time. As Zedner notes, this 'tells us much of both the role of women in managing and attempting to eke out an inadequate household budget, and also of the place of petty crime in the economy of the urban female poor' (1994: 37).

In general, women made up a similar proportion of those before the courts for indictable offences, and this declined slightly across the period, from around 27 per cent in 1857 to about 19 per cent in 1890 (Zedner, 1994). However, in the latter part of the century, though the number of women in prisons had declined, they outnumbered men when it came to recidivism; more women were 'hardened habitual' offenders with more than ten previous convictions (Zedner, 1991; Turner, 2011, 2012). From 1857 onwards, the majority of those tried on indictment, both women and men, were before the courts for 'offences against property without violence' – most frequently 'simple larceny' – about 70 per cent of which across the period were committed by women as compared to around half for men. Women were also tried for 'larceny from the person', which often involved prostitutes stealing from clients (though summary convictions for prostitution under the vagrancy laws were also declining), which made up about a quarter of all serious female crime in 1857, but these declined as the century proceeded. Another category of theft for which women were indicted was 'larceny by servants', reflecting the nature of female employment. They also appeared for 'receiving stolen goods' or 'obtaining goods by false pretences and attempts to defraud', the latter increasingly so between the middle and the end of the century (Zedner, 1994).

The second largest category of serious offences for both women and men consisted of 'offences against the person'. In the early period, women made up around 40 per cent of those tried for murder, but this was before the statistics separated out women indicted for infanticide (the murder of an infant under a year old). Thereafter, they made up less than a quarter of those charged with murder. All those charged with infanticide and other related lesser offences (not capital), such as 'concealment of birth', were women (Zedner, 1991, 1994).

Offences against property with violence was the third largest category of offence, though the accused were women in only 2 or 3 per cent of burglaries or housebreaking cases; however, they were often charged with being accomplices or look-outs. A further 3 or 4 per cent were committed for forgery or currency offences, most often for 'uttering' counterfeit coins but also for forgery and coining, which were skilled crimes. Women also made up the majority of offenders committed for brothel-keeping or 'keeping disorderly houses', a category in which they outnumbered men at least until the end of the century (Zedner, 1994). Overall women tended to commit offences that were financially motivated, something, as Zedner points out, that seems 'to belie the widely held notion of female criminals as sexually motivated or driven by impulse to commit irrational, behavioural offences' (ibid.: 40).

Constructions of femininity

By the nineteenth century, new ideas about the roles of men and women in society had emerged; many of the ideas about the home and domesticity and the 'natural position' of women and men were constructed around middle-class notions of family and employment (Davidoff and Hall, 1994). Men, seen as the breadwinners, the earners of household income, would work outside of the home. Women were homemakers; their domestic role was to care for the family. These constructions of femininity, these beliefs or ideas about how people, and especially how women, should act, were underpinned not only by the new work demands of the capitalist economy but also by the patriarchal system of reproduction – the family (Davidoff and Hall, 1987; Clark, 1995).

Women were established in the middle-class ideal as wives and mothers, primary carers of their husbands and children. The husband's earned income would then maintain the family. Alongside this, a set of ideas formed which were based on the notion that women were unable or unsuitable for public life or work outside the home because they were non-aggressive, physically weak, and the only people who could successfully bring up children and manage the household. The 'Angel in the House', the 'ideal woman', was obedient to her husband, dutiful, quiet and passive. Women were to be pure, innocent, submissive and self-sacrificing, patient and gentle, thinking of nothing but the domestic sphere. 'The family was central to middle class morality ... a sanctuary for the preservation of traditional moral and religious values' (Zedner, 1994: 12). A range of literature aimed at middle-class girls detailed the attributes and virtues of the ideal woman in advice books, etiquette manuals and didactic fiction, together with warnings of the consequences should they stray from this path.

Unsurprisingly, working-class families 'found that the ideal contradicted the reality'; since men could not earn enough alone to maintain the household, women also needed to work and bring in an income (Clark, 2000: 29; D'Cruze, 1998). Although working-class women may have found these ideals difficult, if not impossible, to live up to, they were not immune from such influences, and research shows the ways in which schooling, female networks in working-class communities and the socialisation of mothers taught women the constraints and boundaries of social norms and 'respectability' (Zedner, 1994; Roberts, 1985).

It is also worth noting that women who were victims of crime were judged against such notions of femininity; thus those who were perceived as unable to maintain their homes or fulfil their duties – due to drunkenness, for example – emerge as victims of violence in cases where the perpetrator was seen as justified in his actions (Clark, 2000; D'Cruze, 1998). Marital violence and the stigma associated with it were assumed to be a feature of the lives of the poor and the working-classes (Hammerton, 1995). Women also used the courts to expose, threaten or shame their husbands or as a means of arbitration (D'Cruze, 1998; Hammerton, 1995). Yet it was also increasingly the case that men (particularly working-class men) accused of domestic violence were castigated for their brutality and uncivilised masculine behaviour (Wood, 2004; Emsley, 2005). 'By the end of the nineteenth century, the exposure of marital misconduct among men of all classes had brought an unprecedented amount of attention to proper ideals of male behaviour in marriage' (Hammerton, 1992: 3).

Deviant and criminal women

Women who committed crime in the nineteenth century and those who wrote about female criminality at this time were seen or were understood within this framework of morality (Zedner, 1994). As we have seen, women figured especially in less serious crimes and predominated in the statistics for certain types of offences. As Zedner points out, all such offences stood or fell by these normative constructions of femininity; they were therefore crimes that were noticed more by the public, and by the police, and as such more likely to result in prosecution. Women who broke the law found that they were judged against these prevailing norms of feminine propriety, and therefore they were seen as 'double deviant' (Heidensohn, 1985; Zedner; 1991, 1994).

Such women were also labelled as 'fallen': 'the epitome of female corruption – fallen from innocence, she had plummeted to the depths of degradation and contaminated all who came near her' (Zedner, 1994: 11). The types of crime committed by women at this time are therefore overladen with notions of female deviancy – infanticidal women or baby farmers, the worst of all mothers, the female poisoner, those who subverted their domestic duties as a wife and mother, and those involved in offences relating to drunkenness, prostitution, sexual promiscuity, all lacking purity, modesty and passivity. This does not necessarily mean that all women were treated harshly, but the way in which they feature in the statistics and in the courts meant that they were perceived in certain ways. Some women were able to fit the prevailing ideals, and this may have affected how they were treated; others were clearly unable to do so. Moreover, it is important to emphasise that, when women did break the law, their behaviour was viewed and regulated in both formal and informal ways.

Those crimes committed by women in the home and those relating to the family or children, though small in number, were also of great concern. Infanticide was an 'exceptionally emotive crime. Not only is this due to the innocence and helplessness of the victims involved, but also because this type of criminality inverts the expected "normal" protective relationship (based on maternal instinct) between a mother and her child' (Kilday, 2010: 61). Although the realities of infant murder cases might well have been quite different, the perception at least was based on ideas about infanticide and its relationship with illegitimacy. While it was recognised that unmarried mothers faced difficulties, both financial hardship in general and the ending of poor relief from 1834 made her situation

> more perilous by more than want. She also faced the shame of her fall: 'the infant at her breast was her stigma, her burden, her curse'. The unmarried mother, it was assumed, would seek above all to conceal her fall from virtue by destroying the evidence of her sin.
>
> (Higginbotham, 1989; see also Kilday, 2010; Arnot, 2000; for legal responses, see Ward, 1999, 2001)

Similarly, contravening the domestic ideal, the 'figure of the domestic poisoner, particularly where she was a woman, was guaranteed to trigger cultural anxieties ensuring that the comparatively small numbers of ... cases would attract much public attention' (D'Cruze and Jackson, 2009: 57; Watson, 2004). During the nineteenth century (as has been the case in the contemporary period), there were a small number of extreme cases where women who have committed serious offences have been viewed as particularly 'monstrous' or 'evil' (D'Cruze and Jackson, 2009; Jewkes, 2011). Two such examples were Mary Ann Cotton (convicted of the poisoning of multiple victims; see Wilson, 2013) and Amelia Dyer (convicted of the murders of multiple children given into her care; for female murderers in general, see Knelman, 1998).

Prostitution

Prostitution was one female offence that drew considerable attention in the nineteenth century. 'Prostitution' was not in itself a criminal offence, but it was often used to point towards specific offences which were related to the sale of sex, such as soliciting, living off immoral earnings or keeping a 'disorderly house'. For the Victorians, prostitutes were the female equivalent of the criminal class (Emsley, 2010). Perceptions of and fears about them were expressed in moral terms, but such women were also seen as consorting with male criminals, distracting the police, helping to 'set up' victims for others to rob or, indeed, committing thefts and robberies themselves from clients or each other (Tobias, 1967). Association with prostitutes was also a common theme in such eighteenth-century criminal biographies as the *Newgate Calendar*, the offender hero being brought into a life of criminality by his association with them or continuing a life of crime to support his lust for them (see Rawlings, 1992, for examples). As Henderson observes, 'it is difficult to overstate the degree of horror with which many writers regarded prostitution's apparent ability to undermine and destroy first the individuals, female and male, most directly involved in the trade, their families, and ultimately the entire social edifice' (1999: 167).

Authors of the nineteenth century, such as William Acton, wrote about the extent and nature of the prostitution problem. Using police returns, he claimed that there were 3,325 brothels and over 8,600 prostitutes in the London area; this included only those known to the police, and thus gave 'but a faint idea of the grand total of prostitution by which we are oppressed' ([1857] 1968: 33, 37). Henry Mayhew and his co-author Samuel Bracebridge estimated there were more than 80,000 in London in 1861, supporting similar claims made in the medical journal *The Lancet* in 1857 (Godfrey and Lawrence, 2005). According to Acton, the causes of prostitution in women were natural desire and sinfulness, idleness, 'vicious inclinations strengthened and ingrained by early neglect, or evil training, bad associates, and an indecent mode of life' ([1857] 1968: 118). While he did recognise the problem of extreme poverty and that women who had 'fallen' found it difficult to obtain an honest living, he also added to the list he constructed of causes the love of dress, drink and amusement.

Prostitution was regarded as the 'great social evil', and such women were subject to considerable societal scorn. Historical research reveals the difficult social and economic position in which they found themselves. Walkowitz (1982) argues that poverty was the principal cause of prostitution. Low wages as well as the seasonal or casual labour markets left some women with few alternatives, and they found prostitution to be a temporary solution to their immediate difficulties. Many poor working-class women were dependent on the local job market in their area. They were often 'the unskilled daughters of the unskilled classes', general and domestic servants, street sellers, mill workers, laundry or charwomen. Some migrated into the town and cities for work, their families unable to support them; others were natives of the city providing for themselves or did not wish to burden their families. Although one of the other major concerns about prostitution was the potential for the vice to corrupt innocent young women, most were young, stayed in the trade only for short periods of time, and were not the victims of middle-class seduction and betrayal or drugged children trapped by white slavers (Walkowitz, 1982; Bartley, 2000).

Policing women and crime

Both the problem of prostitution and the surveillance of prostitutes by the police were highlighted with the passing of the Contagious Diseases Acts (1864–9). Prostitution had previously been the subject of police attention only when it intruded on public decency or disorder. Concern about the spread of venereal disease and the subsequent legislation surrounding this changed the ways in which prostitution was policed, ultimately increasing the surveillance of all working-class women in public spaces. New powers were given to a plain-clothes morals police to stop and arrest women they thought were prostitutes and force them to undergo a genital examination to see whether or not they were infected with venereal disease. These new Acts were in force in garrison and navy towns in England, such as Southampton, Portsmouth, Gosport and Plymouth, where it was said large numbers of men in the armed and naval forces had been struck down by the disease (Walkowitz, 1982; Walkowitz and Walkowitz, 1974).

The Acts were designed to eradicate physical and moral disease. Women who were found to be infected were placed into lock hospitals; those who refused to submit to the examination were imprisoned until they relented. Names of prostitutes were also placed on a special register, which meant that they were required to visit a doctor for further medical examinations twice a month. Those in lock hospitals were held on venereal wards for up to nine months. Prostitutes complained of the brutality of the doctors – the pain of the actual examination as well as the attitudes of those who treated them (Walkowitz, 1982).

In terms of policing, women complained about harassment on the streets as they went about their daily lives; they also argued that lodging-house keepers were reluctant to accommodate women and that lodging houses run by women were regularly targeted for searching by officers. The result of the Acts was not the control of venereal disease but greater regulation and surveillance of working-class women in public spaces, either alone or with others, or with men to whom they were not married. In the end, they merely added to the methods through which women who were seen as stepping outside of accepted feminine norms were regulated and controlled. The Acts epitomised not only a sexual double standard through focusing on the women and not their male clients but also their class bias, as only street-walking or lower-class prostitutes were singled out (Walkowitz, 1982).

The Acts were finally repealed in 1886 after a nationwide campaign for their revocation. One group, the Ladies' National Association, was led by Josephine Butler. Research suggests that, by this time, prostitutes in the areas affected by the Acts were older – perhaps because of their inability to get their names taken off the register or the stigmatisation of the laws; it might also have been because their reputation in the local area provided an obstacle to employment. By the time of the repeal of the legislation, more than a quarter of women working as prostitutes in Devonport were over 31 years old; in 1870 this figure had been less than 10 per cent (Walkowitz, 1982).

But prostitutes were not the only women who were 'police property'. While, as long as they did not flout public decency, prostitutes were tolerated in some districts and areas, 'immoral' women were often picked up on other charges, frequently as drunk and disorderly, and removed from the streets (Walkowitz and Walkowitz, 1974). Those who were fighting and arguing in the streets or involved in various forms of disorderly behaviour were also targets for the police, as were those committing low-level street thefts. As research on female participation in gangs in the late Victorian period has demonstrated, working-class women were prominent and dominant on the streets of their neighbourhoods (Davies, 1999). Women who were out in these public spaces were those most likely to be policed. While overall women committed less crime, and less serious crime, than men, they assaulted other women, they settled disputes, and they robbed or stole – often from men under the guise of sexual availability (Archer, 2011; Williams, 2014; Alker, 2014). Their crimes occurred on streets, in lodging houses, in back-alleys; they took advantage of drunken men by rifling their pockets or grabbing their watches in dark passageways, often to supplement their meagre incomes, and they were apprehended on the streets or when they were trying to pawn the goods they had stolen (Alker, 2014).

When it came to violence on the streets, particularly fighting in local areas, women often knew their opponents; their actions were not random, casual or opportunist, and they quickly moved from verbal abuse to physical violence. They kicked, scratched and punched, stabbed and slashed, often using items that were close to hand such as knives, scissors, forks or domestic utensils (Archer, 2011). Young women did participate in gangs but their involvement in violence was more limited. Female members of 'scuttling' gangs in Manchester and Salford in the late nineteenth century drew widespread condemnation for their behaviour and were deplored as 'vixens', 'viragoes' and 'Amazons' by the local newspapers, though they formed only a small proportion of those convicted of violence. While they participated in collective assaults on local people and on the police, they were often regarded as marginal to the gang. Although magistrates addressed them with stern lectures, they were regarded as more malleable and open to reform (see below; Davies, 1999). Godfrey (2004) has argued that young women were more socially controlled and their role in the gangs was often as girlfriends, hangers-on or trophies; they competed with other girls for boys' affection, and this also aroused conflict within and between neighbourhoods as young men tried to assert their own position (see Davies, 1999, 2006).

Women in the penal system

The development of convict prisons, local prisons and 'semi-penal' institutions across the nineteenth century needs to be understood within the perceptions of female crime and criminality outlined above. The causes of female criminality were also underpinned by the belief in the possibility of reform for many women; as women were 'weaker' and their will was more malleable, they were thought to be more open to change, but this could be achieved only through institutional support.

Alongside prisons there developed a range of other semi-penal institutions – refuges, homes, reformatories and asylums – to support women who manifested criminality, deviance, 'wayward' behaviour, promiscuity, immorality, insanity or alcoholism (Wiener, 1994; Hunt et al., 1989; Bartley, 2000; Barton, 2005; Morrison, 2005, 2008). However, their application and use varied quite significantly across the country. Some women found themselves embroiled in a network of institutions that would envelop their lives, as they spent years within one establishment or were moved from one institution to the next. Others did not experience them at all, despite some obvious similarities in terms of their offending histories with those who did.

Women who had been identified as deviant or criminal needed to be disciplined, resocialised and returned to appropriate femininity; prison regimes would assert this through the use of work and domesticity, regulation and timetable, religion and examples of propriety and virtue (Ignatieff, 1978; Dobash et al., 1986; Sim, 1990; Zedner, 1994). All of this, increasingly in the latter half of the century, was underpinned by the role of medical experts and doctors. Implicit was the widely held belief, increasingly legitimated by the medical profession, that women's deviance or criminality was linked to their biology and sexuality. These views justified the interventions into women's lives through and beyond the penal system (Dobash et al., 1986; Sim, 1990).

Forsythe (1987) argues that, inside prisons, women were seen as creatures of feeling and impulse, highly emotional and volatile. Some were therefore seen as passive victims of circumstance who were highly disturbed and emotional and could be unbalanced by the lack of attention or progression in prison. There was also the view that women would might burst into a frenzy, smashing up their cells, breaking windows, destroying the little prison property they had, while yelling, screaming, shouting or singing (Forsythe, 1987, 1993; Davie, 2010). In the eyes of those in authority there was no explanation for this violent reaction. However, a closer look at the records suggests that many such women were simply expressing their frustration with the prison system and the futility of their situation or were feeling the effects after alcohol consumption; they were resisting within the context of their situation. Similar patterns of resistance could be found in the lock hospitals to which women were sent under the Contagious Diseases Acts (Walkowitz and Walkowitz, 1974).

The authorities used this emotionality as an explanation for all manner of behaviour. They thought women had no regard for or awareness of the consequences of their actions – that they would cut themselves or try to hang themselves merely to get transferred to the hospital wing, that they were like mischievous children, playing tricks or seeking attention. One observer wrote: 'a woman would coolly pound a piece of glass to powder and bring on an internal haemorrhage, twist laces around their necks until respiration ceases or hang themselves in the hope of being cut down in time and taken to the infirmary' (cited in Forsythe, 1987: 129). Looking back now we have different views about how and why women in prison might have behaved in this way. But in the Victorian period the solution was to appeal to the hearts of these women, plugging directly into the views expressed by Elizabeth Fry (1827) that, through understanding and the example of Lady Visitors and female prison staff, they could be returned to femininity and appropriate womanhood.

A less optimistic view was reserved for some women criminals, and this is that they were 'utterly depraved' – a phrase frequently used by commentators of the time – that some were beyond care and help and that they had 'fallen too far' and were 'irredeemably ruined' (Forsythe, 1987). A contemporary journalist wrote that convict women as a class 'are desperately wicked – deceitful, crafty, lewd and void of common feeling ... all the vices under the sun are exemplified in these hundreds of women' (cited ibid.: 129).

From the mid-century the issue of women's sexuality became a key focus of attention for many male scientific experts, and a whole series of behaviours were labelled as disorders of women – illegitimate pregnancy, promiscuity and homo-sexuality were seen as closely associated with the female biological constitution (Dobash et al., 1986; Sim, 1990; Zedner, 1994). They were underpinned by posi-tivist views about the relationship between biology and criminality. However, this should not be overstated, as deviant women were frequently seen as a moral men-ace, and such views 'hark back to an older and far wider assumption that all women are morally weaker because they are biologically and psychologically inferior to men' (Zedner, 1991: 315).

Women in the convict system

Far fewer women experienced the convict prison system. Across the period under examination, the number of women declined from a high of 1,050 committals in 1860 to fewer than a hundred by 1890. In 1880 they made up about one-eighth of those undergoing penal servitude in convict prisons (Zedner, 1991, 1994).

Women convicted and sentenced to penal servitude by the courts were held in local prisons during and after their trial until they were transferred to a convict prison; all these were located in the south of England, mainly in London. When the system was first set up, women were sent to Millbank for periods of separation and then on to one of the public work prisons allocated for women. Brixton was used initially, from 1853 until about 1869 (see Davie, 2010), and Parkhurst, on the Isle of Wight, was also employed between 1864 and 1869. Fulham Refuge was opened in 1856 to hold women; despite being described as a 'refuge' it was a convict prison and should be understood as such. By the 1870s the female convict system was largely fixed: all women went first to Millbank for the first period during which they were under separation. They would then be transferred to Fulham Refuge or Woking (after this prison opened in 1869) for the public works stage. Apart from 'refuge class', the same stages of the progressive system were set down for women as for men.

The period of separation at Millbank was nine months, but unlike men, women were able to gain marks during this stage. The regime under separation for women involved long hours of needlework undertaken in their cells, interrupted only by attendance at the chapel, exercise and some education. At Fulham and Woking, labour consisted of needlework, knitting and laundry work. Some were employed in the daily running of the prison – for example, in the kitchen – and at Woking they also undertook mosaic tiling.

Recent research by Williams (2014) illuminates the backgrounds of convict women from London and Liverpool, who were overwhelmingly habitual petty property offenders. Many tended to have numerous summary convictions before a long sentence of penal servitude, rather than having committed a single serious offence. Their crimes were dictated by the environment and the opportunities that presented themselves; women from London tended to be involved in counterfeiting, or to have committed fraud or thefts from the workplace and shops, while those in Liverpool stole food, domestic items, money or jewellery from people or houses. Violence was rare. Women who were serious offenders lived uncertain and precarious lives of poverty, disadvantage and deprivation; they experienced menial and poorly paid insecure employment, if not chronic unemployment, poor housing and living arrangements and poor health.

Even once they had progressed through the system far enough to obtain such a privilege, few women convicts received visitors unless they had family or friends in London or the South. Penal records demonstrate that they kept in touch with family and friends through letters. For those with children, letters home reveal a contrasting picture of experiences. No babies or children were permitted in the convict prisons during the nineteenth century. Pregnant women were held in local prison wings until they gave birth and then, after a short period with their child, were sent down to the convict system without them. Children and babies were left with husbands, sisters, mothers or other relatives, were sent to industrial schools (formalised by the Industrial Schools Act 1866), homed through church or charitable organisations and schools, or adopted. It is evident from the letters sent out by convict women in the 1870s to the police or the local priest or chaplain that some had little knowledge of what had happened to their children under such circumstances. Permission to write letters about their children, outside of those regularly allowed by the stage system, was frequently given by the matron or governor when requested. There are also some very sad stories of women learning of the death of a baby or child from a new inmate arriving from their home community or being told that their children had been adopted by another family (Johnston and Godfrey, 2013a).

Licensing and release

The final part of the sentence of penal servitude was slightly different for women than for men (see Chapter 7). Women on licence could be released either through conditional licensing or on a licence to be at large. Conditional licensing applied only to convict women prisoners, and essentially this meant that, after serving a certain proportion of their sentence, they were released to a refuge for a period of six to nine months. Usually they were afforded the opportunity of going to a refuge only once; despite requests from women who had been in the convict system before, these were not usually accepted. Refuges were funded by voluntary subscription and funds raised through the labour of the women inmates, but the government also paid for their maintenance. Various refuges were used from the 1850s onwards, but by the 1870s there were three in use: the Carlisle Memorial

Refuge in Winchester and the Westminster Memorial Refuge in Streatham, London, both for Protestant women, and the East End Refuge in Finchley, London, for Catholics. From what is known of the regimes in these places, although security was said to be nominal, the day-to-day activities were largely similar to those in prison – long hours of laundry work and needlework. Women were paid their gratuity partly in clothing and partly in money when they left the refuge, the aim being to help them either to emigrate or to find suitable employment (Kimberley Commission, PP, 1878–9; Johnston and Godfrey, 2013a).

Women in local prisons

As they committed less crime and less serious offences than men, women were more likely to experience a short sentence in a local prison than one of penal servitude. Even then, however, they made up only about a quarter of those in local prisons (Zedner, 1991, 1994).

As we have discussed in Chapter 6, the reform period of the late eighteenth century resulted in changes in local prisons. Before the Gaols Act 1823, there was little effort to separate prisoners by sex or according to other criteria, such as age, seriousness of offence, or whether convicted or not. The new Act changed all this by introducing classified association – a particular triumph for Elizabeth Fry, who had been campaigning for the separation of female prisoners and their supervision by female staff. Fry had been visiting the women in Newgate prison since 1813, and her campaigning, along with other Quaker women, meant that she was probably better known than John Howard. Fry's (1827) approach to the reform of women in prison was not merely about the prevention of abuse or exploitation of female prisoners under the governance of male warders but was also based on individual appeal from other women. Through the efforts of Lady Visitors, Fry believed that personal relationships could develop and that, through their example, these unfortunate women would turn towards religion and a more virtuous life. Although a number of Lady Visitors committees were set up across the country, some groups found their work resented by local authorities and were forced to give up (Zedner, 1994, 1998).

Accommodation for women in local prisons varied across the country. Some of the smaller prisons may have had only one or two women, yet those in large urban areas such as London, Liverpool, Manchester and Birmingham held perhaps hundreds at any one time. Even in the 1880s the Inspector of Prisons still had concerns about the separation of the sexes in some local prisons, where local authorities who felt there were insufficient numbers to justify the investment were reluctant to commit to alterations to accommodate women.

By the time the local prisons were transferred to government control in April 1878, and some prisons had been closed, there were 69 local prisons, of which 62 had wings for women (*Report of the Commissioners of Prisons*, PP. 1878; 6, Appendix 7: 33–5). However, by the 1930s, after a further decline in the female prison population, the capacity was reduced to Holloway (the only all-female local prison since 1902), five local prisons with wings for women (at Birmingham, Cardiff, Durham,

Exeter and Manchester) and one convict prison and borstal at Aylesbury (*Report of the Commissioners of Prisons and the Directors of Convict Prisons*, PP, 1938: 18; Johnston, 2014).

Semi-penal institutions

By the end of the nineteenth century, while female crime in general had declined and so there were fewer women in local and convict prisons, there was nevertheless an expansion of semi-penal institutions (Wiener, 1994; Barton, 2005) holding women and girls. As Barton notes, these were largely outside of the control of the state; though they had links to government-run establishments or policies, they were usually run by charitable organisations or self-elected committees. As they were separate from the formal judicial system and did not therefore count officially as 'custody', in most cases admission on the part of women was 'voluntary'. Such institutions were keen to have the consent of women who wanted to be reformed and thus they were unlikely to take those who were regarded as difficult – for their continued effectiveness in reforming women helped to maintain their funding. But, while it was 'voluntary' (Dobash et al.,1986), there was pressure from family, the police, friends, charity workers and the clergy for women to consent to admission, and often their alternatives were presented as appalling. They knew that they could be forcibly admitted if they fell too far (for example, unmarried mothers, labelled as 'mentally defective', found themselves as long-term inmates) or they were reminded of the severity of conditions in prison. In the early twentieth century, refuges and reformatories became more involved with the state and the courts. For example, the Inebriate Act 1898, the Probation Act 1907 and the Mental Deficiency Act 1913 enabled drunken women to be confined in reformatories for up to three years (see Morrison, 2005, 2008), young women to be referred to a refuge or reformatory as part of a probation order, and women defined as 'mental defective' (this included those with children out of wedlock who claimed poor relief) to be confined in asylums (Cox, 2013).

Contact with the outside world was largely prohibited inside these semi-penal institutions, as only appropriate and positive role models were encouraged and letters and visitors were monitored and supervised. Discipline was based around the family and the domestic sphere, the rules and regulations being enforced by a 'matron-mother' or a married couple, exerting the influence and protection that many of the inmates were perceived to lack in their family backgrounds and also operating as an appropriate example for women and girls to follow. Those who were immoral or 'wayward' or perceived as at risk, rather than those who had committed criminal offences, were drawn into this system to prevent their progress to imprisonment, therefore widening the net of discipline to confine non-criminal women (Wiener, 1994).

The intention therefore of such institutions was to 'protect' and 'rescue' women, but their use expanded what was already a fairly encompassing system of social control and regulation for working-class women. Barton (2005) and Morrison (2005, 2008) have scrutinised the extent to which semi-penal institutions protected and rescued women and have argued both that female offenders were subject to more intrusive processes of change than males and that those who had fallen too far, who were too confirmed in their behaviour to be saved, were doubly punished for their transgressions.

Case study: Alice Ann Rowlands (NA, PCOM 3, licence no. A45114/7538; Convict Registry Office no. K.8; Local/County Prison Register no. 7109)

Alice Ann Rowlands was born and lived in Liverpool with her parents, Joseph and Alice, and her five brothers and sisters. She found herself in the convict system in the mid-1880s after falling into crime in her early teens and was first in trouble with the police at the age of 12, when she was remanded in custody, then discharged, in relation to stealing money. Unfortunately this encounter with the law would not be the last, and the following year Alice was found guilty of stealing money. As she was then 13 she was sentenced to ten days in prison, to be followed by five years in a juvenile reformatory.

This period in the reformatory seemed rather to accelerate Alice's offending, as less than a month passed following her release before she was back in prison, remanded for riotous behaviour, but then discharged. In the following years she stacked up a few petty offences and short prison sentences: seven days for a workhouse offence; one month for stealing clothing; seven days for drunkenness. Then in December 1882 she was convicted of housebreaking and sentenced to 12 months' imprisonment. Time spent in the workhouse and stealing clothes, probably to gain money from pawnbrokers, suggest that her life was affected by poverty. These previous convictions would be significant. In February 1884, when Alice, now described as a 'frequent offender' (*Liverpool Mercury*, 2 February 1884), was found guilty of larceny by Liverpool Sessions for stealing a shirt and singlet from James Pearson, she received a sentence of five years' penal servitude.

Alice now found herself entering the convict system, having initially been remanded in custody to await trial and sentence in Liverpool. Six weeks later she was removed from Walton prison and sent to Millbank to serve the first part of her sentence under separate confinement. There she worked sewing in her cell. She wrote and received letters from her aunt and her father, who were living in the Toxteth Park area of Liverpool. The convict system checked all of the prisoners' letters and the 'character' of their correspondents. As was regularly the case, Liverpool police were asked to check the claimed relationship of the correspondents; as far as Alice's aunt was concerned, 'nothing was known against her character'.

After six months in Millbank, Alice was removed to Woking prison and set to work in the laundry. During her time there she committed further offences, this time against the prison rules. Between October 1884 and May 1886 she was punished five times. Most offences were related to her interactions with other prisoners and often involved quarrelling or fighting with other women. Her first offence was for provoking another inmate, named Jackson, and fighting with her on their return from chapel; she received one day in close confinement and lost 12 remission marks as a punishment. A couple of months later she was punished for quarrelling with prisoner

Williams while in the infirmary and lost a further 12 remission marks. Throughout her time at Woking Alice was regularly in the infirmary wing for short periods relating to her gynaecological health and to have a non-malignant breast tumour removed.

Nine months later Alice was again in trouble for fighting with another prisoner, named Hand, and for singing in the hall; she received three days in close confinement and again lost 12 remission marks. She also got into trouble for being very rude to the assistant superintendent, who had prevented her from leaving the mosaic room where she was then working; for this she was placed in close confinement for one day. About two months after this altercation Alice was found with a light on in her cell for the purposes of cooking and having two pieces of steel concealed in her petticoat. This was punished more severely than her previous offences: she was demoted from class two to probation class, lost a further 24 remission marks and spent three days in close confinement. Despite this, just over five months later she was released on conditional licence, having served two years and three months of her five-year sentence. As a first-time convict, she was released to Russell House, a refuge in the Streatham area of London.

On 30 July 1887 the Directors of Convict Prisons permitted Alice to leave Russell House. This was to be her final contact with the criminal justice system, and evidence suggests that she was not convicted of any further offences during her lifetime. She returned to Liverpool and established a relationship with and later married Thomas Dowler, who worked as a labourer in the nearby shipyard. The couple had four children, although only two survived infancy, and the family continued to live in the Toxteth Park area of Liverpool. When Alice died in 1905 she was in her mid-forties. According to the 1911 census, her husband Thomas was still working in the shipyard, and he and their two daughters were living together; the elder daughter was married with a small baby and the younger was working as a cake confectioner. Despite her misspent youth, then, Alice desisted from crime, perhaps because of her relationship with Thomas and the greater stability that family life and children offered her – though perhaps she just grew up or simply did not want to go back to prison. Most criminological literature suggests that these are the kind of connections that encourage desistance from crime (Farrall and Calverley, 2006), although this can be difficult to ascertain historically (Godfrey et al., 2010). Penal records show only people's interactions with the criminal justice system or government administration; they reveal nothing about their motivations, emotions or reasoning and only a suggestion of their social circumstances. Alice, or at least something in Alice's life, changed and she continued on a path away from crime and the criminal justice system. Others, on the other hand, were unable to change or were in the grip of addiction, poverty, economic change or decline or changes in the labour market.

9

JUVENILE OFFENDERS

Responding to the problem of juvenile crime

From the late eighteenth century onwards, there was a marked shift in attitudes towards and policies directed at juvenile offenders (King and Noel, 1993; King, 1998). It is prudent to note that the concern about juvenile crime has a much longer history, at least to the sixteenth century, when specific concerns about young offenders can be identified (Griffiths, 1996), but a body of research which focuses predominantly on the late eighteenth century through to the mid-Victorian period suggests that, despite the exact origins of this concern, by the nineteenth century there was an expanding discourse about juvenile crime and methods to tackle the problem. Why exactly this occurred is debatable. Juvenile crime had not been regarded before the nineteenth century as a separate social problem, but by then it was 'a major focus of anxiety among the propertied classes' and separate policies were developed to respond to it (King and Noel, 1993; King, 1998: 116). This may not have been the 'invention' of the problem of juvenile crime, as some have suggested (Magarey, 1978) but, as Shore (2000) argues, more a reconceptualisation, in which a new language emerged, with a particular response to, and understanding of, the juvenile offender. As Radzinowicz and Hood put it, 'the concept of the young offender, with all that implies for penal policy, is a Victorian creation' (1990: 133). This chapter will discuss the concerns about and responses to juvenile crime and will focus in particular on Victorian penal policies directed at young offenders and the development of separate policies and institutions for their punishment.

The causes of juvenile crime

In 1816, a *Report of the Committee for Investigating the Causes of the Alarming Increase in Juvenile Delinquency in the Metropolis* was published, perhaps one of the first reports to deal solely with crime committed by juvenile offenders. The committee responsible for it was made up largely of Quaker reformers, many of whom were already active in campaigning about criminal justice or other social issues; members included William Crawford (later a highly influential prison inspector), Thomas Fowell Buxton (a campaigner against capital punishment), Peter Bedford (a philanthropistfrom Spitalfields) and Samuel Hoare (a Quaker banker and brother-in-law of Elizabeth Fry) (Stack, 1979; Shore, 2000).

Although there are problems with the criminal statistics at this time, concerns about juvenile crime came to the fore around the end of the Napoleonic Wars in 1815, and evidence does suggest an increase in those aged under sixteen being indicted for felony (Shore, 2000). At the very least there was a belief that this was the case. The committee would later evolve and form the Society for the Improvement of Prison Discipline and Reformation of Juvenile Offenders, which in 1818 proclaimed that 'juvenile delinquency has of late years increased to an unprecedented extent, and is still rapidly and progressively increasing' (cited in Horn, 2010: 9).

Committee members visited and collected interviews from hundreds of juvenile boys imprisoned across the city. They claimed that, across London, there were thousands of boys under the age of 17 in prisons, who daily engaged in crime. These individuals associated with older thieves and with girls who lived through prostitution. As we have seen in Chapter 1, the committee viewed the increase in juvenile crime as a problem emanating largely from poor communities and from bad or absent parenting. Its members believed that young criminals were poorly educated, were exposed to immorality and kept bad company. Juvenile crime, then, was the result of a poor environment – poverty and lack of employment or education – but also of immorality – of parental neglect, drink, gambling and Sabbath-breaking (*Report of the Committee* …, 1816). Typical vignettes of young criminals they interviewed were:

> K. L. aged 13 years. Cannot read. His parents are living. Associating and gambling with some boys in the street, he was led in time to join them in committing depredations. He was committed for stealing some property placed at the outside of a shop door. He was convicted, and sentenced to be flogged.
>
> …
>
> S. T. aged 17 years. Has a father and mother in very low circumstances: has received no education. About two years since he lost his situation as an errand boy. From that period he has been out of employment. He first became initiated into vice by forming an acquaintance with bad characters in the streets, and gambling with them. They soon led him into criminal practices, and he now subsists by depredations.
>
> …
>
> W. X. aged 12 years. Has a father only living, his mother having been dead about a twelvemonth: since which this lad has been engaged in bad practices, his father being very often from home. He became acquainted with a gang

of depredators, and began with them to pick pockets. The father has been in the habit of chastising this boy with cruelty, which has had a tendency to harden him. He now commits depredations for a subsistence.

(Ibid.: 31–2)

Attitudes towards and commentary on juvenile crime tended to focus on the iniquitous urban environment, particularly London, and, within this, largely on pickpockets or thieves (Shore, 2000). As Shore argues, commentators often concentrated on the immorality or sinfulness of children rather than considering their poverty or debilitating environment: 'the figure of the pickpocket, or small juvenile burglar, sneaking in at a window pointed out by his adult accomplice, was an easier quarry than the vast, petty, menial, thievery and pilfering that was committed by many children' (Shore, 2002a: 55).

However, the committee members were also critical of the criminal justice system and saw this as a secondary cause of juvenile crime. The severity of the criminal law as well as the defective state of the police and of prison discipline, they claimed, 'powerfully contribute to increase and perpetuate the evil' (*Report of the Committee ...*, 1816: 10–11). Specifically, they were referring to the uncertainty in the criminal law, as police officers (concentrating on the rewards for apprehending more serious criminals) sometimes released minor petty offenders rather than taking action against them, which might have prevented future crimes; on the other hand, youngsters placed in prison could be corrupted by hardened criminals.

The juvenile offender raised particular concerns and anxieties, and this was also related to the changing way in which children were seen in society (Cunningham, 1995, 2006). Humanitarian and educational reformers had succeeded in removing children from some workplaces and had limited their working hours (for example, the Factory Act 1833, which prohibited the selective employment of children under the age of nine and restricted the working day to eight hours for those aged nine to 13). Related to this was a successful campaign which began to promote the schooling of children during their formative years, though it was fully implemented and regulated only by the Education Acts of the 1870s and 1880s. It was based on the notion that children needed protection from certain aspects of the adult world to which they had hitherto been exposed. During the nineteenth century, attitudes towards children and childhood were constructed and reconstructed, and this fuelled concerns about the delinquent child (Hendricks, 2002). Between 1780 and 1840 a new view of childhood was constructed: the wage-earning child was no longer the norm, and childhood now constituted a distinct set of characteristics requiring protection and fostering through formal education. The delinquent child, and those who were poor or neglected, displayed all the qualities seen as the antithesis of the innocent, dependent, middle-class notion of childhood.

By mid-century, these views were widely held. The leading reformer and campaigner Mary Carpenter argued that she did not need to 'demonstrate the immense importance of the juvenile portion of the community to the future, and even to the present welfare of the state, – or to show the need of education to prepare the young to be good citizens and useful members of the community' (1851: 1). Discussion about the legislative changes regarding juvenile offenders in the 1850s would confirm these beliefs; the notion of childhood was extended beyond the age of seven (before this only children under seven were incapable of criminal intent) to 14, as the juvenile offender became a separate category for recognition (Hendricks, 2002). Carpenter (1851) made a distinction between what she called the 'perishing' classes and the 'dangerous' classes: the perishing classes were those who were 'at risk', who, through poverty, destitution, ignorance and the circumstances in which they were growing up, might fall into crime or immorality without a helping hand; the dangerous classes were those young people who had already been convicted or imprisoned and lived through criminality. Both of these groups were seen as in need of care and protection, either to prevent them from falling into crime in the first place or to restore them to 'the true position of childhood' (cited in Hendricks, 2002: 29).

Juveniles, criminalisation and the criminal justice system

Changing attitudes towards children also resulted in changes in the law and in the operation of criminal justice system with regard to young offenders. Legally, children under the age of seven were incapable of committing crime. In the eighteenth century, those above seven were subject to the same laws and the same punishment as adults. But by the nineteenth century we see the introduction of *doli incapax*: children aged between seven and 14 were held to be incapable of committing crime unless it was proved that they acted with malice. If this was the case – and 'proof was frequently forthcoming' (Radzinowicz and Hood, 1990: 133) – then they were *doli capax* – capable of committing crime and so subject to the law and all subsequent punishments available. Those over the age of 14, at least in theory, were treated the same as adult offenders (May, 1973; Knell, 1965).

Magarey (1978) has argued that new laws, notably the Vagrancy Act 1824 and the Malicious Trespass Act 1827, also drew larger number of young people into the criminal justice process. Widened definitions of 'rogues and vagabonds', and the criminalisation of a number of petty types of behaviour that were more likely to be committed by this group, meant more children and young people were charged and prosecuted for minor offences. These revisions to the law led to an influx of juvenile criminals to the petty sessions courts.

Similarly, by the mid-nineteenth century, directive policies about juvenile offenders had an effect; the Juvenile Offenders Act 1847 instructed that all those under the age of 14 be tried in the petty sessions court in cases of simple larcenies up to the value of 5 shillings, and this was quickly followed by the Juvenile Offenders Act 1850, which increased the age to 16. The 1847 Act also set a maximum penalty of three months' imprisonment, though this could include hard labour or whipping; if appropriate, the case could be dismissed or result just in a whipping (Horn, 2010). The Criminal Justice Act 1855 further stated that all cases of simple larceny be tried in the petty sessions court. The cumulative result of these new laws was a noticeably larger number of juveniles appearing before the courts – perhaps because of the cheaper, quicker process for the victim or because the victim or police were more inclined to prosecute in a lower court, where penalties were less severe. It has also been suggested that this resulted in an increase in the use of the whip on juvenile offenders (Philips, 1977).

Collectively, these two developments are the basis for Susan Magarey's (1978) argument that the criminalisation of petty behaviours and changes in the way in which juveniles appeared before the courts 'created' or 'invented' the problem of juvenile delinquency. She maintains that they formed an image of a large and increasing amount of juvenile crime which alarmed the commentators of the period. As noted earlier, King (1998) and Shore (2002a) locate this change three decades earlier, in the 1810s. Therefore, by the 1840s, the problem of juvenile crime had been identified and documented and the young offender placed within the broader notion of the 'criminal class':

> there is a youthful population in the Metropolis devoted to crime, trained to it from infancy, adhering to it from Education and Circumstances, whose connections prevent the possibility of reformation, and whom no Punishment can deter; a race 'sui generis', different from the rest of Society, not only in thoughts, habits, and manners, but even in appearance, possessing, moreover, a language exclusively of their own.
>
> (Miles, 1839, cited in Shore, 2002a: 1)

Punishing the juvenile offender

As we have seen, during the late eighteenth and early nineteenth century there was a movement away from bodily punishments towards a greater use of imprisonment. There was also a shift towards a greater belief in the ability of prison to change the individual rather than just holding or detaining them (Foucault, 1991). Responses to juvenile offenders and child criminals need to be understood within this broader shift. At least in the early years, legislation such as the Gaols Act 1823 did not make any special differentiation in prisons on the basis of age; offenders were classified according to their gender and the category of offence. While there were plenty of commentators already exploring the need to address the punishment of juveniles, the growing use of policies inside prisons which emphasised the use of classification, later separation and a system of categorization, highlighted the age differentials and led to policies directed specifically at the young offender.

The first-time offender needed protection from being corrupted by the more hardened adult or habitual criminals during their imprisonment, and nowhere was this view more prevalent than in discussions of the juvenile offender. The Society for the Improvement of Prison Discipline in 1817, for example, was convinced of the need to separate young people to avoid moral contamination. The Brougham Committee of 1847 argued that 'the contamination of a gaol ... as usually managed may often prove fatal, and must always be hurtful to boys committed for a first offence, and thus for a very trifling act they may become trained in the worst of crimes' (cited in McConville, 1981: 334). The potentially corruptive influence of the prison environment was recognised in the Gaols Act 1823, and different categories of criminals (petty, serious, tried, untried, sentenced, unsentenced) were ordered to be placed into different classes or wards of prisons according to their status and gender, but at this time the age of the offender was not one of the classifications in use.

There were two ways in which the criminal record of a juvenile offender gave cause for concern: first, though committing largely petty offences, youngsters were often seen as beginning a life of crime; second was the futility of the criminal justice system, but particularly the use of short-term confinement in local prisons, in its efforts to address such behaviour (Tobias, 1967). The use of imprisonment must not further corrupt the juvenile criminal but put a stop to their offending and to the possibility of their developing into an adult offender. This was a core rationale of juvenile punishment policy and would define its direction in subsequent decades; by the beginning of the twentieth century, a separate juvenile justice system had come into being.

The debate between the use of the separate system and the silent system also touched on the question of age: could or should children and juveniles be treated in the same way as adults? While adults were subjected to long terms of physical and mental isolation in the government prisons of Millbank and Pentonville, could this also be endured by young people? Some commentators felt that such disciplinary regimes were not appropriate, and Margaret May argues that the debate about 'cellular isolation clearly revealed the mental and physical differences between children and adults' (1973: 12). This led prison inspectors to conclude that 'so marked is the distinction in the feeling and habit of manhood and youth that it is quite impractical to engraft any beneficial plan for the lengthened confinement of boys upon a system adapted to adults' (Crawford and Russell, cited ibid.). Changes in the use of imprisonment and the application of reformatory methods in the disciplinary prison brought to the fore the apparently unique needs of the young offender.

While some established schools or homes for juvenile offenders or the poor, destitute or vagrant child had existed since at least the mid-eighteenth century – for example, the Marine Society (founded in 1756) – they developed on an ad hoc basis into the nineteenth century. The various ventures of the Philanthropic Society (which in 1848 established the Farm School at Redhill in Surrey, often seen a 'model' for reformatory movement), the Warwickshire justices' Stretton home, Elizabeth Fry's girls' reform home in Chelsea, and the Society for the Suppression of Juvenile Vagrancy (later the Children's Friend Society) all operated at different periods, as did the Refuge for the Destitute, which was used for juvenile offenders well into the 1830s (King, 2006). In general, these societies or homes were maintained by public subscription and were usually lent impetus by a group of philanthropic, evangelically minded or Quaker gentlemen and ladies or interested magistrates (not dissimilar and often overlapping with an interest in prison and punishment reform more generally). Some of these groups encouraged emigration, sent juveniles to sea or encouraged them to take up a trade, while others tried to create a family atmosphere in which to school offenders (Radzinowicz and Hood, 1990). But, it was still overwhelmingly the case in the early nineteenth century that most juvenile offenders were sent to the same prisons as adults, to serve short periods in local gaols or houses of correction, while others were transported and some were sentenced to death.

As we have seen in Chapter 4, the use of capital punishment between the end of the eighteenth and the early nineteenth century changed significantly and, as such, it is probably not surprising that, of the 103 youths under under the age of 14 who were sentenced to death at the Old Bailey between 1801 and 1836, none were executed; all had their sentences commuted to either transportation or imprisonment (Knell, 1965). The case of John Any Bird Bell, a 13- or 14-year-old hanged in Maidstone in 1831 for murdering a boy of the same age seems rather to be an exception. However, newspaper reports of this case highlight the typical narratives of the time surrounding children's violence, parental neglect or misuse (often on the part of the mother), early delinquency and callousness, together with an unusual or unpleasing physical appearance (Shore, 2002a). Prosecution of cases of violent crime by juveniles was very infrequent; very few children were indicted at higher courts for such offences, and extreme or exceptional cases are used 'as a conduit through which are expressed societal doubts about the role and future of youth' (ibid.: 67; also see D'Cruze et al., 2006; Stevenson et al., 2003).

It was not until the Children's Act 1908 that the death penalty was abolished for all persons under the age of 16. Given the decline in the number of capital offences over the nineteenth century – effectively only murder after the 1860s – many young people who engaged in criminality were unlikely to the types of offence to which these laws then applied and, in any case, were very unlikely to face execution. This shows some evidence that young offenders were beginning to be treated differently in the early part of the nineteenth century, even though there was no special provision for them; the government continued to use short prison sentences and to transport juvenile offenders overseas.

The first government experiment with a juvenile prison establishment in England came in the late 1830s. As we have seen in Chapter 7, the Inspectors of Prisons were advocating the use of the separate system. Even though the adult project at Millbank had largely failed, they maintained their faith in the system as a reformatory philosophy and turned their attention to applying it to the juvenile criminal. Following the initial rationale of Millbank, Parkhurst prison on the Isle of Wight was chosen to house juvenile offenders who had been sentenced to transportation for a period of separate imprisonment before they were sent overseas.

Parkhurst prison for juveniles, 1838–1864

Parkhurst prison, the first entirely separate establishment for juvenile offenders, received its first inmates during December 1838. As a government project, it was overseen by a supervisory committee of visitors (namely Lord Yarborough,

J. P. Kay, the prison inspector William Crawford (who had been member of the 1816 committee) and Captain Joshua Jebb, later Surveyor-General of the Convict Prisons (McConville, 1981)). In the end, the project was relatively short lived. Parkhurst was closed as an institution for young offenders in 1864 and became part of the convict system holding female prisoners sentenced to penal servitude (Stack, 1979).

The Select Committee on Gaols and Houses of Correction in 1835 (see Chapter 6) had recommended the establishment of a juvenile prison to deter youngsters and to train them to make a better life in the colonies; this also addressed some of the perceived deficiencies with transportation. McConville maintains that it had long been thought that 'youthful offenders were more open to beneficial influences than the mature', but they also made up a large proportion of those sentenced to transportation (in 1840, 47 per cent were under the age of 21) (1981: 204).

The Act establishing Parkhurst made provision for both sexes, but only boys were ever held at the prison. Most of the boys sent there were under sentences of transportation, and their conduct during their time at the prison would decide their fate in the Antipodes, determining whether they arrived as free emigrants, under a conditional pardon, or to be confined in government prison. However, in the early years, and again when the use of transportation had declined, juveniles serving prison sentences were also sent to the establishment (Stack, 1979). It was recognised that the goals of deterrence and reform were difficult to attain together, though the aim was to do so through an extensive system of trade training and education, plus the incentive of an easing disciplinary system (McConville, 1981). The first report acknowledged:

> In carrying the first of these objects into effect, the utmost care must be taken to avoid any species of discipline which is inconsistent with the habits and character of youth, or calculated in any degree to harden and degrade. The second object can only be effected by a judicious course of moral, religious and industrial training, but the means adopted for this purpose should not be of such a nature as to counteract the wholesome restraints of the corrective discipline …. There should be nothing, throughout the arrangements at Parkhurst, of a tendency to weaken the terrors of the law, or to lessen in the minds of the juvenile population at large (or their parents) their dread of being committed to prison.
>
> (Reports Relating to Parkhurst Prison, 1839,
> cited in Stack, 1979: 391, and McConville, 1981: 204)

Both Stack and McConville agree that the regime at Parkhurst was severe and based on the principle of 'less eligibility', despite the committee's claims that they did not wish to harden or degrade youths. This is apparent from the regime, which initially called for leg irons, silence, minimal diets, strict surveillance by prison officers, and strongly marked prison dress in an attempt to obtain the required level of deterrence. At first it was also thought unwise to have an infirmary; boys could feign sickness to gain the comparative luxuries of the hospital ward. Later the regime was eased, leg irons were removed, an infirmary was built and diets were improved, but the committee, reflecting wider views about this issue at the time, remained committed to 'less eligibility'. Most of the boys committed to Parkhurst, the majority teenagers from large urban areas, the perceived centres of juvenile criminality and corruption, stayed in the prison for two or three years before being transported to Australia or New Zealand (Stack, 1979).

From the 1840s the separate system of discipline was implemented. Its rationale, as for adult offenders, was that periods of isolation would offer time for reflection; this would cool the passions of prisoners, make them disposed to the instruction offered to them and allow for reflection on 'the folly of their former self-willed and vicious conduct' (Stack, 1979: 394). All new inmates were sent to the probationary ward, where they spent four months in isolation —confined in a cell by night and day – except for chapel, school and exercise. Then the younger children were sent to the junior ward and the older ones to the general ward.

From the 1850s, individuals would spend five stages in the ward under a progressive system adapted from the adult convict system. Depending on his ward and class, satisfactory behaviour would earn him a small monetary gratuity, ranging from 2d to 6d. Good behaviour also earned inmates the reward of being able to write a letter home and a ration of pudding after dinner on Sunday (Stack, 1979). This period also marked the beginning of the demise of Parkhurst, by this time 'unmistakably and unequivocally ... simply a prison for younger convicts' (Radzinowicz and Hood, 1990: 154). No boys were sent abroad from Parkhurst after 1853, and after 1856 all were all serving prison sentences of one or two years and were released unconditionally on completion. By this time, though, there had been significant moves in other parts of the penal system to accommodate juvenile criminals, best exemplified by the reformatory and industrial schools movement.

Reformatories and industrial schools

Pressure for legislation from the government to address juvenile offending reached a height at the end of the 1840s and the early 1850s – 'a deluge of "speech and pamphlet philanthropy" swept the country' (Radzinowicz and Hood, 1990: 172). Opinion was divided on many central elements, particularly the controversy between deterrence and reformation, along with the duty of the state and the role of philanthropists. Some saw discipline, rules and regulations as having a key role; others thought only religion could bring about reformation. Some thought only first offenders should be sent to reformatories, to nip criminality in the bud, yet others maintained these should be reserved only for hardened juvenile criminals for whom other punishments had failed to work. Whipping and sentences of imprisonment were also debated. Some thought these punishments quicker and cheaper for first offenders, and necessary for the punishment element; others were absolutely opposed to the use of either (Radzinowicz and Hood, 1990). Stack (1994) locates these views broadly within two groups – the 'humanitarians' – namely Mary Carpenter, Matthew Davenport-Hill and W. C. Osborn – and the 'hardliners' – T. B. Lloyd-Baker, Sydney Turner and Jelinger Symons.

After initial attempts to form an acceptable Bill failed, the Select Committee on Criminal and Destitute Children and two national conferences in Birmingham gave impetus to the movement and to the idea that reformatories would be established through voluntary effort but with both financial support and certification from the government (Radzinowicz and Hood, 1990). In the end, the Youthful Offenders (Reformatory Schools) Act 1854 enabled the establishment of reformatory schools for those under the age of 16 convicted of crime. The reformatory school sentence would be a period of between two and five years after an initial 14 days' imprisonment in a local prison. Reformatories would be certified by the government (a government inspector was established in 1857) and financial maintenance would be sought from the parents, but all other costs would be met by the state.

A couple of years later, the Industrial Schools Act 1857 established schools for vagrant and destitute children. The aim of these schools was to address those children aged between seven and 14 who might be in danger of falling into crime and delinquency; they could be committed by a magistrate for as long a period as thought necessary, but not beyond their fifteenth birthday. While there appeared to be quite clear boundaries on paper between these schools and reformatories, in practice the lines were a little more blurred. This was also partly because of the changing categories of young people who could be committed to industrial schools. Initial take-up was modest, but an amendment in 1861 drew in a larger group of children: those under 14 found begging or receiving alms; those found wandering or without a settled home or means of subsistence; those 'frequenting the company of reputed thieves'; those committed by parents as beyond their control; and those under 12 committed by magistrates after conviction for a criminal offence. Yet more changes occurred through the Industrial Schools (Consolidation) Act 1866, which widened the categories of eligible children still further, to orphans, children whose parents were undergoing penal servitude, refractory children, and children of criminal parents who were unsuitable for the workhouse (Radzinowicz and Hood, 1990; Stack, 1994; Shore 2008). Nonetheless, collectively the development of reformatories and industrial schools 'marked a radical change in penal policy. For the first time in a legislative enactment Parliament recognised juvenile delinquency as a distinct social phenomenon and accepted responsibility not only for young offenders, but also for children who ... required care and protection' (May, 1973: 7).

The operation and development of reformatory schools was reasserted in 1866 by an amending act, the Reformatory Schools (Consolidation) Act. The initial preliminary prison sentence of 14 days was cut to ten days. No child under the age of ten was to be committed (unless they had a previous conviction punishable by penal servitude or imprisonment or were sentenced by a higher court), and the powers of the state, the inspector and managers were more clearly defined. Although the establishment of industrial schools had been slow, that of reformatories was the opposite: after the initial Act in 1854, ten were established in 1855 and a further 17 in 1856; by 1860 there were 48 reformatories certified by the government holding 4,000 young offenders. Yet while the number of new reformatories stalled to not more than 53 institutions in the latter decades of the nineteenth century, the building of industrial schools, after a slow start, accelerated. There were only 18 in 1859 and 25 in 1866, but the widening of the categories of eligible children initiated an expansion – to 50 by 1871 and 99 by 1884. Although only 1,668 juveniles were in industrial schools in 1864, the net widened to encompass over 20,000 children by 1885 and 24,500 by 1893 (Radzinowicz and Hood, 1990). Shore argues that this 'journey from the reformatory school for juvenile offenders in the mid-nineteenth century seems to have transformed into the industrial school for the refractory working-class by the latter part of the century' (2008: 169).

Reformatories were unevenly distributed across the country; most committals came from Yorkshire, Lancashire, Middlesex, Surrey and Warwickshire. Similarly, most industrial schools were located in the industrialising areas of the north of England, in the Midlands or in London. The cost to the government of both rose substantially across the period as voluntary contributions, which had at first been substantial, ebbed away (Radzinowicz and Hood, 1990).

The regime in the reformatory was determined largely by the views of the local benefactors involved, and thus varied across the country. Though the prison for young offenders in Mettray in France was often cited by many reformers as an exemplar of what could be achieved (e.g., Davenport-Hill, 1848; Carpenter, 1851), conditions in England were often poles apart and practice varied in different institutions. Schooling started at six in the morning, to be followed by eight hours of work; more education or religious teachings took place before bed (often sleeping rooms with hammocks) at eight or nine in the evening. Diets was sparse and punishments were often fines or withdrawal of privileges, though this was underpinned by the use of the cane and the birch. Industrial schools had very similar rules and regulations: inmates would be fed, clothed and educated, but the emphasis was on industrial training (Radzinowicz and Hood, 1990).

In practice those sent to reformatories were overwhelmingly first offenders. More than half of those committed between the early 1860s and the end of the 1880s fell into this category and, in the early years, a quarter were under the age of 12. Of those with previous convictions, the majority had only one. Even hardliners such as Reverend Sydney Turner (by this time, Inspector of the Reformatory Schools) thought the reformatories were being over-used and complained that they were 'for those who are not curable by a less expensive or protracted system of treatment' (cited in Radzinowicz and Hood, 1990: 184). It was also the case that those committed were likely to be sent for longer terms – less than 10 per cent were sent for two years and more than 40 per cent for the full five years; by the 1890s, over three-quarters were committed for more than four years.

Undoubtedly, the development of reformatories and industrial schools led to greater social control of poor or working-class children and young adults; more juveniles were drawn into the system, where they stayed for much longer periods of time than ever would have been the case in a local prison; intervention also took place much earlier, as many were sent to a school on their first conviction and became subject to the discipline, routine and labour of the daily institutional regime (Foucault, 1991; Platt, 1969; Morris and Giller, 1987). For Platt (1969: 176), those identified as the 'child savers' in the reformatory movement were 'in no sense humanists or libertarians'; reform was not possible without discipline. The over-whelming majority of juvenile offenders were prosecuted for petty and minor crimes, so it is certainly the case that a

> lack of willingness to overlook the crimes of children, … the decreasing use of acquittal verdicts and the growth of the secondary punishments implies a conscious inclination to draw children into the criminal justice system, sug-gesting to some extent the problem … was exacerbated, though not created, by the policy-makers of the time.
>
> (Shore, 2002a: 150)

Case study: juvenile offenders in mid-nineteenth-century Shropshire

As outlined in the above discussion, take-up of reformatory schools varied across the country. In predominantly agricultural Shropshire, the magistrates were very aware of the prevailing views on the problem of juvenile crime. Their initial discus-sions were prompted by the Juvenile Offenders Bill which was before Parliament in 1847. The magistrates were much in favour of the proposals, supporting its main objectives – 'to ensure the more speedy trial of juvenile offenders and to avoid the evils of their long term imprisonment previously to Trial' (SA, QA 2/1/3, Visiting Justices Reports (VJR): 37).

A couple of years later they received a communication from the Philanthropic Farm School at Redhill, Surrey, relating to the reform of juvenile offenders (the chaplain of the Philanthropic Society was Reverend Sydney Turner, later Inspector of Reformatory and Industrial Schools). The average number of individuals under the age of 16 committed to Shrewsbury prison during each of the preceding five years was 75. However, during the year beginning Michaelmas 1850, the number had increased – 46 having been committed up to April 1851. The terms of imprisonment for juveniles were generally short, and there were not a large number of young people held at prison at any one time. Conscious of prevailing views, the justices agreed that, where possible, juveniles should be separated from older offenders, but in practice this was difficult to carry out unless youngsters were confined alone. Sharing the views of other commentators on the isolation of juvenile prisoners, the magistrates feared that separate confinement was not suited to the minds of youth and were concerned that serious injury to the offenders' intellect might result from lengthy periods of isolation. They also worried that less hardened boys might be contaminated by more hardened boys if they were placed in wards rather than with specially selected adults, as cur-rently occurred. They concluded that, where it was necessary to commit a juvenile offender on a summary conviction to prison, this should be for a short term, and that males aged under 14 should be whipped to deter future offending (SA, QA 2/1/3, VJR: 109–10), thus drawing on the provisions of the 1847 Act.

The Shropshire magistrates also took a slightly different view on financial assistance and support from the families of young offenders. They supported the Philanthropic Society's suggestion that magistrates be given powers to make relatives pay for juveniles in prison, though they thought this inoperable in Shropshire. They argued that 'no doubt in London and other large towns cases do occur frequently where the parents are in good circumstances and have neglected their offspring', but this was not the case in Shropshire. When a relative could be found, they commented, they were often among the poorest in the county, thus making clear a distinction between poverty and immorality or neglect (SA, QA 2/1/3, VJR: 111). In addition, the Philanthropic Society suggested lengthening the terms of imprisonment for second and third offences. The Shropshire justices disagreed with this proposal if the terms were to be served in county gaols. Juveniles would leave prison in a worse state of mind than when they entered, they thought, and required different management to adult offenders. Unless they were transferred to a prison such as Parkhurst or an institution such as the Philanthropic Farm, they stood very little chance of reform (ibid.). The magistrates further supported the Philanthropic Society's view that juvenile offenders who were abandoned or orphaned should be sent to a reformatory and that the directors of these establishments should have certain powers of detention. However, as in many other counties across England, they were less keen on the expense falling on the county or the borough rate, suggesting instead that the union or parish could be charged with a portion of the cost (ibid.: 112).

After the passing of the Reformatory Schools Act in 1854, a committee was appointed to consider the possibility of forming a reformatory for juvenile offenders in the county (SA, QA 2/1/3, VJR: 165). Those appointed were Sir Baldwin Leighton, Bart., W. W. Whitmore, Esq., G. Pritchard, Esq., T. W. Wylde Browne, Esq., Reverend H. Burton and Reverend D. Nihill, all of whom were active members of the Shropshire magistracy; Nihill had been the chaplain-governor of Millbank before moving to the county (Johnston, 2005b). The committee thought a reformatory desirable but, rather than recommending one for Shropshire alone, hoped it might be able to unite with some of the adjoining counties in establishing an institution. Hitherto, about £58 per year was available for sending prisoners to reformatories, and this sum had been sufficient. Nevertheless, the justices hoped that the gaol charity would receive an increase in subscriptions, as magistrates and the public had become more aware of the problem.

The committee did, though, recommend the formation of district pauper schools, as distinct from prisons. The pauper school would bring a large number of children together, and education, together with religious and moral training, could be given in a more efficient manner and at less financial cost. It was believed that, 'by removing the Pauper child from the contamination, which under the present system in too many instances surround him, a great check may be given to crime' (SA, QA 2/1/3, VJR: 171–5). In the following quarter, eight juvenile offenders were committed to the county prison and one female prisoner was sent to the Philanthropic Society. A petition regarding district schools was also presented to the House of Commons by Wylde Browne and seconded by Whitmore. It read:

The petitioners, both from judicial and general acquaintance with the subject of juvenile delinquency are led to the conviction that, with a view to due protection of the public from depredation and to rescue children from ruin by precluding their growth in criminal habits, which in their future career may be formidable to society, legislation measures, more comprehensive and effectual than at present exist, are becoming highly expedient.

(Ibid.: 178)

The proposers thought that juvenile criminals and those children at risk could be addressed by district pauper schools (as distinct from union workhouses), and they submitted results from experiments that supported the compulsory formation of such schools. They requested the House of Commons pass a Bill for both the prevention of crime and the reform of juvenile offenders through the use of pauper district schools and reformatories (ibid.).

At an adjourned session in the county, further discussions resolved that Shropshire should unite with another county, or with private individuals, to establish a reformatory, and a committee (consisting of Leighton, Wylde Brown and Whitmore) was appointed to communicate with interested parties (SA, QA, 2/1/3, VJR: 184). The three men visited the reformatory at Saltley, which had been established to receive juvenile offenders from Birmingham and Warwickshire. Saltley reformatory had been opened in 1852 by Charles B. Adderley (later Lord Norton), an active member of the reformatory movement. Its buildings were about to be enlarged, and the committee requested that it be allowed to unite with the Saltley committee, that the Quarter Sessions Court estimate the likely sums to be raised by voluntary subscriptions, and that a public meeting or circulars should be sent to those most likely to assist (ibid.: 189). At the June Session 1856, the gaol chaplain reported that 21 boys had been sent to reformatories since 1840. Of these, four had been apprenticed, three had emigrated, two had run away, two had been sent home as 'unfit for Refuge', four had been transported, one was 'living by stealing', and another had died. The remaining four boys were still in the reformatory.

The amount of money subscribed towards providing a reformatory in the county was £827 11s 0d – not enough to erect an establishment for the county alone. The committee recommended that a circular be sent to the subscribers requesting them to pay their subscriptions; the resulting money would then be invested and the interest paid to the gaol charity fund and used to send boys to reformatories. When a juvenile was sent to a reformatory instead of prison, he should initially be remanded in the gaol, and the chaplain would then arrange to send him to a reformatory (SA, QA 2/1/3, VJR: 204). But it was also the case that magistrates in the county continued to send youngsters to prison for a whipping without a sentence of imprisonment, as permitted under the 1847 Act. However, the magistrates found this provision impractical, as delays sometimes occurred in obtaining a surgeon, so they recommended a short sentence of imprisonment should be given as well (SA, QA 2/1/4, VJR: 8).

In the summer of 1858 the magistrates finally entered into an agreement with the Philanthropic Society. They agreed to pay 2s 6d per week for maintenance and a shilling for rent for each male juvenile offender under the age of 14. However, they were limited to sending only six boys in the subsequent 12 months and to no more than 12 boys at any one time (SA, QA 2/1/4, VJR: 27). Records show that, across the period 1857 to 1877, the numbers of young people in Shropshire committed under the Juvenile Offenders Act 1847 fluctuated. On average there were about ten per year between 1858 and 1863; this peaked at 19 in 1871, then gradually declined to around ten per year. By 1877, when the local prison was centralised, there were around 13 (Johnston, 2004, 2005c).

Shropshire was perhaps typical of the largely agricultural counties in its response to the perceived problem of juvenile crime; it did not have a large enough problem or sufficient funds to warrant the construction of a reformatory of its own. But the magistrates were not ignorant of the concerns or debates of the day: their discussions covered many of the same issues that no doubt were being had up and down the country. On the one hand, they were keen to unite with other counties to form a reformatory, and some even went as far as to propose their own solutions to Parliament. Yet it is also clear that they continued to use short sentences and whipping to punish juveniles. Given the restricted numbers that could be sent to a reformatory, some young offenders would have spent substantial periods in Shrewsbury prison awaiting removal. And considering the relatively stable population of the county and the lack of large-scale industrialisation and urbanization, it is perhaps surprising that they were so keen on these discussions, though it was probably the result of the endeavours of a small group of active and influential magistrates on the county bench who were concerned with many aspects of criminal justice and the poor law (Johnston, 2005b).

Juvenile punishment in the late nineteenth century

The extent to which child imprisonment was reduced by the use of reformatory and industrial schools is also more complex to estimate than might first appear. Though the number of children in prisons was reduced, from 53,752 in 1856–60 to 43,854 in 1871–5, the new system did not simply replace the old (Stack, 1994). The 'hardliners' were successful, in that the government continued to use the preliminary prison sentence before the reformatory sentence. However, overall success could be placed with the humanitarians: they may well have been successful in 'creating an atmosphere hostile to child imprisonment' that persuaded victims or the police not to prosecute or the courts not to pass sentences of imprisonment (ibid.: 73). Overall only a small proportion of young people under the age of 16 convicted of crimes were ever sent to reformatories, so the chances that these institutions significantly reduced child criminality as a whole seems unlikely (Stack, 1994). Reformatory and industrial schools did not stop the flow of juvenile offenders to prison. While boys were kept out of prison by being removed from circulation for long periods, they frequently spent long periods in local prisons while reformatory places were found for them (McConville, 1981).

Child imprisonment continued alongside other forms of punishment, most notably the use of training ships, which were classified neither as reformatories nor as industrial schools (Shore, 2008). Training ships such as the *Akbar* and the *Clarence* were moored on the Mersey, the *Wellesley* on the Tyne, the *Exmoor* off Essex and the *Cornwall* on the Thames; all were intended to train young working-class lads for the navy. Throughout the late nineteenth and into the twentieth century, the ships were controversial; public attention was drawn to a range of issues, including 'mutinies' on the *Akbar* and the *Clarence* in the late 1880s, excessive violence, floggings and the poor treatment of boys on the *Wellesley*. Another 'scandal' in 1910 on the *Akbar* (by then a nautical training school) also revealed ill-treatment. While some have suggested the report concerning this was a 'whitewash', which Churchill (then Home Secretary) was unhappy about, it did lead to the Departmental Committee into the Reformatory and Industrial Schools in 1913 (Shore, 2008; Radzinowicz and Hood, 1990; Horn, 2010).

More than 30,000 children were confined in reformatory and industrial schools by the turn of the century, equating to one in every 230 juveniles between the ages of five and 15 (Watson, 1896, cited in Radzinowicz and Hood, 1990: 181). John Watson described the web of 'agencies at work towards the elevation and reformation of unfortunate and incorrigible children', including the day industrial schools, truant schools, certified industrial schools, reformatories, and prison 'when all these influences fail' (1896: 275, cited in Shore, 2008: 169). Overall, by the First World War, there were an estimated '208 schools: 43 reformatories, 132 industrial schools, 21 day industrial schools and 12 truant schools' (Radzinowicz and Hood, 1990: 182).

It is important to note that it was still the case until at least the end of the nineteenth century that young people served short sentences in local prisons, and this was recognised as a continuing problem by the Gladstone Committee of 1895, which recommended the establishment of borstals. This was not addressed until the Children's Act of 1908, which established a separate court system for young offenders, formally abolished the death penalty for those under 16 and established a new institution for punishment, the borstal training system. Reformatories and industrial schools also continued to be used until 1933, when they were replaced by the approved schools system (for the punishment of juveniles in the twentieth century, see Bailey, 1987; Cox, 2013; Forsythe, 1990; Humphries, 1981; Shore, 2008; Wills, 2005, 2008).

By the latter decades of the nineteenth century the changing ideas about youth and adolescence and concerns about youth crime and delinquency took on new forms: the 'razor' or 'scuttling' gangs of the urban environment (Davies, 1998, 1999, 2009, 2011), the 'hooligan' (Pearson, 1983), and the greater criminalisation of what were largely working-class youth leisure activities (Gillis, 1975). These ideas and perceived threats meant another shift in the way in which young people were conceived, as adolescence replaced or at least joined with class as the perceived cause of misbehaviour and delinquency (Gillis, 1975; Cunningham, 1995; Hendricks, 2002, 2006).

CONCLUDING REMARKS

By the end of the period under discussion, there had been some major changes and transitions in the criminal justice system. Across England, policing was more organised, and executions, which now took place behind the walls of local prisons, were carried out only in cases where people were found guilty of murder. A system of convict prisons had been developed, and this operated to contain those offenders sentenced for more serious offences, for which, instead of being transported overseas, they would serve long periods of imprisonment.

It was also the case that the central government had much greater involvement in the criminal justice and penal system in 1880 than it did in 1815, but change was slow and protracted. Government involvement brought much more bureaucracy, particularly within the penal system, though this was also evident in policing and in the monitoring of offenders. From the early nineteenth century onwards, we have observed the role that reformers, campaigners and social enquiry played in the identification of the perceived problem of crime and the ways in which responses developed. Though the 'correlation between social problem and administrative remedy is seldom exact … [there was] a silent metamorphosis taking place within such long-established arms of government … as new areas of administration were placed under or, we might even say, grew into their jurisdiction' (MacDonagh, 1958: 55); this was the case especially with the organs of criminal justice within the Home Office. By the latter part of the century, the police and the Home Office were driven by bureaucratic imperatives; these supported their goal to remove or limit the possibilities of temptation to crime or immorality by regulating the 'purveyors of immoral behaviour' (released convicts, alcohol licensing, prostitution, bookmakers, for example), and therefore they 'sought more powers and gradually refined and supplemented the regulative machinery' (Petrow, 1994: 296). However, this process and bureaucratic administration has provided crime historians and criminologists with a wealth of information on the administrators' views of the system as well as on the people that were processed by it.

By 1880, the police were established across the whole of England. The policeman – and the police as a body – had a stronger identity, and, despite the drawbacks in terms of discipline and respectability, a career in the force offered a regular income and status, as well as a pension, to a working-class man (Emsley, 1996, 2008). The Inspectors of Constabulary continued to press for greater uniformity and centralisation, defining the activities and role of the police and what constituted police efficiency (Emsley, 2008). As part of the 'policeman- state', they increasingly took on the role of prosecutors and would do so in eight out of ten cases by the start of the First World War (Godfrey, 2014). Within this aspect of their work they now had a much greater influence on the degree and extent to which cases were processed by the criminal justice system, and by the early twentieth century they also surveyed an increasing number of regulatory offences passed by the legislature.

The public displays of punishment – whipping, the use of pillories and execution – had all disappeared from sight. As McConville observes, by the end of the nineteenth century, hangings carried out inside prisons were 'tended by near-anonymous functionaries who conducted themselves with the undertaker's decorum and discretion – a death penalty with which all could easily live' (1995: 431). Similarly, Gatrell (1994) argues that the end of the graphic spectacle of prisoners being executed before a mass audience and the reduction in capital crimes by the end of the 1860s effectively muted the abolitionist cause for a century, as both of these factors allowed the death penalty to be retained until the 1960s.

Yet it was not just the obvious markers of the ultimate penalty for criminality that were curtailed. By the late nineteenth century the prison system, both local and convict, was an increasingly secret world. Prisons were much more cut off from the rest of society than they had been in the 1810s or the 1820s; even the movement of prisoners between courts and prisons or transfers between prisons were the subject of complaints to the Home Office about the public 'seeing' convicts handcuffed at train stations or waiting with prison officers by transports (Wiener, 1994; Pratt, 2002, 2004).

Centralisation allowed the interest, diversity and inconsistent practices in the local prison system to be overcome, but it replaced them with a highly bureaucratic and closed-off administration. Edmund Du Cane, then the chairman of the Prison Commission, proceeded with policies aimed at uniformity and economy in the local prison system and fashioned a highly deterrent, complex and austere regime. In subsequent years, this administration would increasingly be called into question for its stringency, its high rates of recidivism, and problems with groups of prisoners to whom such harshness could not be applied (the young, women, especially those with babies, and the mentally ill, for example), as well as a lack of accountability on the part of the chairman. But the severe deterrent regime would remain in place at least until the recommendations of the Gladstone Committee's investigation into prisons in 1895 (see also Harding, 1988; Forsythe, 1990; McConville, 1995; Pratt, 2002, 2004).

The numbers in the convict system declined as the nineteenth century drew to a close. Although there were on average 10,300 convicts per day in 1880, this fell to around 8,300 in 1885, to 4,900 in 1890 and to around 3,250 by the time of the

Gladstone Committee's report in 1895 (*Report of the Commissioners of Prisons*, PP, 1880, 1885, 1890, 1895); the number of convict prisons in use was reduced to five. As noted above, the 1890s saw a movement against the severity of the regimes and the rigid control in prisons that had held sway under the leadership of Edmund Du Cane since 1878 (Harding, 1985; Forsythe, 1990). The Gladstone report recommended an amelioration of the regimes in both convict and local prisons. Not only was there a shift in attitudes towards punishment at this time (Garland, 1985); it may also have been the case that the smaller convict population made the changes more acceptable. In convict prisons, periods of separation were gradually reduced for different classes of prisoner at the turn of the twentieth century, though they were not abolished until 1930. Educational and recreational classes were introduced and conversation was per-mitted in certain circumstances both at meal times and during exercise, but this was the beginning of a long and protracted process which lasted into the 1920s and 1930s (Forsythe, 1990, 1995; see also Hobhouse and Brockway, 1922; Rutherford, 1984; Brown, 2013). The sentence of penal servitude was finally abolished in 1948.

Reformatory efforts at the end of the nineteenth and beginning of the twenti-eth century were concerned largely with particular groups of offenders – juveniles, the mentally ill, and those sentenced for preventive detention – and alternative sentencing removed certain groups from prison (Garland, 1985). By this time, the numbers in the convict system had also declined, particularly as far as women were concerned. Changes in the disciplinary regimes in convict prisons had begun to occur slowly. But the majority of prisoners, of both sexes, continued to be those who were held in local prisons, where little changed until the 1920s and 1930s (Forsythe, 1990; Johnston, 2008c, 2014). The men and women who experienced local imprisonment were not deemed worthy of any special attention, though, from the latter decades of the nineteenth century, recidivism, and female recidivism in particular, was a major cause for concern. It remained the case that most women in local prisons were serving short sentences for petty crimes, but a proportion of them, particularly older women with convictions for drunkenness, spent their lives in and out of local prisons with little or no means of support outside (Godfrey *et al.*, 2007; Turner, 2011, 2012). The archipelago of semi-penal institutions expanded in this period, engulfing the lives of (some) deviant women and girls for long periods (D'Cruze and Jackson, 2009; Barton, 2005; Bartley, 2000; Cox, 2013), but others continued to spend their lives passing through the 'revolving door' of local prisons.

By the 1880s, the prison system had been fashioned into a bureaucratic organi-sation for 'grinding men good' in a way that was certainly not the case in 1815. From around the 1840s we can identify individual prisons or areas that operated to ensure a 'just measure of pain', but not all were like this. It was only from the late 1850s and the 1860s, when we observe the greater shift towards deterrence and severe penal regimes, that prison really came to envelop the lives of those subject to them. A significant shift in penal philosophy occurred in local prisons from 1865, by which time the convict system was also in full-scale operation, though some of the many local prisons continued to try to hold on to their diverse practices for at least the following three decades (Forsythe, 1987; Forsythe 1993; Zedner, 1994;

McConville, 1998b, 1995). While in the convict system there were at least progressive stages and a realistic prospect of release on licence, the regimes by the 1860s and 1870s were undoubtedly grinding. Those who experienced one sentence of penal servitude had a chance of recovering their lives, as has been seen in a number of the case studies in this book, but those who served multiple sentences or were committed for a number of years in their middle years were unlikely to recover – the cycle of reoffending or age, poor health and infirmity preventing them from retrieving a 'normal' life (Johnston and Godfrey, 2013a).

While the sentences in local prisons were on average short, the nature of the regimes was severe; as McConville (1995) has explored, a longer sentence (less than two years) in a local prison was probably harsher than the same period in the convict system, as there was no licensing or chance of remission until 1898. The destructive effect of the local prisons was the cumulative result of multiple short sentences, and the problem of recidivist offenders was recognised at mid-century and soon became a pressing issue. Although the total daily average prison population in 1877, at the time the local prisons were centralised, was 20,361, the high number of commitments reveals a different picture – and a problem overwhelmingly located in the local prison system, where there were 187,412 commitments. This number peaked at 192,235 in 1879, and remained above a yearly average of 185,000 during the early 1880s, but began to decline towards the end of the decade. By the time of the Gladstone Committee in 1895 the total daily average population was 14,394 and the total number of commitments was 160,117 (Johnston and Godfrey, 2013b).

Views about criminality in 1880 were still based largely on ideas about individual morality, but there were growing ideas, particularly with reference to certain types of offending, that were underpinned by Social Darwinism and the relationship between biology, heredity and criminality. Positivist criminology, as it was known, did influence some criminal justice and penal policies (Garland, 1985, 1990) – for example, legislation concerning habitual drunkenness and policies which emphasised categories such as 'mental defective' and, to some extent, those held under preventive detention. However, some ideas about the biological make-up of offenders and hereditary criminality can be seen in the views of commentators during the mid-century, if not before, and they did not necessarily translate into the methods or mechanisms for dealing with such people in local or convict prisons (Forsythe, 1995). 'The English never fully accepted the idea that criminals were a separate species of mankind, and they regarded even the worst of them as having some hope of redemption' (Radzinowicz and Hood, 1980: 1317; see also Emsley, 2010; Godfrey *et al.*, 2010). While there might not have been wholesale adoption of the kinds of hereditary arguments rehearsed in other countries in Europe, views about criminals in England towards the latter decades of the century were underpinned by notions of degeneracy and physical or mental deficiencies.

The criminal classes were still thought to exist, but in smaller numbers, and they were not seen as the threat they had been in the middle of the nineteenth century, at least in part due to the perception that their numbers had been reduced through surveillance and monitoring. Those problem groups that remained were often referred to as the 'rough' or the 'residuum' – not just criminals, but the poor, lunatics, vagrants, and those described as the lowest and least productive of society on account of biological, physical or mental weakness or degeneracy. It was this term, the 'residuum' or the 'rough', that was in common usage, in various forms, from the 1880s until the Second World War (Stedman Jones, 2013; Godfrey and Lawrence, 2005; Godfrey, 2014) and, of course, in relation to urban street crime, the scuttling gangs and the 'hooligans' who became the folk devils of the end of the nineteenth century (Davies, 1998, 1999, 2009; Pearson, 1983).

REFERENCES

Archival documents

National Archives, Kew, London (NA)

HO 9 – Home Office:	Convict Prison Hulks: Registers & Letter Books, 1802–1849		
HO 20 – Home Office:	Prisons Correspondence and Papers		
HO 20/8	Miscellaneous Documents 1839		
HO 24 – Home Office:	Prison Registers and Returns, England and Wales		
HO 24/20	Volume 1	1860	Returns for the County of Shropshire
HO 24/21	Volume 2	1861	Returns for the County of Shropshire
HO 24/22	Volume 3	1862	Returns for the County of Shropshire
HO 24/23	Volume 4	1863	Returns for the County of Shropshire
HO 24/24	Volume 5	1864	Returns for the County of Shropshire
HO 24/25	Volume 6	1865	Returns for the County of Shropshire
HO 24/26	Volume 7	1866	Returns for the County of Shropshire
HO 24/27	Volume 8	1867	Returns for the County of Shropshire
HO 24/28	Volume 9	1868	Returns for the County of Shropshire
HO 24/29	Volume 10	1869	Returns for the County of Shropshire
PCOM 3 & 4	Registers of Male and Female Convicts on Licence (1853–1877)		

Shropshire Archives, Shrewsbury (SA)

Quarter Sessions Records

QA 2/1/1	Visiting Justices Reports 1823–1838
QA 2/1/2	Visiting Justices Reports 1838–1845
QA 2/1/3	Visiting Justices Reports 1845–1857

QA 2/1/4   Visiting Justices Reports 1857–1871
QA 2/1/5   Visiting Justices Reports 1871–1878
QA 2/3   Miscellaneous Documents – Box 1
                Rules and Regulations Salop Gaol 1843 (SGROR)
QS/13/1   Reports of Prisoners by the Chaplain
D34.6   *Narrative of the Life of Thomas Williams*, Eddowes, Shrewsbury, 1815
Kelly's Directory of Shropshire, 1863
Kelly's Directory of Shropshire, 1870

Parliamentary papers (PP)

1810–11 (199) *Report from the Committee on the Laws relating to Penitentiary Houses* [Holford Committee].

1814–15 (326) *Papers relating to Convict Hulks in the Rivers Thames and Medway, and in Portsmouth and Langston Harbours.*

1824 (104) *Gaols: Copies of all Reports, and of the Schedules* (B) *transmitted to the Secretary of State, from the several counties, cities and towns, in England and Wales, under the provisions of the act of 4 Geo. IV. c. 64, commonly called the Gaol Act.*

1831–2 (547) *Report from Select Committee on Secondary Punishments*, together with the minutes of evidence, an appendix, and index.

1834 (559) *Report from the Select Committee on Inquiry into Drunkenness*, with minutes of evidence and appendix.

1834 (593) *Penitentiaries (United States): Report of William Crawford, Esq., on the Penitentiaries of the United States, addressed to His Majesty's Principal Secretary of State for the Home Department.*

1835 (438) (439) (440) (441) *Select Committee of House of Lords on Gaols and Houses of Correction in England and Wales*, first report; second report; third report; fourth and fifth reports, minutes of evidence, appendices, index.

1837–8 (669) *Report from the Select Committee on Transportation*, together with the minutes of evidence, appendix, and index [Molesworth Committee].

1839 (169) *First Report of the Commissioners appointed to Inquire as to the Best Means of Establishing an Efficient Constabulary Force in the Counties of England and Wales* [Constabulary Force Commissioners].

1850 (632) *Select Committee on Prison Discipline*, report, proceedings, minutes of evidence, appendix, index [Grey Committee].

1852–3 (386) *Capital Convictions: Return of the Number of Persons Capitally Convicted in England and Wales, from the Year 1838 to 1852, both Inclusive; Specifying the Offences and Sentences, and Whether and how Carried into Effect, by Execution or Otherwise.*

1854 (1808) *Report of the Commissioners appointed to Inquire into the Condition and Treatment of the Prisoners Confined in Leicester County Gaol and House of Correction*, together with the minutes of evidence.

1861 (286) *Report from the Select Committee on Transportation*, together with the proceedings of the committee, minutes of evidence, appendix, and index.

1863 (499) *Select Committee of House of Lords on State of Prison Discipline in Gaols and Houses of Correction*, report, proceedings, minutes of evidence, appendix, index [Carnarvon Committee].

1863 (3190) (3190-1) *Report of the Commissioners appointed to Inquire into the Operation of the Acts* (16 & 17 Vict. c. 99. and 20 & 21 Vict. c. 3.) *relating to Transportation and Penal Servitude*, Vol. 1: report and appendix.

1864 (467) *Convict Prison Dietaries: Copy of the Reports of a Committee appointed to Inquire into the Dietaries of Convict Prisons.*

1866 (3590) *Report of the Capital Punishment Commission,* together with the minutes of evidence and appendix.

1870 (131) *Game Laws (Convictions): Return of the Number of Convictions under the Game Laws in Separate Counties in England and Wales, for the Year 1869.*

1873 (289) *Photographs of Criminals: Statements of the Number of Photographs of Convicted Criminals sent from the Prisons of each County and Borough to London from the Time the Act of 1870 Came into Force to 31 December 1872, etc.*

1878 (C.2174) *First Report of the Commissioners of Prisons,* with appendix.

1878–9 (C.2442) (C.2442-1) *Second Report of the Commissioners of Prisons,* with appendix.

1878–9 (C.2368) (C.2368-1) (C.2368-2) *Royal Commission to Inquire into the Working of the Penal Servitude Acts,* report, minutes of evidence, appendix, index [Kimberley Commission].

1880 (C.2733) (C.2733-1) *Third Report of the Commissioners of Prisons,* with appendix.

1885 (C.4567) (C.4567-1) *Eighth Report of the Commissioners of Prisons,* with appendix.

1890 (C.6191) (C.6191-1) *Thirteenth Report of the Commissioners of Prisons,* with appendix.

1893–4 (188) *Death Sentences (England and Wales): Return of Persons Sentenced to Death for the Crime of Murder in England and Wales from 1 January 1884 to 31 December 1892.*

1895 (C.7880) (C.7880-1) *Eighteenth Report of the Commissioners of Prisons,* with appendix.

1895 (C.7702) (C.7702-1) *Report from the Departmental Committee on Prisons,* report, minutes of evidence, appendices, index [Gladstone Committee].

(1938) *Report of the Commissioners of Prisons and the Directors of Convict Prisons for the year ending 1936,* Cmd. 5675.

Secondary sources

'A Prison Matron' [F. W. Robinson] (1862) *Female Life in Prison, in Two Volumes.* London: Hurst & Blackett.

'A Prison Matron' [F. W. Robinson] (1866) *Prison Characters: Drawn from Life, with suggestions for Prison Government, in Two Volumes.* London: Hurst & Blackett.

Acton, W. ([1857] 1968) *Prostitution.* London: MacGibbon & Kee.

Alker, Z. (2014) 'Street violence in mid-Victorian Liverpool'. Unpublished PhD thesis, Liverpool John Moores University.

Anderson, C. (2000) *Convicts in the Indian Ocean: Transportation from South Asia to Mauritius, 1815–1853.* Basingstoke: Palgrave Macmillan.

Anderson, C. (2012) *Subaltern Lives: Biographies of Colonialism in the Indian Ocean World, 1790–1920.* Cambridge: Cambridge University Press.

Anderson, S. (2005) '(Re)presenting scandal: Charles Reade's advocacy of professionalism within the English prison system', in B. S. Godfrey and G. Dunstall (eds), *Crime and Empire 1840–1940: Criminal Justice in Local and Global Context.* Cullompton: Willan, pp. 145–58.

Anderson, S., and J. Pratt (2008) 'Prisoner memoirs and their role in prison history', in H. Johnston (ed.), *Punishment and Control in Historical Perspective.* Basingstoke: Palgrave Macmillan, pp. 179–98.

Anon (1812) 'Remarks on a late execution at Shrewsbury', *The Philanthropist,* 2: 206–8.

Archer, J. E. (1989) 'Under cover of night: arson and animal maiming', in G. E. Mingay (ed.), *The Unquiet Countryside.* London: Routledge.

Archer, J. E. (1999) 'Poaching gangs and violence: the urban–rural divide in nineteenth-century Lancashire', *British Journal of Criminology,* 39(1): 25–38.

Archer, J. E. (2000) *Social Unrest and Popular Protest in England, 1780–1840*. Cambridge: Cambridge University Press.

Archer, J. E. (2010) *'By a Flash and a Scare': Arson, Animal Maiming, and Poaching in East Anglia, 1815–1870*. London: Breviary Stuff.

Archer, J. E. (2011) *The Monster Evil: Policing and Violence in Victorian Liverpool*. Liverpool: Liverpool University Press.

Archer, J. E., and J. Jones (2003) 'Headlines from history: violence in the press, 1850–1914', in E. A. Stanko (ed.), *The Meanings of Violence*. London: Routledge, pp. 17–31.

Arnot, M. (2000) 'Understanding women committing new-born child murder in Victorian England', in S. D'Cruze (ed.), *Everyday Violence in Britain, 1850–1950: Gender and Class*. Harlow: Longman, pp. 55–69.

Bailey, V. (1987) *Delinquency and Citizenship: Reclaiming the Young Offender 1914–1948*. Oxford: Clarendon Press.

Bailey, V. (1993) 'The fabrication of deviance: "dangerous classes" and "criminal classes" in Victorian England', in J. Rule and R. Malcolmson (eds), *Protest and Survival: The Historical Experience*. London: Merlin, pp. 221–56.

Ballinger, A. (2000) *Dead Woman Walking: Executed Women in England & Wales, 1900–1955*. Aldershot: Ashgate.

Bartley, P. (2000) *Prostitution: Prevention and Reform in England, 1860–1914*. London: Routledge.

Barton, A. (2005) *Fragile Moralities and Dangerous Sexualities: Two Centuries of Semi-Penal Institutionalisation for Women*. Aldershot: Ashgate.

Bartrip, P. (1981) 'Public opinion and law enforcement: the ticket of leave scares in mid-Victorian Britain', in V. Bailey (ed.), *Policing and Punishment in Nineteenth-Century Britain*. London: Croom Helm, pp. 150–81.

Baugh, G. C. (ed.), (1979) *A History of Shropshire*, Vol. 3. Oxford: Oxford University Press for the Institute of Historical Research [Victoria County Histories].

Bean, P., and J. Melville (1989) *Lost Children of the Empire: The Untold Story of Britain's Child Migrants*. London: Harper Collins.

Beattie, J. M. (1975) 'The criminality of women in eighteenth-century England', *Journal of Social History*, 8(4): 80–116.

Beattie, J. M. (1986) *Crime and the Courts in England, 1660–1800*. Oxford: Clarendon Press.

Beattie, J. M. (2002) *Policing and Punishment in London, 1660–1750: Urban Crime and the Limits of Terror*. Oxford: Oxford University Press.

Beier, A. L. (2005) 'Identity, language, and resistance in the making of the Victorian "criminal class": Mayhew's convict revisited', *Journal of British Studies*, 44: 499–515.

Bosworth, M. (2000) 'Confining femininity: a history of gender, power and imprisonment', *Theoretical Criminology*, 4(3): 265–84.

Braithwaite, J. (2001) 'Crime in a convict republic', *Modern Law Review*, 64(1): 11–50.

Branch Johnson, W. (1957) *The English Prison Hulks*. London: Phillimore.

Briggs, J., C. Harrison, J. McInnes and D. Vincent (1996) *Crime and Punishment in England*. London: UCL Press.

Brodie, A., J. Croom and J. O. Davies (2002) *English Prisons: An Architectural History*. Swindon: English Heritage.

Brooke, A., and D. Brandon (2004) *Tyburn: London's Fatal Tree*. Stroud: Sutton.

Brown, A. (2003) *English Society and the Prison: Time, Culture and Politics in the Development of the Modern Prison, 1850–1920*. Woodbridge: Boydell Press.

Brown, A. (2008) 'Challenging discipline and control: a comparative analysis of prison riots at Chatham (1861) and Dartmoor (1932)', in H. Johnston (ed.), *Punishment and Control in Historical Perspective*. Basingstoke: Palgrave Macmillan, pp. 199–214.

Brown, A. (2013) *Inter-War Penal Policy and Crime in England: The Dartmoor Convict Prison Riot, 1932*. Basingstoke: Palgrave Macmillan.

Brown, A., and E. Clare (2005) 'A history of experience: exploring prisoners' accounts of incarceration', in C. Emsley (ed.), *The Persistent Prison: Problems, Images and Alternatives*. London: Francis Boutle, pp. 49–73.

Brown, A., and C. Maxwell (2003) 'A "receptacle of our worst convicts": Bermuda, the Chatham prison riots and the transportation of violence', *Journal of Caribbean History*, 37(2): 233–55.

Callow, E. (attrib.) (1877) *Five Years' Penal Servitude by One Who Endured It*. London: Richard Bentley & Son.

Carlyle, T. ([1850] 2008) *Latter-Day Pamphlets*. Project Gutenberg.

Carpenter, M. (1851) *Reformatory Schools, for the Children of the Perishing and Dangerous Classes, and for Juvenile Offenders*. London: C. Gilpin.

Causer, T. (2011) '"The worst types of sub-human beings"? The myth and reality of the convicts of the second penal settlement at Norfolk Island, 1825–1855', *Islands of History* [Sydney], pp. 8–31.

Clark, A. (1995) *The Struggle for the Breeches: Gender and the Making of the British Working Class*. London: Oram.

Clark, A. (2000) 'Domesticity and the problem of wife-beating in nineteenth-century Britain: working-class culture, law and politics', in S. D'Cruze (ed.), *Everyday Violence in Britain, 1850–1950*. Harlow: Pearson, pp. 27–40.

Clay, J. (1846) *Chaplain's Twenty-Third Report of the Preston House of Correction, presented to the Magistrates of Lancashire, 1846*. Preston: Clarke.

Cohen, S. (1972) *Folk Devils and Moral Panics*. London: MacGibbon & Kee.

Cohen, S. (1985) *Visions of Social Control: Crime, Punishment and Classification*. Cambridge: Polity.

Cohen, S., and A. Scull (eds) (1983) *Social Control and the State*. London: Martin Robertson.

Coleman, R., and M. McCahill (2011) *Surveillance and Crime*. London: Sage.

Collins, P. (1962) *Dickens and Crime*. London: Macmillan.

Constantine, S. (2008) 'Child migration: philanthropy, the state and the empire', *History in Focus*, no. 14, www.history.ac.uk/ihr/Focus/welfare/articles/constantines.html (accessed 12 June 2014).

Cooper, D. (1974) *The Lesson of the Scaffold*. London: Allen Lane.

Cox, D. J. (2008) *Foul Deed and Suspicious Deaths in Shrewsbury and around Shropshire*. Barnsley: Wharncliffe.

Cox, D. J. (2010) *'A Certain Share of Low Cunning': A History of the Bow Street Runners, 1792–1839*. Cullompton: Willan.

Cox, D. J. (2014) *Crime in England, 1688–1815*. London: Routledge.

Cox, D. J., B. Godfrey, H. Johnston and J. Turner (2014) 'On licence: understanding punishment, recidivism and desistance in penal policy, 1853–1945', in V. Miller and J. Campbell (eds), *Transnational Penal Cultures*. London: Routledge, pp. 184–201.

Cox, P. (2013) *Bad Girls in Britain: Gender, Justice and Welfare, 1900–1950*. Basingstoke: Palgrave Macmillan.

Critchley, T. A. (1978) *A History of Police in England and Wales*. London: Constable.

Crone, R. (2012) *Violent Victorians: Popular Entertainment in Nineteenth-Century London*. Manchester: Manchester University Press.

Cunningham, H. (1995) *Children and Childhood in Western Society since 1500*. Harlow: Longman.

Cunningham, H. (2006) *The Invention of Childhood*. London: BBC Books.

Davenport-Hill, M. D. (1848) *Report of a Charge delivered to the Grand Jury of the Borough of Birmingham, Michaelmas Quarter Sessions for 1848: by the Recorder*. London: Charles Knight.

Davidoff, L., and C. Hall (1987) *Family Fortunes: Men and Women of the English Middle Class 1780–1850*. London: Routledge.

Davie, N. (2010) 'Business as usual?: Britain's first women's convict prison, Brixton 1853–1869', *Crimes and Misdemeanours*, 4(1): 37–52; www.pbs.plymouth.ac.uk/solon/JournalVol4Issue1.htm.

Davies, A. (1998) 'Youth gangs, masculinity and violence in late Victorian Manchester and Salford', *Journal of Social History*, 32: 349–69.

Davies, A. (1999) '"These viragoes are no less cruel than the lads": young women, gangs and violence in late Victorian Manchester and Salford', *British Journal of Criminology*, 39(1): 72–89.

Davies, A. (2006) 'Youth, violence, and courtship in late Victorian Birmingham: the case of James Harper and Emily Pimm', *History of the Family*, 11(2): 107–20.

Davies, A. (2009) *The Gangs of Manchester*. Preston: Milo.

Davies, A. (2011) 'Youth gangs and late Victorian society', in B. Goldson (ed.), *Youth in Crisis?: Gangs, Territoriality and Violence*. London: Routledge.

Davis, J. (1980) 'The London garotting panic of 1862: a moral panic and the creation of a criminal class in mid-Victorian England', in V. A. C. Gatrell, B. Lenman and G. Parker (eds), *Crime and the Law: A Social History of Crime in Western Europe since 1500*. London: Europa, pp. 190–213.

Day, S. P. (1858) *Juvenile Crime: Its Causes, Character, and Cure*. London: J. F. Hope; available at http://hdl.handle.net/2027/uc2.ark:/13960/t4cn71z1z (accessed 9 January 2015).

D'Cruze, S. (1998) *Crimes of Outrage; Sex, Violence and Victorian Working Women*. London: UCL Press.

D'Cruze, S., and Jackson, L. (2009) *Women, Crime and Justice in England since 1660*. Basingstoke: Palgrave Macmillan.

D'Cruze, S., S. Walklate and S. Pegg (2006) *Murder: Social and Historical Approaches to Understanding Murder and Murderers*. Cullompton: Willan.

DeLacy, M. (1981) '"Grinding men good": Lancashire's prisons at mid-century', in V. Bailey (ed.), *Policing and Punishment in Nineteenth-Century Britain*. London: Croom Helm, pp. 182–216.

DeLacy, M. (1986) *Prison Reform in Lancashire 1700–1850*. Stanford, CA: Stanford University Press.

Devereaux, S. (1999) 'The making of the Penitentiary Act, 1775–1779', *Historical Journal*, 42(2): 405–33.

Devereaux, S. (2009) 'Recasting the theatre of execution: the abolition of the Tyburn ritual', *Past and Present*, no. 202: 127–74.

Dickens, C. ([1849–50] 1994) *David Copperfield*. London: Penguin.

Dobash, R. P., R. E. Dobash and S. Gutteridge (1986) *The Imprisonment of Women*. Oxford: Blackwell.

Elliott, D. J. (1984) *Policing Shropshire 1836–1967*. Studley: Brewin Books.

Emsley, C. (1996) *The English Police: A Political and Social History*. 2nd ed., London: Longman.

Emsley, C. (2005) *Hard Men: Violence in England since 1750*. London: Hambledon.

Emsley, C. (2008) 'The birth and development of the police', in T. Newburn (ed.), *Handbook on Policing*. Cullompton: Willan.

Emsley, C. (2009) *The Great British Bobby*. London: Quercus.

Emsley, C. (2010) *Crime and Society in England, 1750–1900*. 4th ed., Harlow: Longman.

Evans, R. (1982) *The Fabrication of Virtue: English Prison Architecture, 1750–1840*. Cambridge: Cambridge University Press.

Farrall, S., and A. Calverley (2006) *Understanding Desistance from Crime*. Milton Keynes: Open University Press.

Feeley, M., and D. Little (1991) 'The vanishing female: the decline of women in the criminal process, 1687–1912', *Law & Society Review*, 25(4): 719–57.

Ferguson, R. (1847) 'Pentonville prisoners', *Quarterly Review*, 82: 175–206.

Fiddler, M. (2008) 'Panopticon', in Y. Jewkes and J. Bennett (eds), *Dictionary of Prisons and Punishment*. Cullompton: Willan, pp. 196–7.

Forsythe, B. (1993) 'Women prisoners and women penal officials, 1840–1921', *British Journal of Criminology*, 33: 525–40.

Forsythe, B. (1995) 'The Garland thesis and the origins of modern English prison discipline: 1835 to 1939', *Howard Journal*, 34(3): 259–73.

Forsythe, B. (2001) 'Suffering, faith and penitence amongst British prisoners 1835 to 1860: the application of theology', *Howard Journal*, 40(1): 14–25.

Forsythe, W. J. (1983) *A System of Discipline: Exeter Borough Prison, 1819–1863*. Exeter: Exeter University Press.

Forsythe, W. J. (1987) *The Reform of Prisoners, 1830–1900*. London: Croom Helm.

Forsythe, W. J. (1990) *Penal Discipline, Reformatory Projects and the English Prison Commission 1895–1939*. Exeter: Exeter University Press.

Foster, D. (1974) 'Class and county government in early nineteenth-century Lancashire', *Northern History*, 9: 48–61.

Foucault, M. (1991) *Discipline and Punish: The Birth of the Prison*. London: Penguin.

Fry, E. (1827) *Observations on the Visiting, Superintending, and Government of Female Prisoners*. London: John and Arthur Arch.

Garland, D. (1985) *Punishment and Welfare: A History of Penal Strategies*. Aldershot: Gower.

Garland, D. (1990) *Punishment and Modern Society*. Oxford: Clarendon Press.

Garland, D. (2002) *The Culture of Control: Crime and Social Order in Contemporary Society*. Oxford: Oxford University Press.

Gatrell, V. A. C. (1980) 'The decline of theft and violence in Victorian and Edwardian England', in V. A. C. Gatrell, B. Lenman and G. Parker (eds), *Crime and the Law: A Social History of Crime in Western Europe since 1500*. London: Europa, pp. 238–338.

Gatrell, V. A. C. (1990) 'Crime, authority and the policeman-state', in F. M. L. Thompson (ed.), *The Cambridge Social History of Britain 1750–1950*, Vol. 3. Cambridge: Cambridge University Press, pp. 243–310.

Gatrell, V. A. C. (1994) *The Hanging Tree: Execution and the English People 1770–1868*. Oxford: Oxford University Press.

Gatrell, V. A. C., and T. B. Hadden (1972) 'Criminal statistics and their interpretation', in E. A. Wrigley (ed.), *Nineteenth-Century Society: Essays in the Use of Quantitative Methods for the Study of Social Data*. Cambridge: Cambridge University Press, pp. 336–96.

Gibbs, M. (2001) 'The archaeology of the convict system in Western Australia', *Australasian Historical Archaeology*, 19: 60–72.

Gillis, J. (1975) 'The evolution of juvenile delinquency in England 1890–1914', *Past and Present*, 67: 96–126.

Godfrey, B. (2004) 'Rough girls, 1880–1930: the "recent" history of violent young women', in C. Alder and A. Worrall (eds), *Girls' Violence: Myths and Realities*. Albany: SUNY Press.

Godfrey, B. (2008) 'Changing prosecution practices and their impact on crime figures, 1857–1940', *British Journal of Criminology*, 48(2): 171–90.

Godfrey, B. (2011) 'The "convict stain": desistance in the penal colony', in J. Rowbotham, M. Muravyeva and D. Nash (eds), *Shame, Blame and Culpability: Crime and Violence in the Modern State*. London: Routledge, pp. 96–109.

Godfrey, B. (2014) *Crime in England, 1880–1940*. London: Routledge.

Godfrey, B., and D. Cox (2008) 'The "last fleet": crime, reformation and punishment in Western Australia', *Australian and New Zealand Journal of Criminology*, 41(2): 236–58.

Godfrey, B., and D. Cox (2013) *Policing the Factory: Theft, Private Policing and the Law in Modern England*. London: Bloomsbury.

Godfrey, B., and P. Lawrence (2005) *Crime and Justice, 1750–1950*. Cullompton: Willan.

Godfrey, B., D. Cox and S. Farrall (2007) *Criminal Lives: Family, Employment and Offending*. Oxford: Oxford University Press.

Godfrey, B., D. Cox and S. Farrall (2010) *Serious Offenders*. Oxford: Oxford University Press.

Godfrey, B., S. Farrall and S. Karstedt (2005) 'Explaining gendered sentencing patterns for violent men and women in the late Victorian period', *British Journal of Criminology*, 45: 696–720.

Godfrey, B., P. Lawrence and C. A. Williams (2008) *History and Crime*. London: Sage.

Gray, D. D. (2013) *London's Shadows: The Dark Side of the Victorian City*. London: Bloomsbury.

Greenwood, J. (1869) *The Seven Curses of London*. London: Stanley Rivers.

Griffiths, A. (1875) *Memorials of Millbank, and Chapters in Prison History*, 2 vols. London: Henry S. King.

Griffiths, P. (1996) *Youth and Authority: Formative Experience in England, 1560–1640*. Oxford: Clarendon Press.

Hamilton, P., and R. Hargreaves (2001) *The Beautiful and the Damned: The Creation of Identity in Nineteenth-Century Photography*. Aldershot: Lund Humphries.

Hammerton, A. J. (1992) *Cruelty and Companionship: Conflict in Nineteenth-Century Married Life*. London: Routledge.

Harding, C. (1988) '"The inevitable end of a discredited system?": the origins of the Gladstone Committee Report on Prisons, 1895', *Historical Journal*, 31: 591–608.

Harding, C., and L. Wilkins (1988) 'The dream of a benevolent mind: the late Victorian response to the problem of inebriety', *Criminal Justice History*, 9: 189–207.

Harding, C., W. Hines, R. Ireland and P. Rawlings (1985) *Imprisonment in England and Wales: A Concise History*. Beckenham: Croom Helm.

Hart, J. (1955) 'Reform of the borough police, 1835–1856', *English Historical Review*, 70: 411–27.

Hay, D. (1975) 'Property, authority and the criminal law', in D. Hay, P. Linebaugh, J. G. Rule, E. P. Thompson and C. Winslow (eds), *Albion's Fatal Tree: Crime and Society in Eighteenth-Century England*. London: Allen Lane, pp. 17–64.

Heidensohn, F. (1985) *Women and Crime*. Basingstoke: Macmillan.

Henderson, F. ([1869] 2007) *Six Years in the Prisons of England*. Charleston, SC: BiblioBazaar.

Henderson, T. (1999) *Disorderly Women in Eighteenth-Century London: Prostitution and Control in the Metropolis, 1730–1830*. Harlow: Longman.

Hendricks, H. (2002) 'Constructions and reconstructions of British childhood: an interpretative survey, 1800 to the present', in J. Muncie, G. Hughes and E. McLaughlin (eds), *Youth Justice: Critical Readings*. London: Sage, pp. 22–44.

Hendricks, H. (2006) 'Histories of youth crime and justice', in B. Goldson and J. Muncie (eds), *Youth Crime and Justice*. London: Sage, pp. 3–16.

Henriques, U. R. Q. (1972) 'The rise and decline of the separate system of prison discipline', *Past and Present*, 54: 61–93.

Hibbert, C. (1957) *The Road to Tyburn*. London: Longmans, Green.

Higginbotham, A. R. (1989) '"Sin of the age": infanticide and illegitimacy in Victorian London', *Victorian Studies*, 32(3): 319–37.

Himmelfarb, G. (1984) *The Idea of Poverty: England in the Industrial Age*, New York: Knopf.

Hirst, J. (1998) 'The Australian experience: the convict colony', in N. Morris and D. J. Rothman (eds), *The Oxford History of the Prison: The Practice of Punishment in Western Society*. Oxford: Oxford University Press, pp. 235–65.

Hirst, J. (2008) *Convict Society and its Enemies: A History of Early New South Wales.* New York: ACLS.

Hitchcock, T., and R. Shoemaker (2010) *Tales from the Hanging Court.* London: Bloomsbury.

Hobhouse, S., and A. F. Brockway (1922) *English Prisons To-Day.* London: Longmans, Green.

Holland, H. W. (1862) 'Professional thieves', *Cornhill Magazine*, 6: 640–53.

Holland, H. W. (1863) 'The science of garotting and housebreaking', *Cornhill Magazine*, 7: 79–92.

Hopkins-Burke, R. (2003) 'Policing bad behaviour: interrogating the dilemmas', in J. Rowbotham and K. Stevenson (eds), *Behaving Badly: Social Panic and Moral Outrage – Victorian and Modern Parallels.* Aldershot: Ashgate, pp. 63–76.

Horn, P. (2010) *Young Offenders: Juvenile Delinquency 1700–2000.* Stroud: Amberley.

Housman, A. E. ([1896] 1987) *A Shropshire Lad.* Ludlow: Palmers Press.

Howard, J. ([1777] 1929) *The State of the Prisons in England and Wales.* London, Dent.

Hughes, R. (1996) *The Fatal Shore: A History of the Transportation of Convicts to Australia, 1787–1868.* London: Harvill Press.

Humphries, S. (1981) *Hooligans or Rebels? An Oral History of Working-Class Childhood and Youth, 1889–1939.* Oxford: Blackwell.

Hunt, G., J. Mellor and J. Turner (1989) 'Wretched, hatless and miserably clad: women and the inebriate reformatories from 1900–1913', *British Journal of Sociology*, 40(2): 244–70.

Ignatieff, M. (1978) *A Just Measure of Pain: The Penitentiary in the Industrial Revolution.* London: Macmillan.

Ignatieff, M. (1983) 'State, civil society and total institutions: a critique of recent social histories of punishment', in S. Cohen and A. Scull (eds), *Social Control and the State.* London: Martin Robertson, pp. 75–105.

Ireland, R. W. (2002) 'The felon and the angel copier: criminal identity and the promise of photography in Victorian England and Wales', in L. A. Knafla (ed.), *Policing and War in Europe.* London: Greenwood Press, pp. 53–86.

Ireland, R. W. (2007) *'A Want of Order and Good Discipline': Rules, Discretion and the Victorian Prison.* Cardiff: University of Wales Press.

Jager, J. (2001) 'Photography: a means of surveillance? Judicial photography, 1850 to 1900', *Crime, Histoire & Sociétés/Crime, History & Societies*, 5(1): 27–51.

Jewkes, Y. (2011) *Media and Crime.* London: Sage.

Jewkes, Y., and H. Johnston (2007) 'The evolution of prison architecture', in Y. Jewkes (ed.), *Handbook on Prisons.* Cullompton: Willan, pp. 174–96.

Johnston, H. (2004) 'The transformations of imprisonment in a local context: a case-study of Shrewsbury in the nineteenth century'. Unpublished PhD thesis, University of Keele.

Johnston, H. (2005a) 'Discovering the local prison: Shrewsbury prison in the nineteenth century', *Local Historian*, 35(4): 230–42.

Johnston, H. (2005b) 'The Shropshire magistracy and local imprisonment: networks of power in the nineteenth century', *Midland History*, 30: 67–91.

Johnston, H. (2005c) 'Policing, punishment and social institutions in the nineteenth century: the role of the Shropshire magistracy', in D. J. Cox and B. S. Godfrey (eds), *'Cinderellas and Packhorses': A History of the Shropshire Magistracy.* Almeley: Logaston Press, pp. 43–64.

Johnston, H. (2006) '"Buried alive": representations of the separate system in Victorian England', in P. Mason (ed.), *Captured by the Media: Prison Discourse in Popular Culture.* Cullompton: Willan, pp. 103–21.

Johnston, H. (2008a) 'Less eligibility', in Y. Jewkes and J. Bennett (eds), *Dictionary of Prisons and Punishment.* Cullompton: Willan, pp. 151–2.

Johnston, H. (2008b) 'Moral guardians?: prison officers, prison practice and ambiguity in the nineteenth century', in H. Johnston (ed.), *Punishment and Control in Historical Perspective.* Basingstoke: Palgrave Macmillan, pp. 77–94.

Johnston, H. (2008c) 'Reclaiming the criminal: the role and training of prison officers in England, 1877–1914', *Howard Journal of Criminal Justice*, 47(3): 297–312.

Johnston, H. (2013) 'Architecture and contested space in the development of the modern prison', in J. Simon, N. Temple and R. Tobe (eds), *Architecture & Justice: Judicial Meanings in the Public Realm*. Aldershot: Ashgate, pp. 23–36.

Johnston, H. (2014) 'Gendered prison work: female prison officers in the local prison system, 1877–1939', *Howard Journal of Criminal Justice*, 53(2): 193–212.

Johnston, H., and B. Godfrey (2013a) *The Costs of Imprisonment: A Longitudinal Study*, ESRC End of Award Report, RES-062-23-3102. Swindon: ESRC.

Johnston, H., and B. Godfrey (2013b) 'Counterblast: the perennial problem of short prison sentences', *Howard Journal of Criminal Justice*, 52(4): 433–7.

Johnstone, G. J. (1996) 'From vice to disease? The concepts of dipsomania and inebriety, 1860–1908', *Social and Legal Studies*, 5: 37–56.

Johnstone, G. J., and T. Ward (2010) *Law and Crime*. London: Sage.

Kermode, J., and G. Walker (eds) (1994) *Women, Crime and the Courts in Early Modern England*. London: UCL Press.

Kilday, A. M. (2010) 'Desperate measures of cruel intentions?: infanticide in Britain since 1600', in A. Kilday and D. Nash (eds), *Histories of Crime: Britain, 1600–2000*. Basingstoke: Palgrave Macmillan, pp. 60–79.

King, P. (1987) 'Newspaper reporting, prosecution practice and perceptions of urban crime: the Colchester crime wave of 1765', *Continuity and Change*, 2: 423–54.

King, P. (1998) 'The rise of juvenile delinquency in England, 1780–1840: changing patterns of perception and prosecution', *Past and Present*, 160: 116–66.

King, P. (2003) 'Moral panics and violent street crime, 1750–2000', in B. Godfrey, C. Emsley and G. Dunstall (eds), *Comparative Histories of Crime*. Cullompton: Willan, pp. 53–71.

King, P. (2006) *Crime and the Law in England, 1750–1840*. Cambridge: Cambridge University Press.

King, P., and Noel, J. (1993) 'The origins of "the problem of juvenile delinquency": the growth of juvenile prosecutions in London in the late eighteenth and early nineteenth centuries', *Criminal Justice History*, 14: 17–41.

Knell, B. E. F. (1965) 'Capital punishment and its administration in relation to juvenile offenders in the nineteenth century and its possible administration in the eighteenth', *British Journal of Criminology, Delinquency and Delinquent Behaviour*, 5(2): 198–207.

Knelman, J. (1998) *Twisting in the Wind: The Murderess and the English Press*. Toronto: University of Toronto Press.

Laqueur, T. W. (1989) 'Crowds, carnivals and the state in English executions, 1604–1868', in A. L. Beier, D. Cannadine and J. M. Rosenheim (eds), *The First Modern Society: Essays in English History in Honour of Lawrence Stone*. Cambridge: Cambridge University Press, pp. 305–55.

Lee, M. (2007) *Inventing Fear of Crime: Criminology and the Politics of Anxiety*. Cullompton: Willan.

Linebaugh, P. (1975) 'The Tyburn riot against the surgeons', in D. Hay *et al.* (eds), *Albion's Fatal Tree: Crime and Society in Eighteenth-Century England*. London: Allen Lane, pp. 65–118.

Linebaugh, P. (1977) 'The Ordinary of Newgate and his *Account*', in J. S. Cockburn (ed.), *Crime in England 1550–1800*, London: Methuen, pp. 246–69.

Linebaugh, P. (1993) *The London Hanged: Crime and Civil Society in the Eighteenth Century*. London: Penguin.

Locker, J. P. (2004) '"This most pernicious species of crime": embezzlement in its public and private dimensions, *c.*1850–1930'. Unpublished PhD thesis, Keele University.

Locker, J. P. (2005) '"Quiet thieves, quiet punishment": private responses to the "respectable" offender, *c.*1850–1930', *Crime, History and Societies*, 9(1): 9–31.

Locker, J. P. (2008) 'The paradox of the "respectable offender": responding to the problem of white collar crime', in H. Johnston (ed.), *Punishment and Control in Historical Perspective*. Basingstoke: Palgrave Macmillan, pp. 115–34.

Lombroso, C. ([1876] 2006) *The Criminal Man*. Durham, NC: Duke University Press.

Lombroso, C., and G. Ferrero (1895) *The Female Offender*. London: Unwin.

McConville, S. (1981) *A History of Prison Administration, 1750–1877*. London: Routledge & Kegan Paul.

McConville, S. (1995) *English Local Prisons: Next Only to Death, 1860–1900*. London: Routledge.

McConville, S. (1998a) 'The Victorian prison: England, 1865–1965', in N. Morris and D. J. Rothman (eds), *The Oxford History of the Prison: The Practice of Punishment in Western Society*. Oxford: Oxford University Press, pp. 117–50.

McConville, S. (1998b) 'Local justice: the jail', in N. Morris and D. J. Rothman (eds), *The Oxford History of the Prison: The Practice of Punishment in Western Society*. Oxford: Oxford University Press, pp. 266–94.

MacDonagh, O. (1958) 'The nineteenth-century revolution in government: a re-appraisal', *Historical Journal*, 1(1): 52–67.

McDonald, J., and R. Shlomowitz (1989) 'Mortality on convict voyages to Australia, 1788–1868', *Social Science History*, 13(3): 285–313.

McGowen, R. (1983) 'The image of justice and reform of the criminal law in early nineteenth century England', *Buffalo Law Review*, 32: 89–125.

McGowen, R. (1986) 'A powerful sympathy: terror, the prison, and humanitarian reform in early nineteenth century Britain', *Journal of British Studies*, 25: 312–34.

McGowen, R. (1987) 'The body and punishment in eighteenth century England', *Journal of Modern History*, 59(4): 651–79.

McGowen, R. (1990) 'Getting to know the criminal class in nineteenth-century England', *Nineteenth Century Contexts*, 14(1): 33–54.

McGowen, R. (1994) 'Civilising punishment: the end of public execution in England', *Journal of British Studies*, 33: 257–82.

McGowen, R. (1998) 'The well-ordered prison: England, 1780–1865', in N. Morris and D. J. Rothman (eds), *The Oxford History of the Prison: The Practice of Punishment in Western Society*. Oxford: Oxford University Press, pp. 71–99.

McGowen, R. (2000) 'Revisiting *The Hanging Tree*: Gatrell on emotion and history', *British Journal of Criminology*, 40(1): 1–13.

MacLeod, R. M. (1967) 'The edge of hope: social policy and chronic alcoholism 1870–1900', *Journal of the History of Medicine*, 22(3): 215–45.

McWilliams, W. (1983) 'The mission to the English police courts 1876–1936', *Howard Journal*, 23(3): 129–47.

Magarey, S. (1978) 'The invention of juvenile delinquency in early nineteenth century England', *Labour History*, 34: 11–27.

Mair, G., and L. Burke (2012) *Redemption, Rehabilitation and Risk Management: A History of Probation*. London: Routledge.

Marsh, P. (1984) 'Below the castle walls in the 1840s', in B. S Trinder (ed.), *Victorian Shrewsbury: Studies in the History of a County Town*. Shrewsbury: Shropshire Libraries.

Martineau, H. (1865) 'Life in the criminal classes', *Edinburgh Review*, 122: 337–71.

Maxwell-Stewart, H. (2008) *Closing Hell's Gates: Death of a Convict Station*. Sydney: Allen & Unwin.

Maxwell-Stewart, H. (2010) 'Convict transportation from Britain and Ireland', *History Compass*, 8(11): 1221–42.

May, M. (1973) 'Innocence and experience: the evolution of the concept of juvenile delinquency in the mid-nineteenth century', *Victorian Studies*, 17(1): 7–29.

Mayhew, H ([1865] 1985) *London Labour and the London Poor*. London: Penguin.

Mayhew, H., and J. Binny (1862) *The Criminal Prisons of London*. London: Griffin, Bohn.

Melossi, D., and M. Pavarini (1981) *The Prison and the Factory: The Origins of the Penitentiary System*. London: Macmillan.

Mingay, G. E. (1994) *Land and Society in England, 1750–1980*. Harlow: Longman.

Morgan, G., and P. Rushton (1998) *Rogues, Thieves and the Rule of Law: The Problem of Law Enforcement in North-East England, 1718–1800*. London: UCL Press.

Morgan, G., and P. Rushton (2004) *Eighteenth-Century Criminal Transportation: The Formation of the Criminal Atlantic*. Basingstoke: Palgrave Macmillan.

Morris, A., and H. Giller (1987) *Understanding Juvenile Justice*. London: Croom Helm.

Morrison, B. (2005) 'Ordering disorderly women: female drunkenness in England *c*. 1870–1920'. Unpublished PhD thesis, Keele University.

Morrison, B. (2008) 'Controlling the "hopeless": re-visioning the history of female inebriate institutions, 1870–1920', in H. Johnston (ed.), *Punishment and Control in Historical Perspective*. Basingstoke: Palgrave Macmillan, pp. 135–57.

Morrison, W. D. (1891) *Crime and its Causes*. London: Swan Sonnenschein.

One-who-has-endured-it (1878) *Five Years Penal Servitude, by One who has Endured It*. London: Bentley & Son.

Ormsby, J. (1864) 'A day's pleasure with the criminal classes', *Cornhill Magazine*, 9: 627–40.

Owen, ([1808] 1972) *Some Account of the Ancient and Present State of Shrewsbury*. Manchester: E. J. Morton.

Paley, R. (1989) '"An imperfect, inadequate, wretched system?": policing before Peel', *Criminal Justice History*, 10: 95–130.

Pearson, G. (1983) *Hooligan: A History of Respectable Fears*. London: Macmillan.

Petrow, S. (1994) *Policing Morals: The Metropolitan Police and the Home Office, 1870–1914*. Oxford: Clarendon Press.

Philips, D. (1976) 'The Black Country magistracy 1835–1860: a changing elite and the exercise of its power', *Midland History*, 3(3): 161–90.

Philips, D. (1977) *Crime and Authority in Victorian England: The Black Country, 1835–1860*. London: Croom Helm.

Philips, D. (1980) 'A new engine of power and authority: the institutionalisation of law enforcement in England 1780–1830', in V. A. C. Gatrell, B. Lenman and G. Parker (eds), *Crime and the Law: A Social History of Crime in Western Europe since 1500*. London: Europa, pp. 155–89.

Philips, D. (1983) '"A just measure of crime, authority, hunters and blue locusts": the "revisionist" social history of crime and the law in Britain, 1780–1950', in S. Cohen and A. Scull (eds), *Social Control and the State*. London: Martin Robertson, pp. 50–74.

Philips, D. (2003) 'Three "moral entrepreneurs" and the creation of a "criminal class" in England, *c*.1790s–1840s', *Crime, History and Societies*, 7(1): 79–107.

Philips, D., and R. Storch (1999) *Policing Provincial England, 1829–1856: The Politics of Reform*. London: Leicester University Press.

Pick, D. (1996) *Faces of Degeneration: A European Disorder, c.1848–c.1918*. Cambridge: Cambridge University Press.

Platt, A. (1969) *The Child Savers: The Invention of Delinquency*. Chicago: University of Chicago Press.

Pratt, J. (1997) *Governing the Dangerous: Dangerousness, Law and Social Change*. Sydney: Federation Press.

Pratt, J. (2002) *Punishment and Civilisation: Penal Tolerance and Intolerance in Modern Society.* London: Sage.

Pratt, J. (2004) 'The acceptable prison: official discourse, truth and legitimacy in the nineteenth century', in G. Gilligan and J. Pratt (eds), *Crime, Truth and Justice: Official Inquiry, Discourse, Knowledge.* Cullompton: Willan, pp. 71–88.

Priestley, P. (1989) *Jail Journeys: The English Prison Experience since 1918.* London: Routledge.

Priestley, P. (1999) *Victorian Prison Lives: English Prison Biography 1830–1914.* London: Pimlico.

Radzinowicz, L., and R. Hood (1979) 'Judicial and sentencing standards: Victorian attempts to solve a perennial problem', *University of Pennsylvania Law Review*, 127: 1288–349.

Radzinowicz, L., and R. Hood (1980) 'Incapacitating the habitual criminal: the English experience', *Michigan Law Review*, 78(3): 1305–89.

Radzinowicz, L., and R. Hood (1990) *A History of the English Criminal Law and its Administration from 1750*, Vo. 5: *The Emergence of Penal Policy.* London: Stevens.

Rafter, N. H. (1982) 'Hard times: custodial prisons for women and the example of the New York state prison for women at Auburn, 1893–1933', in N. H. Rafter and E. Stanko (eds), *Judge, Lawyer, Victim, Thief: Women, Gender Roles and Criminal Justice.* Boston: Northeastern University Press.

Rafter, N. H. (1983) 'Chastising the unchaste: social control functions of a women's reformatory 1894–1931', in S. Cohen and A. Scull (eds), *Social Control and the State: Historical and Comparative Essays.* Oxford: Martin Robertson.

Rafter, N. H. (1985) *Partial Justice: Women in State Prisons 1800–1935.* Boston: Northeastern University Press.

Rafter, N. H. (1997) *Creating Born Criminals.* Chicago: University of Illinois Press.

Rawlings, P. (1992) *Drunks, Whores and Idle Apprentices: Criminal Biographies of the Eighteenth Century.* London: Routledge.

Rawlings, P. (1999) *Crime and Power: A History of Criminal Justice 1688–1998.* Harlow: Longman.

Rawlings, P. (2002) *Policing: A Short History.* Cullompton: Willan.

Rawlings, P. (2003) 'Policing before the Police', in T. Newburn (ed), *Handbook of Policing*, Cullompton: Willan, pp.41–65.

Reade, C. ([1856] 1901) *It's Never too Late to Mend.* London: Chatto & Windus.

Reiner, R. (1992) *The Politics of the Police.* 2nd ed. Oxford: Oxford University Press.

Report of the Committee for Investigating the Causes of the Alarming Increase in Juvenile Delinquency in the Metropolis (1816) London: J. F. Dove.

Reynolds, E. (1998) *Before the Bobbies: The Night Watch and Police Reform in Metropolitan London, 1720–1830.* Basingstoke: Macmillan.

Roberts, D. (1986) 'The scandal at Birmingham borough gaol 1853: a case for penal reform', *Journal of Legal History*, 7: 315–40.

Roberts, E. (1985) *A Woman's Place: An Oral History of Working-Class Women 1890–1940.* Oxford: Blackwell.

Rogers, H. (2009) 'The way to Jerusalem: reading, writing and reform in an early Victorian gaol', *Past and Present*, 205: 71–104.

Rothman, D. J. (1990) *The Discovery of the Asylum.* 2nd ed. Boston: Little, Brown.

Rowbotham, J. (2010) 'Execution as punishment in England, 1750–2000', in A. Kilday and D. Nash (eds), *Histories of Crime: Britain, 1600–2000.* Basingstoke: Palgrave Macmillan, pp. 180–202.

Rusche, G., and O. Kirchheimer (1939) *Punishment and Social Structure.* New York: Columbia University Press.

Rutherford, A. (1984) *Prisons and the Process of Justice: The Reductionist Challenge.* London: Heinemann.

Saunders, J. (1986) 'Warwickshire magistrates and prison reform, 1840–1875', *Midland History*, 11: 79–99.

Seal, L. (2010) *Women, Murder and Femininity: Gender Representations of Women who Kill*. Basingstoke: Palgrave Macmillan.

Sekula, A. (1993) 'The body and the archive', in R. Bolton (ed.), *The Contest of Meaning: Critical Histories of Photography*. London: MIT Press.

Semple, J. (1993) *Bentham's Prison: A Study of the Panopticon Penitentiary*. Oxford: Clarendon Press.

Shaw, A. G. L. (1998) *Convicts and the Colonies: A Study of Penal Transportation from Great Britain & Ireland to Australia & Other Parts of the British Empire*. Dublin: Irish Historical Press.

Shepherd, J. (2008) 'Symons, Jelinger Cookson (1809–1860)', *Oxford Dictionary of National Biography*, www.oxforddnb.com/index/101026897/Jelinger-Symons.

Shoemaker, R. S. (2004) 'Streets of shame?: the crowd and public punishments in London, 1700–1820', in S. Devereaux and P. Griffiths (eds), *Penal Practice and Culture, 1500–1900: Punishing the English*. Basingstoke: Palgrave Macmillan, pp. 232–57.

Shore, H. (2000) 'The idea of juvenile crime in nineteenth-century England', *History Today*, June, pp. 21–7.

Shore, H. (2002a) *Artful Dodgers: Youth and Crime in Early Nineteenth-Century London*. Woodbridge: Boydell.

Shore, H. (2002b) 'Transportation, penal ideology and the experience of juvenile offenders in England and Australia in the early nineteenth century', *Crime, History and Societies*, 6(2): 81–102.

Shore, H. (2008) 'Punishment, reformation or welfare: responses to "the problem" of juvenile crime in Victorian and Edwardian Britain', in H. Johnston (ed.), *Punishment and Control in Historical Perspective*. Basingstoke: Palgrave Macmillan, pp. 158–76.

Shore, H. (2010) 'Criminality, deviance and the underworld since 1750', in A. Kilday and D. Nash (eds), *Histories of Crime: Britain, 1600–2000*. Basingstoke: Palgrave Macmillan, pp. 120–40.

Sim, J. (1990) *Medical Power in Prisons: The Prison Medical Service 1774–1989*. Milton Keynes: Open University Press.

Sindall, R. S. (1986) 'The criminal statistics of nineteenth-century cities: a new approach', *Urban History*, 13: 28–36.

Sindall, R. S. (1987) 'The London garrotting panics of 1856 and 1862', *Social History*, 12(3): 351–9.

Sindall, R. S. (1990) *Street Violence in the Nineteenth Century: Media Panic or Real Danger?* Leicester: Leicester University Press.

Smith, D. (1982) 'The demise of transportation: mid-Victorian penal policy', *Criminal Justice History*, 3: 21–45.

Smith, F. B. (1979) 'Mayhew's convict', *Victorian Studies*, 22(4): 431–48.

Smith, G. T. (2004) '"I could hang anything you can bring before me": England's willing executioners in 1883', in S. Devereaux and P. Griffiths (eds), *Penal Practice and Culture, 1500–1900: Punishing the English*. Basingstoke: Palgrave Macmillan, pp. 285–308.

Smith, P. (2008) *Punishment and Culture*. Chicago: University of Chicago Press.

Southerton, P. (1993) *Reading Gaol by Reading Town*. Stroud: Alan Sutton/Berkshire Books.

Spierenburg, P. (1984) *The Spectacle of Suffering*. Cambridge: Cambridge University Press.

Spierenburg, P. (1991) *The Prison Experience: Disciplinary Institutions and their Inmates in Early Modern Europe*. New Brunswick, NJ: Rutgers University Press.

Spierenburg, P. (2001) 'Violence and the civilising process: does it work?', *Crime, History & Societies*, 5(2): 87–105.

Spierenburg, P. (2005) 'The origins of the prison', in C. Emsley (ed.), *The Persistent Prison: Problems, Images and Alternatives*. London: Francis Boutle, pp. 27–48.

Stack, J. (1979) 'Deterrence and reformation in early Victorian social policy: the case of Parkhurst prison, 1838–1864', *Historical Reflections*, 6(2): 387–404.

Stack, J. (1994) 'Reformatory and industrial schools and the decline of child imprisonment in mid-Victorian England and Wales', *History of Education*, 23(1): 59–73.

Stanford, T. (2009) 'Who are you? We have ways of finding out!: tracing the police development of offender identification techniques in the late nineteenth century', *Crimes & Misdemeanours*, 3(1): 54–81.

Stedman Jones, G. (2013) *Outcast London: A Study in the Relationship between the Classes in Victorian Society*. London: Verso.

Stevenson, J. (1989) 'Bread or blood', in G. E. Mingay (ed.), *The Unquiet Countryside*. London: Routledge.

Stevenson, J. (1992) *Popular Disturbances in England, 1700–1832*. London: Routledge.

Stevenson, K., J. Rowbotham and S. Pegg (2003) 'Children of misfortune: the parallel cases of child murderers Thompson and Venables, Barratt and Bradley', *Howard Journal of Criminal Justice*, 42(2): 107–22.

Stevenson, S. J. (1986) 'The "habitual criminal" in nineteenth-century England: some observations on figures', *Urban History*, 13: 37–60.

Stockdale, E. (1977) *A Study of Bedford Prison, 1660–1877*. Chichester: Phillimore.

Stockdale, E. (1983) 'A short history of prison inspection in England', *British Journal of Criminology*, 23(3): 209–28.

Storch, R. (1975) 'The plague of blue locusts: police reform and popular resistance in northern England, 1840–1857', *International Review of Social History*, 20: 61–90.

Storch, R. (1976) 'The policeman as domestic missionary: urban discipline and popular culture in northern England, 1850–1880', *Journal of Social History*, 9: 481–509.

Swift, R. (1985) '"Another Stafford Street row": law, order and the Irish presence in mid-Victorian Wolverhampton', in R. Swift and S. Gilley (eds), *The Irish in the Victorian City*. London: Croom Helm, pp. 179–206.

Swift, R. (1988) 'Urban policing in early Victorian England, 1835–1886', *History*, 73: 221–37.

Swift, R. (1992) 'The English urban magistracy and the administration of justice during the early nineteenth century: Wolverhampton 1815–1860', *Midland History*, 17: 75–92.

Swift, R. (1997) 'Heroes or villains?: the Irish, crime, and disorder in Victorian England', *Albion*, 29(3): 399–421.

Swift, R. (2005) 'Behaving badly?: Irish migrants and crime in the Victorian city', in J. Rowbotham and K. Stevenson (eds), *Criminal Conversations: Victorian Crimes, Social Panic, and Moral Outrage*. Columbus: Ohio State University Press, pp. 106–25.

Symons, J. C. (1849) *Tactics for the Times: As Regards the Condition and Treatment of the Dangerous Classes*. London.

Taylor, D. (1997) *The New Police in Nineteenth-Century England*. Manchester: Manchester University Press.

Taylor, D. (1998) *Crime, Policing and Punishment in England, 1750–1914*. London: Macmillan.

Taylor, D. (2002) *Policing the Victorian Town: The Development of the Police in Middlesbrough c.1840–1914*. Basingstoke: Palgrave Macmillan.

Taylor, D. (2010) *Hooligans, Harlots and Hangmen: Crime and Punishment in Victorian Britain*. Oxford: Praeger.

Tennant, M. (2014) 'Fields of struggle: a Bourdieusian analysis of conflicts over criminal justice in England, c.1820–50', *Social History*, 39(1): 36–55.

Thomas, J. E. (1972) *The English Prison Officer since 1850*. London: Routledge & Kegan Paul.

Thompson, E. P., and E. Yeo (eds) (1971) *The Unknown Mayhew*. New York: Pantheon.

Tobias, J. J. (1967) *Crime and Industrial Society in the Nineteenth Century*. Harmondsworth: Penguin.

Tomlinson, M. H. (1978a) '"Not an instrument of punishment": prison diet in the mid-nineteenth century', *Journal of Consumer Studies and Home Economics*, 2: 15–26.

Tomlinson, M. H. (1978b) '"Prison palaces": a re-appraisal of early Victorian prisons, 1835–1877', *Historical Research*, 51: 60–71.

Tomlinson, M. H. (1981) 'Penal servitude 1846–1865: a system in evolution', in V. Bailey (ed.), *Policing and Punishment in Nineteenth-Century Britain*. London: Croom Helm, pp. 126–49.

Turner, J. (2011) 'Punishing women 1880–1905', *Howard Journal of Criminal Justice*, 50(5): 505–15.

Turner, J. (2012) 'Summary justice for women: Stafford borough, 1880–1905', *Crime, History & Societies*, 16(2): 55–77.

Walkowitz, J. R. (1982) *Prostitution and Victorian Society*. Cambridge: Cambridge University Press.

Walkowitz, J. R. (1992) *City of Dreadful Delight: Narratives of Sexual Danger in Late-Victorian London*. Chicago: University of Chicago Press.

Walkowitz, J. R., and D. J. Walkowitz (1974) '"We are not beasts of the fields": prostitution and the poor in Plymouth and Southampton under the Contagious Diseases Acts', in M. S. Hartman and L. Banner (eds), *Clio's Consciousness Raised: New Perspectives on the History of Women*. London; Harper & Row, pp. 192–225.

Ward, T. (1999) 'The sad subject of infanticide: law, medicine and child murder, 1860–1938,' *Social & Legal Studies*, 8: 163–80.

Ward, T. (2001) 'Legislating for human nature: legal responses to infanticide, 1860–1938', in M. Jackson (ed.), *Infanticide: Historical Perspectives on Child Murder and Concealment, 1550–2000*. Aldershot: Ashgate.

Watson, K. (2004) *Poisoned Lives: English Poisoners and their Victims*. London: Hambledon.

Webb, S., and B. Webb (1963) *English Prisons under Local Government*. London: Longmans, Green.

Weinberger, B. (1981) 'The police and the public in mid-nineteenth century Warwickshire', in V. Bailey (ed.), *Policing and Punishment in Nineteenth Century Britain*. London: Croom Helm, pp. 65–93.

Whiting, J. R. S. (1975) *Prison Reform in Gloucestershire, 1776–1820*. London: Phillimore.

Wiener, M. J. (1994) *Reconstructing the Criminal: Culture, Law and Policy in England, 1830–1914*. Cambridge: Cambridge University Press.

Wiener, M. J. (2004) *Men of Blood: Violence, Manliness, and Criminal Justice in Victorian England*. Cambridge: Cambridge University Press.

Wilde, O. ([1898] 2002) *De Profundis, The Ballad of Reading Gaol and Other Writings*. London: Wordsworth.

Williams, C. A. (2010) 'Policing the populace: the road to professionalisation', in A. Kilday and D. Nash (eds), *Histories of Crime: Britain, 1600–2000*. Basingstoke: Palgrave Macmillan, pp. 160–79.

Williams, L. (2014) '"At large": women's lives and offending in Victorian Liverpool and London'. Unpublished PhD Thesis, University of Liverpool.

Wills, A. (2005) 'Delinquency, masculinity and citizenship 1950–1970', *Past and Present*, 187: 157–85.

Wills, A. (2008) 'Resistance, identity and historical change in residential institutions for juvenile delinquents, 1950–1970', in H. Johnston (ed.), *Punishment and Control in Historical Perspective*. Basingstoke: Palgrave Macmillan, pp. 215–34.

Wilson, D. (2002) 'Millbank, the Panopticon and their Victorian audiences', *Howard Journal*, 41(4): 364–81.

Wilson, D. (2013) *Mary Ann Cotton: Britain's First Female Serial Killer*. Hook: Waterside Press.

Wilson, D. (2014) *Pain and Retribution: A Short History of British Prisons, 1066 to the Present*. London: Reaktion Books.

Wilson, S. (2010) 'Fraud and white-collar crime: 1850 to the present', in A. Kilday and D. Nash (eds), *Histories of Crime: Britain, 1600–2000*, Basingstoke: Palgrave Macmillan, pp. 141–59.

Wood, J. C. (2004) *Violence and Crime in Nineteenth-Century England: The Shadow of our Refinement*. London: Routledge.

Woolnough, G. (2013) 'The policing of petty crime in Victorian Cumbria, 1856–1902'. Unpublished PhD thesis, Keele University.

Young, J. (1971) *The Drugtakers*. London: MacGibbon & Kee.

Zedner, L. (1991) 'Women, crime and penal responses: a historical account', *Crime and Justice*, 14: 307–62.

Zedner, L. (1994) *Women, Crime and Custody in Victorian England*. Oxford: Oxford University Press.

Zedner, L. (1998) 'Wayward sisters: the prison for women', in N. Morris and D. J. Rothman (eds), *The Oxford History of the Prison: The Practice of Punishment in Western Society*. Oxford: Oxford University Press, pp. 295–324.

INDEX

desistance from crime 135
detectives 52–3
deterrence: imprisonment 9, 33, 34, 93,
    94, 96, 103, 113–14, 153, 154; juvenile
    crime 143, 144; public punishment 58,
    61, 68; transportation 74, 78, 79, 83
Devereaux, S. 64
deviancy 124–5, 129, 130
Devon 97
Dickens, Charles 28, 111
diet, prison 20–1, 98, 103–4, 114–16
'disciplinary society' 4
discipline 97–8
disorderly behaviour 49, 121, 128
Dobash, R. P. 4
doli incapax 139
domestic violence 5, 124
Droitwich 47
drunkenness 7, 8, 17–19, 155; case
    studies 23, 41, 42, 86, 134; children
    14; convicts in Australia 84, 86;
    imprisonment for 98; policing of
    everyday life 49–50, 51; prisoner
    reports 16; rural areas 21; women 121,
    122, 124, 125, 133, 134, 154
Du Cane, Edmund 39, 99, 153, 154
Duncombe, T. 76–7
Durham 97, 132
Dyer, Amelia 125

Education Acts (1870s/1880s) 138
Elias, Norbert 4–5
elites 2, 54
employment 84, 86; children 138; women
    131, 132; *see also* labour
Emsley, C. 30, 44, 60, 74
entertainment 14, 15–16
evangelicalism 92
Exeter 132–3

Factory Act (1833) 138
Farm School, Redhill 141, 147
fear 2, 30
femininity 123–4
Ferguson, Robert 109
Fielding brothers 45
fines 7, 18, 22, 23, 24, 41, 146
first-time offenders 106–7, 117, 118–20,
    140–1, 144, 146
flogging 34, 79, 82, 116, 151; *see also*
    whipping
food riots 21
forgery 118, 123
Forsythe, W. J. 71, 129

Foucault, M. 4
France 30, 53, 146
fraud 14, 118, 119, 131
free will 12
Fry, Elizabeth 66, 88, 89, 90, 129,
    132, 141
Fulham Refuge 112, 130

'gallows' literature 15
Galton, Francis 39
gambling 14, 16, 137
game laws *see* poaching
gangs 47, 53, 128, 137–8, 151, 156
Gaol Fees Abolition Act (1815) 89–90
gaols *see* local prisons
Gaols Act (1823) 90, 91, 100, 132, 140–1
Garland, D. 4
'garrotting panic' 30–4, 86
Gatrell, V. A. C. 2, 3, 61, 62, 153
gentry 7, 54
Gibraltar 73, 77, 113
Gladstone Committee 99, 151, 153–4, 155
Gloucester 107
Gloucestershire 52
Godfrey, B. 6, 35, 84, 128
government control 49, 106, 107, 152; *see
    also* centralisation
Graham, John 109
Greenfield, Annie 7–8, 39, 40–2
Greenwood, James 15–16, 18
Grey, George 49, 83
Grey Committee (Select Committee on
    Prison Discipline) 92, 93–4
Griffiths, Arthur 114
Grindley, Joseph 65

Habitual Criminals Act (1869) 35–6, 38
'habitual' offenders 7, 26, 29, 35–9;
    convict prisons 117; police monitoring
    51–3; prisons 96; women 122
Hammerton, A. J. 124
hard labour 94–5, 96–7, 98, 103, 104,
    116, 139
Harding, William 85–6
Harris, Ann 65
Hart, J. 46
Haycock, John 100
Hayward, Samuel 65
Henderson, Frank 114, 116
Henderson, T. 126
heredity 39, 155
Hertfordshire 57
Higginbotham, A. R. 125
Hirst, J. 80